Global Business

Globalization has been under extreme pressure in the wake of the financial crisis. Multinational firms are weighing the costs and benefits of international scale and scope, and are increasingly under pressure to hire local, to source local, and to pay taxes domestically. At the same time, global competitive pressures have intensified.

This book reviews international business practices from the multinational firm perspective, and provides pathways forward concerning competitiveness and sustainability in global markets. What sets this book apart from others is that the benefits and pitfalls of globalization are addressed. Chapter coverage focuses on the functional areas of the business and how they are impacted by international expansion. Practical case studies supplement chapter coverage and highlight both positive and negative developments in the global business arena. Readers should expect to be challenged on what will be the limits of the multinational firm in the future, and how multinational firms can continue to prosper while at the same time adhere to sustainable business initiatives.

Equally useful to both undergraduate and graduate students of international business as well as professional development programs, *Global Business: Competitiveness and Sustainability* provides a necessary tonic for dealing with today's troubled seas of globalization.

Riad A. Ajami is currently Professor of International Management and Global Strategy at the Raj Soin College of Business at Wright State University, USA. Professor Ajami is the Editor-in-Chief of the *Journal of Asia-Pacific Business* and Editor-in-Chief of the Haworth International Business Press Series in Asia-Pacific Business. He has appeared on national television and radio, including, among others, Nightline, the PBS News Hour, NBC News, CNN, National Public Radio and CBS Radio.

G. Jason Goddard is Vice President at Wells Fargo Bank, where he has been a commercial lender for over 20 years. He obtained his MBA from the University of North Carolina at Greensboro, USA. Mr. Goddard is currently Adjunct Professor at Wake Forest University and UNC-Greensboro, and is the Associate Editor of the *Journal of Asia-Pacific Business*, where he has authored numerous articles. Mr. Goddard teaches the investment real estate course at Wake Forest University, USA, and has taught international business and international finance at UNCG and in Ludwigshafen Germany at the University of Applied Sciences.

Global Business
Competitiveness and Sustainability

Riad A. Ajami and G. Jason Goddard

LONDON AND NEW YORK

First published 2018
by Routledge
2 Park Square, Milton Park, Abingdon, Oxon OX14 4RN

and by Routledge
711 Third Avenue, New York, NY 10017

Routledge is an imprint of the Taylor & Francis Group, an informa business

© 2018 Riad A. Ajami and G. Jason Goddard

The right of Riad A. Ajami and G. Jason Goddard to be identified as
authors of this work has been asserted by them in accordance with sections
77 and 78 of the Copyright, Designs and Patents Act 1988.

All rights reserved. No part of this book may be reprinted or reproduced or
utilised in any form or by any electronic, mechanical, or other means, now
known or hereafter invented, including photocopying and recording, or in
any information storage or retrieval system, without permission in writing
from the publishers.

Trademark notice: Product or corporate names may be trademarks or
registered trademarks, and are used only for identification and explanation
without intent to infringe.

British Library Cataloguing-in-Publication Data
A catalogue record for this book is available from the British Library

Library of Congress Cataloging-in-Publication Data
Names: Goddard, G. Jason, author. | Ajami, Riad A., author.
Title: Global business : competitiveness and sustainability / G Jason
Goddard and Riad Ajami.
Description: First Edition. | New York : Routledge, 2018. | Includes
bibliographical references and index.
Identifiers: LCCN 2017026403| ISBN 9781138551794 (hardback) | ISBN
9781315147734 (ebook)
Subjects: LCSH: International business enterprises--Management. | Export
marketing. | Double taxation. | Diversity in the workplace--Management.
Classification: LCC HD62.4 .G624 2018 | DDC 658/.049--dc23
LC record available at https://lccn.loc.gov/2017026403

ISBN: 978-1-138-55179-4 (hbk)
ISBN: 978-1-315-14773-4 (ebk)

Typeset in Bembo
by Saxon Graphics Ltd, Derby
Printed and bound by CPI Group (UK) Ltd, Croydon, CR0 4YY

This work is dedicated to the students of tomorrow; may they be able to help us toward a sustainable, global society.

Alya, Carter, Michelle, Layal
and Leila Goddard

Contents

List of illustrations	*xi*
Preface	*xiii*

1 Global business: competitiveness and sustainability   1

Introduction 1
Globalization: detractors and supporters 2
Global business: the balance of competitiveness and sustainability 6
Thematic definition of the field of international business 11
Discussion and conclusion 13
Discussion questions 13
Bibliography 14

2 International marketing   16

Chapter objectives 16
What must be done: the international marketer's dilemma 16
To centralize or decentralize: the first key decisions 17
Product decisions 20
Pricing decisions 28
Placement decisions: distribution of products 33
Summary 37
Discussion questions 37
Bibliography 38
Appendix: A checklist for export marketing 40

3 International finance   45

Chapter objectives 45
Financing international business 45
Working capital management 45
Capital budgeting and financial structure of an MNC 53
Letters of credit in international trade 56
International capital markets 57

viii *Contents*

Emerging markets 68
Summary 69
Discussion questions 70
Bibliography 70

4 International accounting   **72**
Chapter objectives 72
What is accounting? 72
Differences in accounting practices among countries 73
Policy formation and harmonization 80
Special accounting problems 83
Other international accounting issues 90
Summary 92
Discussion questions 92
Bibliography 93

5 International taxation   **94**
Chapter objectives 94
Why taxes? 94
Types of taxes 96
Tax compliance and tax enforcement 99
Special issues and problems in international taxation tax havens 105
Tax incentives for international business 108
Summary 111
Discussion questions 111
Bibliography 112

6 International staffing and labor issues   **113**
Chapter objectives 113
Organizing a multinational corporation 113
International staffing 114
Managerial staffing 117
Choosing branch managers: selection criteria 120
Training branch managers 122
Compensating branch managers 123
Repatriating branch managers 124
Ethical issues 125
International labor issues 126
Summary 137
Discussion questions 138
Bibliography 138
Appendix: Managerial grid – free questionnaire sites   *140*

Contents ix

7   Managing operations and technology   **141**

Chapter objectives 141
Operations, technology, and international competition 141
Designing the local operations system 147
Production and operations management 148
International technology 153
Management information systems 161
Summary 167
Discussion questions 169
Bibliography 169

8   Global case studies   **171**

Competitiveness Cases:
 Myanmar: the last global frontier (G. Jason Goddard) 172
 Attractiveness of global markets (Van R. Wood et al.) 176
 Increasing market share at Acme Industries (Gregory M. Kellar) 193
 Hedging with foreign exchange (Anonymous) 199
Sustainability Cases:
 Lilly Pharmaceuticals: triple bottom line and values-based leadership
  (Joseph A. Petrick) 205
 International real estate investor (G. Jason Goddard) 213
 Cooperative workforce development: public–private sustainable linkages
  (Jennifer Winner & Riad A. Ajami) 222
 Privilege Capital (Martina Roskova) 230

Glossary   *241*
Index   *249*
About the authors   *260*

Illustrations

Exhibits

1.1	World gross domestic product trends 1990–2015	3
1.2	World gross national income (GNI) per capita trends 1990–2015	4
1.3	FDI inward stock by region and economy 1990–2015	5
1.4	Global consumer convergence spectrum	7
1.5	Global efficiency vs. local responsiveness	7
1.6	Environmental pressures: local responsiveness vs. global integration	8
1.7	The linkage of MNC types to strategic orientation, assets and capabilities	9
1.8	International Business teaching: The intersection of global structure and functional dimensions	12
2.1	Obstacles to standardization in global markets	36
3.1	Effect of trade account movements on working capital needs for a small business	46
3.2	Name that Eurobond!	60
3.3	Market capitalization of select world stock exchanges 2005–2015	66
4.1	Sony's sales by area and product group	78
4.2	Nestle sales by product group	79
4.3	Nestle sales by region	79
4.4	Exchange rates employed in different translation methods for specific balance sheet items	86
4.5	Translating a firm's functional currency into a reporting currency	87
5.1	Example of the application of VAT	97
5.2	Corporate tax rate table	100
5.3	Tax havens of the world	107
6.1	Various staffing models: advantages and disadvantages	127
6.2	Annual rate of change for manufacturing productivity, compensation, unit labor costs, and unemployment rates	131
6.3	The Managerial Grid	136
7.1	Maritime piracy statistics	152
7.2	Licensing as a preferred strategy	157

xii *Illustrations*

7.3	Typical information flow between an MNC and its subsidiaries	164
8.1	Gregory Fuller's notes on Myanmar	174
8.2	Regions/countries examined for export potential	180
8.3	Stage 1: Market size analysis results	181
8.4	Stage 2: PEST Analysis Results	182
8.5	Stage 3: Country attractiveness/competitive strength analysis results	185
8.6	Harrell & Kiefer country plotting matrix	185
8.7	Stage 3: Country attractiveness/competitive strength analysis	187
8A	Stage 1: Market size analysis	189
8B	Stage 2: PEST analysis	190
8C	Stage 3: Country attractiveness variable rankings	191
8D	Stage 4: Competitive strength variable rankings	192
8.8	Parent-subsidiary relationships for Silicatec	200
8.9	Economic data from *The Economist* June 13, 2015 pg. 88	215
8.10	30-year views for 3-Month LIBOR, prime rate and 10-Year US Treasuries as of April 17, 2015	217
8.11	Menger satisfaction scale	218
8.12	Shackle possibility curve	220
8.13	Complex project management of market expansion	234

Tables

8.1	Inflation rates in India	196
8.2	Competitive offerings	196
8.3	Expansion projections	196
8.4	IT implementation plans	197
8.5	Capital cost plans	198
8.6	Breakeven analyses	198
8.7	Sub C's foreign currency exposure	201
8.8	Historical price and earnings data	203
8.9	Effect on share price of Euro decline	203

Boxes

Perspective 2.1	International grocery store example	20
Perspective 2.2	Cross-cultural advertising mistakes	25
Perspective 6.1	The managerial grid	135
Perspective 7.1	International piracy	152

Preface

This book serves as a call to arms for global business. **Globalization**, the process by which businesses or other organizations develop international influence or start operating on an international scale, has been recently pilloried in the popular press as a wave of populist sentiment has swept the globe. This sentiment has led to calls for national protectionist trade policy, and for the roll-back of many of the benefits that the global economy has experienced in recent decades. Thankfully, this anti-globalization sentiment is not condoned in most populations, and certainly is not popular in the majority of business entities. A primary focus for this book is the discussion of emerging global issues and the response of multinational firms to deal with the concerns of our global society and economy, global sustainability, and multi-national corporate activities.

The current backdrop of the debate on the benefits of globalization provides context for the times in which we live, as the focus of this book is centered on the balancing act between competitive strategies for success on the one hand, and sustainable business practices on the other. There have been numerous examples in recent years of corporate success leading to excess, often with the drive for increased revenue in the short run damaging the reputation of the firm in the long run. While the drive for profit has been the focus of the populist rhetoric, in many cases just as important an element has been the over-reach of governments attempting to regulate industry for the putative amelioration of the global marketplace. Regulation leads to increased cost for business, which will either be passed on to the consumer or will lead to efforts to increase revenue by the affected firm. As governments consider a more nationalistic approach to trade, these various national and international regulations could thwart profitable ventures throughout the world, so a managed approach which considers the implications of sustainability on competitive strategy becomes of paramount importance.

In the chapters that follow, we present a return to fundamentals for international business with an eye on the ever-changing landscape and the seas of change. International business and multinational corporate activities have grown significantly during the past four decades. The rapid and continuous growth of cross border linkages has contributed to the importance of our xiv *Preface*

understanding of the study of international business operations and global markets. Some of the case studies in this book offer a prescription for success in this new global marketplace, while others provide the necessary tonic for mistakes made in the past. Moreover, the richness of the case studies presents real-world examples of issues facing multinational firms and global society and present a bridge between globalization, multi-national corporate strategies, and issues of social concern and global sustainability. Sustainability runs through the heart of this book. This sustainability is not just defined in environmental terms, but also in the broader sense of corporate reputation, responsibility, and the limits therein. Whether threats to competitiveness and sustainability come from land, air or sea, the common thread is that corporate action must be in the long-run interests of shareholders and stakeholders alike. The global business that is able to achieve sustainable competitive advantage has the highest hopes of successfully steering through today's troubled seas of globalization.

Numerous academic and professional colleagues, and global public policymakers, have given the authors invaluable assistance in the preparation of this book. Our deep appreciation goes to the many who are too numerous to mention by name from Wright State University, particularly Professors Dr. Greg Kellar and Dr. Joseph Petrick. Our deep appreciation also goes to the following: Dr. Kamel Abdallah, a leading and insightful businessman and academician, working across the globe, and currently living in France and the United Arab Emirates; Hanne Nørreklit, Aarhus School of Business, Denmark; Frederic Herlin, formerly of the Center for Creative Leadership, Brussels; Ram Baliga and Tom Taylor, Wake Forest University; Frank Lord Partridge III, NC School of the Arts; Todd Parrish, Salem College; David Church, Wells Fargo; and the supporting team from the Center for Global Business at Wright State University, particularly Susan E. Meindl, managing editor of the *Journal of Asia-Pacific Business*, for research support. Moreover, the team from the Center for Global Business includes a number of research affiliates, particularly Ohoud Ibrahim M. Alakhdhar, for her knowledge and ability to translate significant documents relating to the global oil industry, Arab Organization of Petroleum Exporting Countries (AOPEC), and other original documents related to the emerging economies of the Gulf States. Her earlier journalistic training was important for clarifying some of our views on emerging economies and the global oil industry, among others. The authors would also like to gratefully acknowledge the contributions of our case study authors not yet mentioned, among them Martina Roskova of Privilege Capital, Dr. Van Wood, VCU, Whitney Harrison and Jesse Myrick of the VCU School of Business Graduate Program, and Ms. Jennifer Winner, Air Force Research Laboratory. Finally, the authors would like to thank Susan Resko for the cover design which helps us illustrate that opportunity exists for the best of fishing in troubled waters.

Riad A. Ajami and G. Jason Goddard, May 2017

1 Global business
Competitiveness and sustainability

I carry in my world that flourishes the worlds that have failed.

(Rabindranath Tagore)

Chapter objectives

This chapter will:

- Define the strategic orientation of this book
- Discuss the required shift in focus for global business educators
- Preview subsequent chapters and case studies

Introduction

Globalization has received much criticism in recent years. Populist rhetoric in the United States and Britain has joined forces with **xenophobic** political movements in Europe to present the case against the continued integration of world economies. At the heart of much of this rhetoric has been a focus on mass migratory flows of people across borders but globalization has also been blamed for the increase in inequality of incomes over the last decades.

Forgotten in this populist blitzkrieg have been the successes of globalization in contributing to rising wages in developing countries as well as rising standards of living in the developed world. Globalization begets global business as internationally active corporations have been the primary arbiter of global market penetration and the rise in global economic integration and inclusiveness.

When done correctly, global business can and does lead to a more sustained growth and provides benefits to consumers worldwide. Global business competition is generally good for consumers, as prices typically fall and quality typically rises, as sovereign consumers render their vote as to the winners and losers in the global marketplace by their purchasing decisions. Where global business has gone awry is when the profit motive comes before providing sustainable solutions for consumers. Rather than retreating from global market integration, it is the opinion expressed in this book that increased inclusion and

2   *Global business*

promise are only possible when markets are integrated, when competition is free, and when sustainability is the overarching goal for the world economy.

Globalization: detractors and supporters

Given the reported retreat of globalization in recent years, it is worth reviewing just how successful market integration has been. Exhibit 1.1 shows world gross domestic product trends in five-year intervals from 1990 to 2015.

For ease of comparison, the compound annual growth rate over the period is shown at the far right of Exhibit 1.1. All areas of the world experienced positive GDP growth since 1990, with Asia, the Middle East and North Africa, and other developing areas of the world exhibiting a higher growth trajectory than world averages. High income areas such as in Europe and North America experienced growth less than world averages during this same time period. Based on the data shown in Exhibit 1.1, collective cognitive dissonance toward globalization in the developed world may have its origin in these slower relative growth rates. For workers displaced from their jobs owing to foreign competition, the temporary set-back could be ripe for anti-globalization sentiment.

Exhibit 1.2 takes a different view of the same time period. Rather than showing results based on GDP performance, Exhibit 1.2 shows world gross national income (GNI) per capita trends. The percentage column for each year illustrates how a particular region compares to the world average in terms of GNI per capita.

What this chart makes clear is that any cognitive dissonance regarding globalization experienced in the developed world is unfounded. While high income countries may have grown at slightly less than the world averages from 1990 to 2015, the dollar difference in per capita income is staggering when comparing high income countries with the rest of the world. Instead of globalization harming the lives of global citizenry, the figures in Exhibit 1.2 support the conclusion that a more sustainable level of growth is being experienced relative to the past. It should be noted that in Exhibit 1.1 the percentage of high income country GDP has fallen from 78% of the world total in 1990 to 64% of the world total in 2015. Viewed in light of the GNI per capita figures shown in Exhibit 1.2, this lesser share of world GDP by high income countries is hardly deleterious to citizens of the developed world. The analogy of "a rising tide raises all boats" seems most appropriate.

Exhibit 1.3 further supports the thesis that globalization promotes sustainability rather than disaffection. When foreign direct investment (FDI) inward stock is viewed from 1990 to 2015, global inclusiveness is clearly illustrated.

Other than China, which has received much higher foreign direct investment than world averages, the majority of regions are within a percentage point or two of the world average compound annual growth rate over the surveyed period. Based on this table, no area of the world is being ignored by economic

	1990	%	1995	%	2000	%	2005	%	2010	%	2015	%	25 Year CAGR %
World GDP	22,563,112	100%	30,658,939	100%	33,321,292	100%	47,121,204	100%	65,612,000	100%	73,502,341	100%	5.04%
East Asia & Pacific	4,723,765	21%	8,196,923	27%	8,134,973	24%	10,109,794	21%	16,673,982	25%	21,281,190	29%	6.47%
Europe & Central Asia	8,834,247	39%	10,742,682	35%	9,923,996	30%	16,620,602	35%	20,831,861	32%	19,985,557	27%	3.46%
Latin America & Caribbean	1,166,399	5%	1,910,007	6%	2,262,083	7%	2,844,746	6%	5,335,582	8%	5,298,318	7%	6.51%
Middle East & N. Africa	543,762	2%	707,678	2%	965,694	3%	1,523,380	3%	2,742,640	4%	3,113,598	4%	7.54%
North America	6,575,111	29%	8,270,122	27%	11,030,553	33%	14,267,952	30%	16,583,523	25%	19,503,407	27%	4.63%
South Asia	411,962	2%	485,124	2%	619,218	2%	1,053,910	2%	2,093,719	3%	2,666,094	4%	8.09%
Sub-Saharan Africa	306,872	1%	337,323	1%	367,685	1%	685,043	1%	1,355,385	2%	1,572,873	2%	7.05%
Low Income	96,261	0%	84,193	0%	113,343	0%	159,882	0%	289,212	0%	392,904	1%	6.04%
Low & Middle Income	3,671,225	16%	4,995,310	16%	5,948,892	18%	9,774,453	21%	20,614,148	31%	26,532,486	36%	8.59%
Middle Income	3,580,606	16%	4,912,371	16%	5,838,774	18%	9,616,509	20%	20,324,551	31%	26,139,582	36%	8.64%
Lower Middle Income	918,521	4%	1,137,002	4%	1,337,274	4%	2,179,330	5%	4,601,541	7%	5,820,363	8%	8.00%
Upper Middle Income	2,661,818	12%	3,776,431	12%	4,502,630	14%	7,438,380	16%	15,726,206	24%	20,319,219	28%	8.84%
High Income	18,876,079	84%	25,640,772	84%	27,352,382	82%	37,325,946	79%	45,004,571	69%	46,985,247	64%	3.87%

Exhibit 1.1 World gross domestic product trends 1990–2015 (World Bank, 2016)

	1990	%	1995	%	2000	%	2005	%	2010	%	2015	%	CAGR %
World	4,192	18%	5,216	18%	5,441	16%	7,306	16%	9,355	19%	10,433	19%	3.87%
East Asia & Pacific	2,753	12%	4,058	14%	3,762	11%	4,910	11%	7,233	15%	9,602	18%	5.34%
Europe & Central Asia	9,710	41%	11,970	42%	12,397	36%	19,078	42%	24,350	50%	24,147	45%	3.87%
Latin America & Caribbean	2,309	10%	3,586	13%	4,034	12%	4,523	10%	7,989	16%	8,939	16%	5.80%
Middle East & N. Africa	2,422	10%	2,422	9%	2,890	8%	4,169	9%	6,943	14%	8,207	15%	5.22%
North America	23,786	100%	28,312	100%	34,750	100%	45,132	100%	48,513	100%	54,217	100%	3.49%
South Asia	383	2%	382	1%	451	1%	701	2%	1,191	2%	1,533	3%	5.95%
Sub-Saharan Africa	599	3%	545	2%	505	1%	803	2%	1,281	3%	1,628	3%	4.26%
Low Income	293	1%	222	1%	230	1%	306	1%	502	1%	620	1%	3.17%
Low & Middle Income	808	3%	1,004	4%	1,133	3%	1,707	4%	3,315	7%	4,479	8%	7.40%
Middle Income	851	4%	1,072	4%	1,216	4%	1,846	4%	3,616	7%	4,925	9%	7.59%
Lower Middle Income	490	2%	519	2%	554	2%	858	2%	1,531	3%	2,035	4%	6.11%
Upper Middle Income	1,174	5%	1,607	6%	1,881	5%	2,881	6%	5,889	12%	8,186	15%	8.43%
High Income	18,619	78%	24,075	85%	25,619	74%	34,479	76%	39,538	81%	41,366	76%	3.38%

Exhibit 1.2 World gross national income (GNI) per capita trends 19910–2015

(World Bank World Bank website link, 2016)

Region/economy	1990	%	1995	%	2000	%	2005	%	2010	%	2015	%	25 Year CAGR %
World	2,196,997.5	100%	3,565,317.8	100%	7,488,448.9	100%	11,457,442.0	100%	20,189,655.2	100%	24,983,214.1	100%	10.66%
Developed economies	1,687,518.9	77%	2,711,005.6	76%	5,791,253.6	77%	8,565,673.5	75%	13,443,849.9	67%	16,007,397.6	64%	9.83%
Europe	932,445.9	42%	1,405,636.0	39%	2,466,198.8	33%	4,684,299.1	41%	8,171,968.4	40%	8,782,483.4	35%	9.80%
European Union	885,533.3	40%	1,329,453.7	37%	2,345,798.5	31%	4,426,957.0	39%	7,357,768.2	36%	7,772,955.8	31%	9.47%
North America	652,444.2	30%	1,128,907.2	32%	3,108,255.0	42%	3,456,620.1	30%	4,406,182.5	22%	6,344,007.3	25%	9.94%
United States	539,601.0	25%	1,005,726.0	28%	2,783,235.0	37%	2,817,970.0	25%	3,422,293.0	17%	5,587,969.0	22%	10.23%
Developing economies	509,469.9	23%	843,340.5	24%	1,644,214.9	22%	2,635,508.2	23%	6,042,537.7	30%	8,374,427.8	34%	12.37%
Africa	60,678.2	3%	89,316.2	3%	153,484.1	2%	282,574.5	2%	594,608.1	3%	740,436.4	3%	10.99%
Asia	339,675.0	15%	571,679.9	16%	1,027,613.7	14%	1,629,042.3	14%	3,876,875.9	19%	5,886,452.9	24%	12.62%
East and South-East Asia	301,718.9	14%	513,020.6	14%	927,585.3	12%	1,353,175.7	12%	3,016,308.5	15%	4,794,030.8	19%	12.21%
East Asia	240,078.6	11%	365,438.8	10%	695,043.1	9%	919,908.0	8%	1,872,155.4	9%	3,089,139.5	12%	11.23%
China	20,690.6	1%	101,098.0	3%	193,348.0	3%	272,094.0	2%	587,817.0	3%	1,220,903.0	5%	18.52%
Hong Kong, China	201,652.9	9%	227,532.1	6%	435,417.1	6%	493,894.7	4%	1,067,228.0	5%	1,572,605.8	6%	8.93%
Latin America and the Caribbean	107,187.1	5%	179,929.6	5%	460,982.5	6%	719,593.1	6%	1,554,060.3	8%	1,718,595.3	7%	12.26%
South America	74,815.4	3%	127,900.9	4%	308,949.5	4%	428,847.6	4%	1,080,750.5	5%	1,111,253.7	4%	11.90%
Central America	28,495.6	1%	48,392.8	1%	139,668.3	2%	263,158.1	2%	425,493.0	2%	533,182.0	2%	12.98%
Least developed countries (LDCs)	11,046.1	1%	18,722.5	1%	36,833.1	0%	75,520.6	1%	151,272.8	1%	266,046.8	1%	14.18%

Exhibit 1.3 FDI inward stock by region and economy 1990–2015 (UNCTAD, 2016)

Note: Totals exclude the financial centres in the Caribbean

6 *Global business*

integration and its effect has been continued and sustained growth in economies and per capita incomes. For those countries that have received large FDI inflows without the corresponding increase in economic performance, the fault lies not with globalization but with those local governments that are unable or unwilling to capitalize on the opportunities provided by economic integration. Now that we have debunked some primary arguments of the anti-globalization movement, we now turn to the primary focus of this book: success factors for globally active firms.

Global business: the balance of competitiveness and sustainability

Large market participants, such as the Norwegian Sovereign Wealth Fund, have increasingly made investment decisions based on how successful companies are in succeeding commercially while balancing growth with sustainability. Sustainability in our context is not simply an environmental concern, but it also must surely include considerations for product safety, consumer satisfaction, and consumer welfare.

The path to global market integration and commercial success is littered with pot-holes and occasional landmines. Sometimes initial smooth sailing for internationally active firms hits an unexpected resistance, such that it might appear that global economic participants are passengers on a rudderless ship. If the ship is truly without direction, then there is no need for a book such as this. If international expansion inevitably leads to tears, then there are no lessons to be learned from prior mistakes.

Problems in global business in part stem from the fact that global consumers tend to oscillate between desires for convergence and divergence. Convergence is defined as consumers desiring similar goods and services across the globe, while divergence is defined as local taste and preference differences globally. A world of convergence benefits multinational firms that sell similar products across the world. Exhibit 1.4 highlights the global consumer convergence spectrum that businesses face in the marketplace.

As some markets first experience the entry of global competitors, consumers may long for global convergence up until a tipping point is reached. When national cultural identities and institutions are threatened or replaced by the "global other", consumers may retreat into desires of divergence: localism, nationalism, and cultural identity. During these retreats into divergence, the palpable benefits of globalization are conveniently forgotten.

How long the tipping point between convergence and divergence is delayed is a focal point of this book. In some ways, information technology is a leveler in this world, but at the same time there is multiplicity in functional approaches. Within the functions of a global business, there are decisions concerning the level of local responsiveness that is appropriate, realizing that this often contrasts with organizational efficiency.

Exhibit 1.5 illustrates a classic model focusing on global efficiency versus local responsiveness and flexibility.

Global business

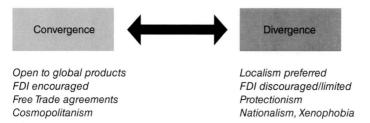

Exhibit 1.4 Global consumer convergence spectrum

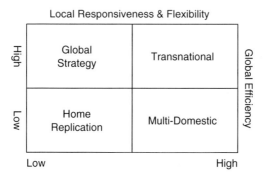

Exhibit 1.5 Global efficiency vs. local responsiveness (adapted from Bartlett and Ghoshal, 1991)

Global efficiencies are cost savings and other synergies created by operating in different foreign markets. Local responsiveness and flexibility concerns the level to which a firm can respond to the divergent needs of its various markets. Typically the two goals are mutually exclusive, however the model does reveal that transnational corporations can be more apt to achieve high levels of global efficiency while also attaining a high level of local responsiveness and flexibility than other strategic orientations.

Firms pursuing a **transnational strategy** attempt to maximize both local responsiveness and overall market integration by seeking the development and dispersion of innovation and knowledge within the entire network. Thus the multinational firm is seen as a network whereby each subsidiary is provided responsibility relative to its capabilities and strategic mission. The multinational's success is furthered by the movement of people within the firm that help facilitate the mutual development and dispersion of innovation and knowledge. In order to remain competitive, the transnational firm selects the strategic model that best fits the environmental pressures faced in order to remain competitive and successful.

Exhibit 1.5 shows that firms focusing on a **global strategy** typically achieve a high level of global efficiency but that the level of local market responsiveness tends to suffer relative to transnational corporations. For example, if a global business utilizes the global strategic orientation, then the typical mode of operation is to pursue market behavior that is successful in the majority of the

8   *Global business*

markets where a firm competes. If those markets are materially diverse, then this strategic orientation can be problematic.

Some global firms that operate in highly divergent markets may pursue the multi-domestic strategy. This option tends to score highly in terms of local responsiveness and flexibility, as the needs of each foreign market are taken into account by the firm when competitive strategy is designed. This approach may be best for firms operating in diverse markets, but there is an associated cost as the benefits of global efficiency are not achieved using this approach.

The final global strategic alternative depicted in Exhibit 1.5 is home replication strategy. This strategic orientation is often employed by firms that are newly global. Firms that are entering foreign markets in order to sell excess inventory abroad may not take the time to cater their marketing and competitive positioning relative to the foreign market environment. This strategic orientation tends to score low on both global efficiency and local responsiveness and flexibility. Unless the foreign market is highly convergent with the home market, this approach is often not successful and there are limited synergistic effects of expanding into global markets.

What should be clear from the preceding discussion is that the selection of foreign markets where a global business may compete goes a long way in determining which strategic orientation is most beneficial. If it is determined that selling a product or service will be most successful in highly divergent markets, then a transnational strategic orientation may be the best option. If a global business can remain successful operating in foreign jurisdictions which are not that divergent, then one of the other strategic alternatives may be acceptable, if only for a period of time. As global businesses gain successes in foreign markets, there will come a time when a tipping point is reached where the foray into divergent markets can no longer be avoided.

Exhibit 1.6 provides a framework for assessing the environmental pressures associated with whether a market is considered convergent (i.e. globally integrated) or divergent (i.e. when the desire for local responsiveness and flexibility is paramount for success).

Exhibit 1.6 links up well with the global consumer convergence spectrum exhibited in Exhibit 1.4. Consumers are individual reflections of the markets where they reside, so as the desire for differences in customer needs and tastes

Pressures for global integration		*Pressures for local responsiveness*
For strategic coordination	*For operating integration*	*AKA flexibility/divergence*
Importance of global customers	Scale economies	Differences in customer needs/tastes
Importance of global competitors	Pressure for cost reductions	Need for substitutes
Investment intensity	Homogeneous needs/tastes	Market distribution structures
	Technology intensity	Host government demands

Exhibit 1.6 Environmental pressures: local responsiveness vs. global integration (adapted from Prahalad and Doz, 1987)

increase, a global firm will fail to respond to this increased pressure for local responsiveness at their peril. If a given firm cannot adequately address the local market desires for distinction, then another competitor will fill the void.

It should be highlighted that the environmental pressures for operating in foreign markets can vary by the function of the business. Consider a situation where the consumer markets of a given set of foreign markets are relatively similar, but where other functional areas contain divergence. A **global firm** may find that from a marketing perspective there is pressure for global integration, but from an accounting perspective there is pressure for divergence. When viewed in a functional context, the strategic orientation of a globally active firm may be different depending on which function of the business (i.e. marketing, accounting, finance, human resources, operations, etc.) is being discussed. While strategic orientation is primarily devised at the overall company level, how the various functions of the business respond to the environmental pressures present in the market and in that functional reality plays a large role in determining which strategic orientation is selected.

Exhibit 1.7 provides a final view of strategic orientation for a global business. The term "multi-domestic" which appeared in Exhibit 1.5 has been updated to "multinational", and the term "home replication" has been updated to "international". The basic message conveyed in Exhibit 1.7 is that there should be a link between strategic orientation and how the assets and capabilities of the global business are utilized and increased.

How these linkages are developed by globally active firms depends on the results of what is known as the strategy formulation process. There are essentially three stages in this process, the first of which is for the company to identify its mission statement and the goals that it wishes to achieve. While this sounds like an innocuous step, it is here where the type of business sought after is defined and where the main objectives for the enterprise are elucidated.

MNC Type	Strategic Orientation	Assets and Capabilities
Multinational	Building flexibility to respond to national differences through strong, resourceful, and entrepreneurial operations	Decentralization and rational self-efficiency
International	Taking advantage of knowledge and capabilities of the managing parent company through world-scale expansion and adaptations	Centralization of sources of competitive capabilities, the rest is decentralized
Global	Achieving cost advantages through centralized operations with global reach	Centralization and global reach
Transnational	Developing global efficiency, international flexibility and world-wide learning simultaneously	Dispersion, interdependence, and specialization

Exhibit 1.7 The linkage of MNC types to strategic orientation, assets and capabilities (adapted from Bartlett and Ghoshal, 2003)

10 *Global business*

Stage two of the strategy formulation process involves firm identification of core competencies and value creating activities. In order to be successful in any market, businesses must identify their unique abilities and how they in fact win business from the competition. Once the scope is widened to include global markets, considerations should be made for environmental differences in the markets that they serve.

Stage three of the strategy formulation process deals with strategy formulation. It is here where the various strategies are decided such as those depicted in Exhibit 1.7. Strategies can be formulated at the corporate level, the business level, and the functional level. Corporate strategies often entail the depth and breadth of the lines of business offered by a given company. Some corporate strategies settle on the focus of a single business, while some corporations opt for the synergistic benefits received from offering a broader set of businesses. This alternative is known as related diversification, whereby a corporation sells products and services that are complementary to each other in an effort to gain economies of scale in production and service offerings. A third corporate strategy is known as unrelated diversification, which is often referred to as being a conglomerate. In this approach, rather than settling on the desire for scale and scope, the conglomerate pursues businesses which are unrelated in an effort to diversify their holdings and insulate the corporate from the whims of the global marketplace.

The second level of strategy formulation is at the business level. For each business pursued by the parent company, the goal here is to identify the appropriate method for achieving success in global markets. Business strategies could center on differentiation, whereby the firm sets itself apart from the competition via the quality or perceived value in the goods and services produced. One can quickly think of numerous industries where this strategy is utilized; anywhere from grocery stores selling higher quality organic produce, to boutique financial firms offering superior service than the average competitor. Another business strategic alternative is cost leadership. Firms opting for this approach seek highly efficient operations in an effort to reduce waste and eliminate redundancy throughout the company. Historically firms in Japan and China have been leaders in this space, but the desire for efficient production knows no geography. A third option for business strategy is for the firm to focus on specific products, groups of customers, or regions of the world in which to sell. Germany has achieved much success in exporting via this approach as the medium sized family owned companies (known in German as the "**Mittelstand**") have flourished by producing upscale typically very narrowly defined products to sell throughout the world. An example would be for something as unexciting as a fan that goes in the back of a refrigerator. The company could manufacture this small product for sale worldwide as a component part in the final product that sits in kitchens across the world. Unexciting but highly profitable!

The third level of strategy formulation is at the functional level. It is the goal of this book to provide strategic considerations for each of the functions of a

Global business 11

business. Chapter 2 provides discussion and analysis around the international marketing function, Chapters 3 through 5 consider competitive strategies in international finance, accounting, and taxation, Chapter 6 provides detail on international staffing and labor issues, and Chapter 7 provides thoughtful consideration for issues dealing with the management of global operations and technology. Each of these chapters highlights decision points related to each business function in light of the balance between competitive pressures and sustainability desires. In the 8th and final chapter, case studies will be presented to provide experiential learning of what was discussed earlier in this book.

Given the book's strategic orientation toward competitiveness and sustainability, each of the case studies in Chapter 8 concerns one or both of these important issues. In terms of cases focusing on competitiveness, "Attractiveness of Global Markets" provides readers with a practical framework for assessing competitive foreign market entry, while "Myanmar: the Last Global Frontier" allows the reader to recommend market entry strategies into Myanmar in the financial services sector. A third case study, "Increasing Market Share at Acme Industries," bridges the gap between competitiveness and sustainability as the firm has a decision to make about expanding from Taiwan into India which reflects on points affecting the competitiveness and profitability of the firm. A fourth case study, "Hedging with Foreign Exchange," provides a practical example of foreign exchange issues faced by global firms.

Some of the global cases in Chapter 8 focus on issues of sustainability. The "Lily Pharmaceuticals" case highlights the successes of a good corporate citizen; in this example, the questions raised refer to the tipping point of the convergence–divergence spectrum. Additional cases focused on sustainability issues include "International Real Estate Investor," which explores how perception differences in valuation and interest rate differences across markets can lead to different market dynamics, and "Cooperative Workforce Development: Public–Private Sustainable Linkages" provides a positive example of partnership creating a sustainable marketplace. Our final case study, "Privilege Capital," puts competitiveness and sustainability together as the reader is asked to explore mergers and acquisitions where the tightrope between global competitiveness and sustainability is now more important than ever.

Thematic definition of the field of international business

The role of international business teaching, despite growing in importance, has been viewed in partial isolation from the various functional areas of business teaching as necessary; however in the preceding two decades, swift and accelerated changes in global competition coupled with corporate leaders' needs for globally conversant managers have placed far-reaching demands on U.S. business schools to alter the curricula and provide for a competent level of international business proficiency.

Teaching within the field of international business embodies two major domains. First, the structural global dimension encompasses business transactions

12 Global business

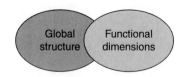

Exhibit 1.8 International Business teaching: The intersection of global structure and functional dimensions (Bear and Ajami, 1995)

involving two or more socio-political or economic factors and the environments which affect such transactions. The structural global dimension includes the global institutional framework of international business as well as economic, human and transnational environmental opportunities and constraints. This dimension also cuts across all the traditional "functional" areas of business as is shown in Exhibit 1.8.

Secondly, the functional dimension of international business focuses upon organizing and managing business operations and transactions. At a narrower level, the focus is upon the comparison of specific business functions such as marketing, finance, and accounting, among others. In addition, the field of international business addresses issues which are dramatically different in degree, if not kind, from the analogous issues in the national or domestic setting, where they raise central and crucial issues for business.

The comparative nature of international business functions allows academicians to judge the universality of theoretical models and conceptual frameworks. Given the complexity of international business environments and operations, it is perhaps not surprising that the field of international business does not operate within a single stable, overarching paradigm which singularly defines the issues for teaching and research. Indeed, the scope of international business is such that it draws upon, and attempts to integrate, the wide range of theory and conceptual frameworks derived from numerous other fields of business and non-business research.

Need for international business proficiency

A primary objective of international business teaching, which parallels the mission of the International Assembly of Collegiate Schools of Business (IACSB), is to sensitize students to the growing significance of the international dimension in business and to familiarize them with the differences and complexities which this dimension necessarily introduces into managerial decision making. Secondly, it is essential to place students' understanding of business theory and practice into a global and comparative context. The apparent success of some non-U.S. business practices and the potential to continuously improve U.S. corporate performance by learning from foreign competitors makes the international perspective in business teaching, more than ever, an indispensable requirement for excellence and relevance in business education.

This book is motivated by the increased level of global economic, political and social interdependencies and thus the need for students to gain a better understanding of the complexities of a global economy.

Discussion and conclusion

Economic viability and competitiveness are closely linked to the ability to understand and operate in a global economy. The international perspective in business teaching, more than ever, is an indispensable requirement for excellence and relevance in business education. It is laudable to underscore the many inroads made in international business proficiency and value-added professional development education, but it is equally vexing to address potential shortcomings of international business curricula.

Clearly, students face numerous challenges in preparing for careers which are dependent on corporate performance factors within a global economy. Global interdependencies whether in the areas of trade, investment, technology transfer, strategic alliance formation, or any other form of linkage are extensive. The U.S. is one of the leading world exporters, second only to China. In 2014, the U.S. exported $1.6 trillion in goods and services, just ahead of Germany at $1.5 trillion, and second only to China at $2.3 trillion. The successes of these three economies came in different areas, as the US has a competitive advantage in large capital goods and services, while Germany focuses on smaller, higher-end exports, and China continues to dominate the lower-priced product export markets.

The U.S. is also the largest single recipient of inward direct foreign investments among the highly industrialized countries; as of 2015, the U.S. figure stood at approximately $5.6 billion. In manufacturing as well as financial services, foreign profits account for roughly 50% of total income for a significant number of *Fortune*'s 500 list. In short, the unit of analysis is no longer the national economy but the international one. "America itself is ceasing to exist as a system of production and exchange separate from the rest of the world" (Reich, 1989).

Employers are beginning to question what value new recruits are adding to an organization and various industry leaders have been appealing to American business schools to train students with the requisite skills appropriate for doing business in a global marketplace. This book offers a fresh perspective on international business education focusing on how to engage in international business and offering case studies highlighting the successes and struggles associated with that effort.

Discussion questions

1 Explain in your own words the concerns raised by detractors of globalization and the benefits raised by its supporters.

14　*Global business*

2　Income inequality has been raised recently as a trouble spot for globalization. Does inequality of income matter if per capita incomes have risen owing primarily to global market integration? Take a position and defend your argument with supporting evidence.

3　Explain the global consumer divergence spectrum and provide examples of how multinational firms can avoid reaching the tipping point where foreign markets react unfavorably to a non-local company.

4　Define the primary types of multinational firms and list examples of companies that fit the strategic orientation shown in Exhibits 1.5, 1.6, and 1.7 of this chapter.

5　Describe the steps of the strategic formulation process. Explain how functional differences in a given company can influence the strategic direction chosen by the globally active firm.

Bibliography

Ajami, Riad A., and G. Jason Goddard. 2013. *International Business: A Course on the Essentials*, 3rd ed., M.E. Sharpe, Armonk, NY and London, England.

Ball, Donald A., Wendell H. McCulloch Jr., Paul L. Frantz, J. Michael Geringer, and Michael S. Minor. 2004. *International Business: The Challenge of Global Competition*, 9th ed., McGraw-Hill Irwin, New York, NY.

Bartlett, Christopher A., and Sumantra Ghoshal. 1991. *Managing Across Borders: The Transnational Solution*, Harvard Business School Press.

Bartlett, Christopher A., and Sumantra Ghoshal. 2003. *Transnational Management: Text, Cases, Readings in Cross-Border Management*, 4th ed., McGraw-Hill, Boston, MA.

Bear, Marcia, and Riad A. Ajami. 1995. International Business Teaching and Literacy: A Multidimensional Assessment, *Journal of Transnational Management Development* 1(4).

Daniels, John D., Lee H. Radebaugh, and Daniel P. Sullivan. 2004. *International Business: Environments and Operations*, 10th ed., Pearson Prentice Hall, Upper Saddle River, NJ.

Eun, Cheol S., and Bruce G. Resnick. 2015. *International Financial Management*, 7th ed., McGraw Hill Education, New York, NY.

Griffin, Ricky W., and Mike W. Pustay. 2005. *International Business: A Managerial Perspective*, 4th ed., Pearson Prentice Hall, Upper Saddle River, NJ.

Luthans, Fred, and Jonathan P. Doh. 2009. *International Management: Culture, Strategy, and Behavior*, 7th ed., McGraw Hill Irwin, New York, NY.

O'Sullivan, John. 2016. Special Report: The World Economy, *The Economist*, October 1.

Prahalad, C. K., and Yves L. Doz. 1987. *The Multinational Mission: Balancing Local Demands and Global Vision*, The Free Press, New York, NY.

Raab, Gerhard, Riad A. Ajami, Vidyaranya B. Gargeya, and G. Jason Goddard. 2008. *Customer Relationship Management: A Global Perspective*, Gower Publishing, Surrey, UK and Burlington Vt., USA.

Raab, Gerhard, G. Jason Goddard, Riad A. Ajami, and Alexander Unger. 2010. *The Psychology of Marketing: Cross-Cultural Perspectives*, Gower Publishing, Surrey, UK and Burlington, Vt., USA.

Reich, Robert B. 1989. As the World Turns, *The New Republic*, May 1: 23–28.

Shenkar, Oded and Yadong Luo. 2004. *International Business in an Age of Globalization*, John Wiley & Sons, Hoboken, NJ.

UNCTAD, FDI/MNE database, www.unctad.org/fdistatistics, accessed October 15, 2016.

Wild, John J., Kenneth L. Wild, and Jerry C. Y. Han. 2006. *International Business: The Challenges of Globalization*, 3rd ed., Pearson Prentice Hall, Upper Saddle River, NJ.

World Bank database, http://data.worldbank.org, accessed 18 Oct. 2016.

2 International marketing

> Misfortune can often be turned to good account if men are sufficiently alert in assigning cause.
>
> (John Kenneth Galbraith)

Chapter objectives

This chapter will:

- Review the key elements in creating and maintaining a viable marketing mix in the international business arena.
- Contrast the views of product standardization and product differentiation, and which types of products best benefit from local adaptation.
- Discuss the issues surrounding the question of centralized versus decentralized marketing management in a worldwide market.
- Discuss the major marketing mix decisions: product, promotion, pricing and distribution within the international business context.

What must be done: the international marketer's dilemma

Marketing is one of the most important areas of operation for multinational corporations. With the internationalization of business, MNCs face increased competition at home from both foreign and domestic competitors and internationally as the MNC seeks to enter new markets. In developing a competitive strategy, firms utilize the marketing process to identify, create and deliver products or services that are in demand and that customers are willing to buy. When performed successfully, the marketing process identifies profitable areas in which resources should be focused, increases sales revenues, generates profits, and creates a long-term, sustainable, competitive advantage for the MNC. When performed inadequately, the results can be disastrous.

The basic marketing-mix decisions consist of four separate but interconnected functions. These are the **four Ps of marketing**: **product, price, promotion**, and **placement**. Companies satisfy consumer needs by developing and manufacturing the goods desired in that market; educating potential clientele

International marketing 17

regarding the existence and qualities of those products; assuring that product cost is balanced between quality and price; and ensuring that adequate volumes of products are distributed to sales outlets or customers in a timely fashion.

While these marketing sub-functions are complex enough on the domestic level, internationalization significantly increases their complexity. Foreign markets are not only physically removed but also differ culturally. Specific cost structures in the foreign market may dictate special pricing, distribution channels found in the domestic environment may be unavailable in the foreign market, portions of the product may need to be modified to meet local tastes, and promotional methods may need to be adjusted to local media. Thus, every single function of the marketing mix may require modification, or at least fine-tuning, in order to do business in the foreign locale.

International marketing entails operating simultaneously in different environments, coordinating these international activities, and learning from the experiences gained in one country to make marketing decisions in other countries. The international marketing firm must make important strategic global decisions about what to sell in which markets. Thus, the company requires huge amounts of accurate and timely information on the nature, economic condition, and consumer needs of the foreign market. The company must understand the conditions of the foreign market, and the competitive movements of other firms operating in that environment. As a result, the MNC must rely heavily on conducting appropriate and accurate assessments to determine whether these potential markets will prove profitable despite the added costs.

To centralize or decentralize: the first key decisions

In developing a successful international marketing program, a firm must make several key decisions about its prospective strategy in world markets. Two crucial issues are:

1 Whether or not the marketing program can or should be standardized across all markets or adapted individually to each separate market.
2 Whether marketing should be centralized in company headquarters or decentralized to individual market locations or foreign manufacturing subsidiaries.

It may be human nature that prompts management to attempt to standardize the marketing function throughout the world, because it greatly simplifies the complexity of marketing and probably provides significant cost benefits to a firm. Selling the same product throughout the world achieves greater efficiencies and scale economies in many areas of operation. Production runs can be longer, thus lowering unit costs. Research and development expenses normally required to adapt the product to each foreign market can be eliminated. Specific creative work required for adapting advertising and promotional campaigns for

18 *International marketing*

the foreign market are not required, nor are specialized sales training programs. Pricing standardization obviates the need for calculating different prices in individual markets.

The major drawback of standardization involves the risk of market loss by not being attuned to individual differences in consumer tastes or local behavior. This cost is difficult to assess, and it is only through definitive, exhaustive market research that a firm can determine whether its standardized marketing program is losing customers.

In general, the question of standardization or adaptation is related to the nature of the product or service. Industrial products sold to other firms or businesses or to governments can be sold relatively unchanged throughout the world. Dynamic random access memory chips (DRAMs), for example, are an important part of the personal computer and are in standard use in the manufacture of computers in the United States, Europe, Japan, and Southeast Asia. In contrast, consumer goods, including such items as automobiles, furniture, and clothing, are tied intricately to personal taste preferences or fads and require more adaptation.

Deciding the degree of standardization also relates to the degree of comparative differences between the two environments in their cultures, physical attributes, institutional infrastructure, and political and economic composition. The greater the degree of difference between a foreign market and the domestic marketers, the more likely it is that the attributes or promotion of a product are inappropriate. For example, although there are distinctive differences between markets in the United States and Canada, products would be more likely to pass unchanged from one to the other, which would be far less true if the two cultures differed significantly, such as the United States and Nigeria.

Similarly, firms must make decisions about the planning, implementation, and control processes involved in their world marketing programs. Should programs be created, developed, and implemented from headquarters, or from onsite subsidiary locations, where personnel are aware of and understand the differences between marketing environments? Proponents of decentralized marketing functions would argue that the advantages of subsidiary involvement in the process are that the local personnel are more familiar with the characteristics and problems of the local target markets and would be better suited to adjusting the marketing mix to suit those necessities and to solve problems. Detractors of this recommendation point out that the MNC, by having a decentralized program, would lose control of the program and that overall corporate costs would be increased through replication of activity in various subsidiary markets.

The pattern that generally emerges is somewhere between these two extremes. Most multinationals have a combination of marketing programs that are, to some degree, both centralized and decentralized, which ensures that the company has control over activities within the subsidiary and the ability to formulate a global marketing program where warranted. It can also pinpoint

International marketing 19

those areas where it is possible to standardize portions of its marketing program across markets. By the same token, however, input from subsidiaries is crucial if the firm is to develop effective marketing programs in individual foreign target markets.

The organizational structure that evolves finds the headquarters of a multinational enterprise taking responsibility for developing the company's philosophy and overall strategy, developing products and product strategies, name brands, and packaging. The foreign subsidiary, on the other hand, takes advantage of invaluable onsite experience and information to tailor the promotion, distribution, and pricing of the product so that it meets the needs or characteristics of the market. When such an intertwining of responsibilities between the headquarters and the subsidiary is created, it is crucial that there be ongoing communication between the two parties. In this way, the MNC can maintain control over its subsidiary's operations and institutionalize efficiencies between headquarters and subsidiaries as well as between the subsidiaries themselves.

Typically, organizations decide among three alternatives regarding their marketing plans: ethnocentric, polycentric, and geocentric. The first alternative is **ethnocentric**. This approach is exhibited when a firm markets its goods and services in foreign markets using the same marketing mix that is used in the domestic markets. This strategy is more often successful when there is very little cultural difference between the home and foreign markets. While this is the least costly of the three alternatives, this approach is risky in markets where there are large cultural differences when compared with the home market of the organization. Sometimes, firms attempt the **polycentric** approach in their marketing mix. These firms attempt to customize the marketing mix in each market in an attempt to meet specific needs of customers in each market. While this strategy could be successful if the company competes in foreign markets with varied cultures, it is the most costly approach of the three alternatives given the customization in each market. The third alternative is the **geocentric** approach. This entails the standardization of the marketing mix, which allows a given firm to offer the same product or service in different markets, and to use essentially the same marketing approach to sell the product or service globally. The difference between this approach and the ethnocentric approach is that the standardized model used in all markets may not necessarily be the same as what had been used in the home market. This approach, which is followed by such companies as Coca-Cola, creates huge economies of scale. But the approach is not without some risk, as if the wrong choices are made in the process of standardizing the marketing approach, the effect of the marketing campaign could be lower than if some customization was offered throughout the areas where the MNC competes.

Perspective 2.1 International grocery store example

The results of varying marketing efforts are easily viewed by consumers in an internationally oriented grocery store. Some products have packaging and a targeted audience for one particular ethnic group, while others have a wider scope. Students are encouraged to visit an international grocery store and to photograph examples of each marketing strategy (i.e., ethnocentric, polycentric, geocentric). Students should then prepare a written assignment pertaining to how the items seen in the grocery store relate to this chapter. If a portion of the next class is used to review these examples, students will be better able to differentiate between the various global marketing strategies. This small exercise helps illustrate that international marketing is everywhere, even in your home town.

Product decisions

When most people think of products, they think of things or services for sale by companies. The physical product as we know it, however, is actually only part of the total product. The total product is the entire package of the physical product and includes its type and form, its brand name, instructions for use, accessories, and even the level of after-sales service. These attributes of the total product help determine the image that the product develops among consumers and the value it provides to purchasers.

Desired product attributes vary among users in different cultures or countries. For example, one classic study conducted on consumer attitudes regarding product attributes of soft drinks found that French, Brazilian, and Indian college students found it important that the drinks not contain any artificial ingredients, while students in the United States ranked taste and availability through vending machines as more important.

There are two general classes of products marketed domestically and internationally: industrial products and consumer goods. Industrial products are goods sold to manufacturing firms, businesses, or governments and include such durables as steel, hardware, machinery, parts, electronic components, and other equipment. Industrial goods tend to be more universal in specifications and are consequently far more frequently standardized than consumer products. Consumer goods, on the other hand, are purchased by a large number of individuals who may vary drastically in their needs and tastes. These goods are frequently mass-merchandise items, including clothing, luxury goods, food products, appliances, and automobiles. Because of differences in taste, such goods far more often require adaptation to personal preferences, differences in culture, education levels, or even fads or fashions within countries than do industrial products.

Product-positioning decisions

The decisions regarding the positioning or development of a product in different markets depends on three crucial factors: the individual characteristics of each market and the environment in which the product will be sold; the functional need for the product (or the use to which it will be employed) in the market; and a company's financial requirements and its competitive position in that foreign market.

The environment of each market can have a profound effect on the optimal product characteristics in that locale. The type of product marketed can be affected by the legal, economic, social, cultural, and physical forces of the targeted market. For example, types of products sold are definitely affected by the physical characteristics of a country, such as geography, terrain, and climate. Automobiles sold in tropical climates, for example, would be less likely to require rust-proofing than those in snowy climates where roads are salted.

Economic forces similarly help determine which products are appropriately marketed in foreign markets, especially if they are tied to levels of economic development. For example, it would be foolish to attempt to market electric-powered products in countries that do not have sufficient or reliable sources of power. Relative income levels and standards of living in each market determine, to a very large extent, the nature of consumer needs in that country, as well as the consumers' definition of appropriate price and product quality. Thus, a marketer must be sure to correctly identify those needs so that the product is not overly sophisticated or is mismatched in other attributes. For example, products such as snack foods, which enjoy high-volume sales in industrialized countries, might be considered luxury goods in a less-developed country and would not find a ready market.

Cultural or sociological forces also have a profound effect on the appropriateness of products in different cultures. In a country with high illiteracy rates, it would, for example, be unwise to package products so that the goods could not be determined easily from photographs on the labels, but care must be taken not to confuse individuals with these illustrations. Take, for example, the experience of a baby food manufacturer that attempted to sell its product in an African nation by using the same label it used in other markets. The label showed a picture of a baby with the type of food spelled out on the jar. Sales were, of course, abysmal, because local consumers interpreted the labels to mean that the jars contained ground-up babies.

Other products are affected by different traditions. For example, package sizes must be smaller in markets in which there is little refrigeration and shopping is done on a daily basis. Some products literally do not suit foreign tastes and must be made saltier or sweeter or offered with different condiments. French fries, for example, in the United States are served with ketchup; in Great Britain, "chips" are served with vinegar. Similarly, brand names may be affected. In Asian markets, such as Taiwan, a very popular brand of toothpaste used to be named "Darkie," but such a brand name would definitely find

22 International marketing

disfavor in American markets, where consumers are conscious of the use of any sort of racial stereotyping.

Even colors hold different meanings in different cultures and must be considered for suitability in product designs. Red, for example, connotes richness or wealth in some countries, but may be considered blasphemous in some African countries. While black symbolizes death or mourning for Americans and Europeans, white has the same connotation in Japan and other Asian nations.

Many products are evaluated by consumers in light of their country of origin. Indeed a great deal of research has been conducted on this topic by a number of marketers. This research has shown that products from Eastern Europe, for example, are seldom rated as being stylish, whereas products from France or Germany are expected to be well-designed.

Different markets have different legal criteria and standards for products. Some of these are standards for safety and content purity. Others have differing requirements regarding labeling. For example, in some countries all contents must be indicated on the package or the source of the contents must be delineated. Other countries may have limits on the types or sources of goods imported into the country, or restrictions regarding the use of brand names or the recognition of copyrights from other countries.

Through an exhaustive analysis of these attributes of foreign market environments, the marketing program can determine the appropriate mix of products for each foreign market. This mix is the variety or assortment of products offered in each quality and price. Thus, a firm might have several established lines that it markets in different locations according to the local needs and desires.

In determining the appropriate product line, a firm also takes into consideration the position of the product in its life cycle. For example, a consumer good in the stage of maturity for domestic home markets may be ripe for introduction into a new market that lags behind home markets in development, but would be expected to behave similarly over time.

Product strategies

A multinational corporation has three different alternatives in targeting the foreign market. It can either extend its product line, or adapt or create an entirely new line of products for the market.

In **product extension**, a firm markets the same products abroad as it does at home, in the expectation that tastes and demands are similar enough to guarantee consumer acceptance. This product strategy is generally used when research determines that crucial characteristics of the domestic and international target markets are similar.

In **product adaptation**, a firm modifies its existing product line to take into account the cultural, legal, or economic differences between domestic and foreign markets. For example, product colors might be switched, electrical

International marketing 23

specifications might be modified to accommodate different voltages, or measurements might be changed to the metric system. Automobiles sold in countries where motorists drive on the left side of the road, such as England and Japan, must be adapted to a right-hand drive.

The third product strategy is **product creation**, specifically for a targeted international market. The product might be within a firm's area of expertise, but is not included in its existing product line. For example, a form of transportation used in Barbados and other Caribbean nations and tropical locales is the moke, a vehicle that resembles a cross between a jeep and a golf cart. This gasoline-powered vehicle is open to the elements but is smaller than conventional vehicles, seats four, and is perfectly suited to the needs of tourists for transportation over short distances on narrow island roads.

Once a firm has made the crucial decisions regarding the appropriate product mix, it needs to decide what message should be communicated about that product and how it should be delivered in its new markets. A firm has many alternatives regarding the content of its **promotion message**. It can either *extend* its message from existing markets or *adapt* its message to the target market, which yields a scenario of five different overall product and promotion strategies for the international enterprise. Their use depends on the features of the product, its expected benefits for buyers, its expected functional use, and its competitive position against other products. These five methods are product extension/message extension; product extension/message adaptation; product adaptation/message extension; product adaptation/message adaptation; and new product.

The easiest method is marketing the same product with the same message. This method of **product extension/message extension** works well when there are few differences between domestic and foreign markets and the product is used for the same purposes. It is also the most profitable, because no additional expenses are incurred for adaptations to individual market areas. Examples of this type of strategy are those used by soft drink manufacturers in world markets who are marketing the same product, a nonalcoholic beverage, which is used for the same purposes, quenching thirst.

In some instances, a firm might market the same product in a foreign target market, but that product may be used for a different function or purpose, and the message regarding its attributes must be adapted for the target market. In such a **product extension/message adaptation** strategy, a company merely changes the message communicated to its consumers. For example, goods that might be considered luxury items used to pursue leisure activities in one market might be necessities in another. For example, bicycles, motor scooters, and cross-country skis might be touted for leisure use in one country, but as being vehicles of basic transportation in another.

In **product adaptation/message extension**, the product is changed but the message is extended. This strategy is effective in markets where the product serves the same functional use but under different environmental conditions, where products must be slightly adapted to suit local tastes. Examples are fast

24 *International marketing*

foods that require different menus or recipes, or vehicles with different tires designed to suit the physical conditions of roads in different markets. This strategy has the advantage of establishing a consistent product image across markets and standardization of the communication message with its associated cost savings.

In **product adaptation/message adaptation**, both the product and the message are changed to meet conditions in foreign target markets where both the characteristics of the market and the use of the product differ from those in domestic spheres. Because the product is put to a different use in the foreign market, it follows that its message differs from that used at home. Under this strategy, however, the firm may still realize some cost benefit in using the same basic research and development or production costs if several of the product attributes are similar.

Developing a **new product** specifically for new markets generally requires communications designed specifically to suit the international market. Sometimes, however, the firm may be able to extend a message if the product developed is serving a slightly different function but one similar to its domestic product line. While this new product strategy is the *most expensive* to follow, it may ultimately yield success in the form of high sales because the firm has developed a product that meets the needs of customer in the target market.

Promotion decisions

As with product decisions, the development of appropriate promotional efforts raises the question of standardization or adaptation. **Promotion** involves reaching potential consumers and providing them with information on the product's existence, attributes, and the needs it satisfies. The **promotional mix**, which includes advertising, personal selling, and sales promotions, must create a relationship between a firm and its customers, as well as enhance long-term sales potential and consumer confidence in the product and the firm. Naturally, the more this promotional program can be standardized, the greater the potential savings to the firm because of achieved efficiencies.

Once a firm has established its target market and defined its characteristics, it then decides on its communications message and which promotional tools and media will be most effective in communicating that message. Great care must be taken to ensure that the content of the message is appropriate to different cultures. Mistakes in this area, such as inappropriate brand names or advertising copy, are very expensive, embarrassing, and unfortunately, all too frequent. For example, General Motors attempted to market its Nova (literally "star") automobile in Mexico without considering that the name when spoken could be interpreted as "*nova*," which means "*no go*" in Spanish. Similarly, Coca-Cola experienced difficulties in China in attempts to market its product under a brand name designed to be the equivalent of the English pronunciation of "Coca-Cola," but the Chinese characters translated literally into "bite the wax tadpole."

Perspective 2.2 Cross-cultural advertising mistakes

The marketing blunders mentioned above are only the tip of the iceberg. The student of international business will also find these examples to be both humorous and educational:

- When Kentucky Fried Chicken entered the Chinese market, to their horror they discovered that their slogan "finger lickin' good" came out as "eat your fingers off."
- When Pepsi entered the Chinese market a few years ago, the translation of their slogan "Pepsi Brings You Back to Life" was a little more literal than they intended. In Chinese, the slogan meant, "Pepsi Brings Your Ancestors Back from the Grave."
- But it's not just in Asian markets that soft drinks makers have problems. In Italy, a campaign for "Schweppes Tonic Water" translated the name into the much less thirst quenching "Schweppes Toilet Water."
- The American slogan for Salem cigarettes, "Salem – Feeling Free," got translated in the Japanese market into "When smoking Salem, you feel so refreshed that your mind seems to be free and empty."
- Things weren't any better for Ford when they introduced the Pinto in Brazil. After watching sales go nowhere, the company learned that "Pinto" is Brazilian slang for "tiny male genitals." Ford pried the nameplates off all of the cars and substituted them with "Corcel," which means horse.
- Sometimes it's one word of a slogan that changes the whole meaning. When Parker Pen marketed a ballpoint pen in Mexico, its ads were supposed to say "It won't leak in your pocket and embarrass you." However, the company mistakenly thought the Spanish word "embarazar" meant embarrass. Instead the ads said "It won't leak in your pocket and make you pregnant."
- Foreign companies have similar problems when they enter English-speaking markets. Japan's second-largest tourist agency was mystified when it expanded to English-speaking countries and began receiving requests for unusual sex tours. Upon finding out why, the owners of the Kinki Nippon Tourist Company changed its name. The company didn't change the name of all its divisions though. Visitors to Japan still have the opportunity to take a ride on the Kinki Nippon Railway.
- When Braniff translated a slogan touting its upholstery, "Fly in Leather," it came out in Spanish as "Fly Naked."
- Coors put its slogan, "Turn It Loose," into Spanish, where it was read as "Suffer From Diarrhea."

26   *International marketing*

- The Dairy Association's huge success with the campaign "Got Milk?" prompted them to expand advertising to Mexico. It was soon brought to their attention the Spanish translation read "Are you lactating?"
- Scandinavian vacuum manufacturer Electrolux used the following in an American campaign: "Nothing sucks like an Electrolux."
- Clairol introduced the "Mist Stick," a curling iron, into Germany only to find out that "mist" is slang for manure.
- An American T-shirt maker in Miami printed shirts for the Spanish market which promoted the Pope's visit. Instead of "I Saw the Pope" (el Papa), the shirts read "I Saw the Potato" (la papa).

Promotional tools

The tools used in promotion include advertising, personal selling, sales promotions, publicity, and public relations.

Advertising methods are similar around the world, primarily because they are based on those developed in the advertising industry in the United States and focus on print, television, and radio advertising. The actual advertising programs may differ, however, because they are directly connected to reaching consumers by addressing their specific cultural values and needs. Where possible, international firms attempt to standardize their advertising in order to achieve savings. Some companies, for example, create a logo that is used internationally, such as McDonald's golden arches.

While companies may wish to develop an advertising program that can be carried across borders, they must be attuned to differences between cultures in order to reach the proper market and deliver the appropriate message. In Japan, for example, more earthier advertisements have been permitted than in the United States, and television and print advertisements include bathroom humor and sexual frankness, such as topless models. Similarly, products banned from being advertised in the United States are advertised in Japan. Imagine the shock of a Westerner encountering explicit ads for such products as tampons, laxatives, hemorrhoid medicines, toilet bowl cleaners, and condoms.

Similarly, an international promotion planner must be apprised of the availability of different types of media in each market. A television campaign suitable for markets in developed countries, where many people own sets, would not reach many potential consumers in poor, developing countries where TV sets are rare. Countries also vary in the availability of their print advertising sources and radio programming and the number of stations. Thus, advertising programs must be developed with the assistance of someone knowledgeable about the available advertising channels in the overseas market. This person helps to identify appropriate media for use in each country and avoid potential problems and mistakes because of cultural insensitivity to the meaning of colors, symbols, and nonverbal and verbal messages being delivered to the buying public. For example, in India owls do not connote wisdom as they do in the United States; they indicate bad luck. In land-poor and urban Hong Kong, consumers could not identify with the Marlboro man's riding the range on horseback. Adaptation of the copy showing him as a stylized urban cowboy with a pick-up truck was found to be far more relevant to consumers.

Onsite resources can also prevent companies from choosing inappropriate media. For example, billboards cannot be used in parts of the Middle East, not because of cultural considerations, but merely because under local weather conditions an outdoor advertisement would last less than two weeks.

Personal selling

Another promotion tool used by international marketers is that of personal selling, where individual salespeople communicate the qualities and characteristics of the products to prospective customers. The use of **personal selling** by firms depends on a number of factors. One of these is product type. Generally personal selling is used more for industrial products, which are purchased by agents for companies or governmental concerns in larger numbers, than for consumer products, which rely on mass merchandizing to stimulate high volumes of sales. An exception is Avon, which has successfully used its own version of personal selling to promote the sale of its lines of cosmetics, fragrances, jewelry, and gifts to customers around the world.

The use of personal selling also depends on the resource characteristics of the target country. In some nations where the costs of labor are low, firms might find it more cost-effective to employ hundreds of sales representatives than to buy expensive and limited air time on a federally controlled television station or attempt to reach a highly illiterate consumer population through media advertising. Still, the use of personal selling may be difficult or impossible in other countries, where street addresses or doorbells are not to be found or where such intrusive hard-sell methods are not welcome.

Even with personal selling, firms attempt to standardize their programs by using the same training programs and recruiting for their sales forces around the world. Indeed, some firms attempt to establish an international sales force in the hope of achieving strategic advantages over competitors. For example, Steelcase Inc., a multinational firm and distributor of office furniture head-quartered in Grand Rapids, Michigan, has trained its global sales force using the same basic program with only slight modifications to accommodate differences between countries. The company believes that this training provides for a uniform sales culture and the generation of additional business opportunities, such as approaching sales prospects working for multinational firms at several locations at the same time. For example, if a sales representative for Steelcase (office furniture) meets with a multinational's purchasing officer for the domestic location, the representative's counterpart can be meeting simultaneously with equipment buyers for the firm's foreign subsidiaries in

28 *International marketing*

overseas locations. An added benefit to the firm is that a consistent training program allows Steelcase to integrate its sales approaches and strategies and coordinate sales activity around the globe.

Sales promotions

Sales promotions are those activities pursued by a firm in an attempt to generate interest in the company's products, greater levels of sales, and enhanced distributor effectiveness. Some of the most popular promotional efforts are those that involve contests or sweepstakes. Other promotions include company sponsorship of sporting or cultural events or participation in trade shows. Sales promotions also come in the form of cents-off coupons on company products, in-store samples and demonstrations of products, and point-of-purchase displays designed to catch the attention of shoppers.

As with the other tools of the promotional mix, these efforts may be constrained by foreign legal requirements, such as limitations on premium amounts and prior government approval of discounts. Some countries may not allow companies to give free gifts. Other constraints may come from the sociocultural aspects of the target market. For example, it may not be worth a company's effort to attempt to stage store demonstrations if the product is sold to consumers in small rural markets rather than in supermarkets. Still, sales promotions may be effective in those markets that have limited opportunities for utilization of the other promotion tools.

Publicity and public relations

Publicity and **public relations** refer to a firm's relationship with entities in its markets other than the buyers of its product, which include non-consuming members of society as well as agents from the various arms of government. Public relations programs are put in place to allow the company a method of communicating about itself, not merely about its products. Thus, public relations departments generally communicate with the press about the activities of the firm, including work with consumer groups and corporate charitable programs, such as scholarship programs or dollar contributions to local charities.

Pricing decisions

Pricing is crucial to the success of any marketing program. An overpriced product may fail to attract customers, and an under-priced product may lower profitability. Pricing must therefore be carefully balanced to achieve the optimum level of sales and revenue. The optimum level can, of course, depend upon the corporate objective, which can vary from maximizing profit to maximizing market share.

Thus, a company may wish to lower prices in order to achieve maximum competitiveness or market share in individual markets, or it may wish to see high prices and, in turn, higher sales revenues figures on its balance sheet. In other situations, a company might be concerned about the relationship between prices charged and taxes payable in high-tax countries. Therefore, an international corporation must review and establish its pricing policies in light of overall short-term and long-term strategic objectives. Consequently, price-setting is customarily carried out as a function at corporate headquarters.

Pricing is a difficult part of the international marketing mix to administer because of its complexities. While a firm may prefer to charge the same price for its goods in all markets, the differences between these markets frequently indicate a need to set different prices in different locales. For example, a company determines an appropriate price for its goods as they are exported across borders. This price may not be appropriate, however, for goods produced by offshore subsidiaries because of differences in relative costs of labor and resources, competitive forces, governmental regulations, and even market strategies. A firm, therefore, would pursue a course where goods are priced according to the exigencies of the local markets, not on an international basis.

Pricing methods

An international marketer considers several crucial factors in determining the appropriate price structure. These factors fall into three general categories: the strategic objectives of the firm, the costs involved in the production of goods, and the competitive forces interacting in the market in relation to consumer demand. The goal of the multinational firm is to develop a competitive pricing structure that will provide for both short-term and long-term profitability, as well as for some flexibility to allow for individual differences between markets.

Cost-based pricing methods

Some pricing methods begin with production costs as a determination point. In **cost–plus pricing**, an additional amount is added to the cost of production to determining appropriate pricing at the next level of distribution. The cost-plus method has the advantages that it is simply administered once all related costs of production are identified. It does not, however, take into account the competitive environment in which the goods are to be sold.

Determination of costs is often also achieved through the use of **average cost pricing**, in which the firm identifies both the variable and fixed costs of production. Variable costs are those that vary with the levels of production. For example, labor or raw materials used in the manufacture of goods are variable costs, while fixed costs are those that do not change regardless of production levels. Some fixed costs are rent, plant and equipment, and basic overhead costs. Through an examination of its cost structure, a firm can determine its average variable costs and average fixed costs to determine a total cost figure upon which prices can be based according to expected levels of production.

30 International marketing

Another easy method of price-setting is using **target return levels** in setting prices. In this method, a company wants to achieve a specific return level in relation to costs or to the original investment. Thus, a fixed percentage or level of monetary return is added to the total costs of the product to determine its ultimate price.

The pricing of goods produced for export must also take into account added costs from their being produced in one country and transported to another. Price escalation in the context of exports refers to the additional costs associated with the movement of the goods from the domestic manufacturer to the foreign consumer, which involves several intermediaries. The escalation occurs because at each level a percentage markup is taken against not only the original factory price, but the aggregate of all markups as well.

These cost-based pricing methods have the distinct drawback of being focused on *short-term objectives* and of *being inflexible*. They are often not integrated into a strategic plan and may or may not provide for a company's long-term benefit by providing for future expenses. For example, cost-based pricing may cover research and development prior to a product's introduction, but it may be insufficient to fund ongoing research essential to the future strength of the company. In addition, such a pricing program may not allow the firm or subsidiary the flexibility necessary to meet the demand or competition in the market.

Demand is, in fact, an important determinant of appropriate prices to be charged in various markets because in market economies, especially for interchangeable commodities, it is the market that ultimately sets the price or value of goods to consumers. The elasticity of demand in relation to income is an important characteristic of markets. Similarly, demand is affected by the prices charged for goods. Some products are highly sensitive to price, and an increase can result in an equal or larger decrease in demand. Other products are not price sensitive and experience no changes in demand regardless of price shifts. It is important, therefore, for international marketers to have a feel for the competitive relationship between prices and demand in foreign marketing environments in order to determine appropriate price levels.

Many firms price their goods entirely in relation to the prices charged within the market by competitors, which is especially true for smaller companies that follow the moves of the market leaders in **oligopolistic markets**, where a few large firms hold the largest portion of the market for certain goods or products. Other firms meet competitive challenges by using factors other than prices, such as offering exemplary service or stressing other attributes of the total product package.

Many firms price their goods entirely in relation to the prices charged within the market by competitors, which is especially true for smaller companies that follow the moves of the market leaders in oligopolistic markets. Other firms meet competitive challenges by using factors other than prices, such as offering exemplary service or stressing other attributes of the total product package.

Some firms use pricing in order to achieve strategic or marketing objectives, de-emphasizing the importance of production costs in setting prices. For example, some firms attempt to reap high profits from their markets; they set high prices for new products to cash in on their novelty value and the fact that competitive products are not yet available. Alternatively, the firm may use pricing to gain market penetration at the expense of profits. In this method, the firm intentionally keeps prices low in order to capture large portions of the market, allowing room for increasing prices once its position is firmly entrenched in the foreign market. Care must be taken in using this approach to avoid being charged by countries with trade actions based on accusations of dumping or predatory pricing.

Dumping, which is considered an unfair trade practice, occurs when exporting nations purposefully under-price their goods for foreign markets only to displace domestic competition and gain market share, with the ultimate objective of raising prices when that position is well established. Dumping pricing differs from market-penetration pricing in that it is lower than the price the exporter charges for the same goods in its own markets or is less than the costs of production.

Transfer pricing

Transfer pricing is a specific concern of multinational firms with production facilities and subsidiaries in many different parts of the world, and is the determination of appropriate prices to be charged between different branches of the same firm that are conducting business between each other. This basic problem with these *intra-company transfers* is one of conflicting objectives by supplier subsidiaries and recipient subsidiary branches. The supplier wishes to charge the branch operations the same price it charges other purchasers in order to boost sales revenues and profit determinations on its balance sheet. By the same token, manufacturing subsidiaries receiving the goods also wish to put their balance sheet in the best light and look for the lowest possible cost for input resources or goods, and greater flexibility in using costs to determine competitive prices in local markets.

Four typical methods of assessing costs in transfer pricing are:

1   Charging the subsidiary buyer for the direct manufacturing costs in order to cover all production costs for the transferred goods.
2   Charging the subsidiary buyer cost-plus-expenses to adjust for production and fixed costs in the manufacture of the goods.
3   Charging prices in accordance with those the subsidiary buyer would pay for the same goods in local markets.
4   Charging the subsidiary buyer according to arm's length, that is, quoting the subsidiary buyer the same price as for all customers. This method has the advantage of dispelling any suspicions that a firm is using pricing policies for any other purposes than for accounting properly for the transfer

32   *International marketing*

of goods and materials between different operating units of the same enterprise.

The objectives of the individual operating units in transfer pricing must also be considered in light of overall multinational corporate objectives. For example, a firm might want to support operations in specific locales by holding costs down until a certain level of market coverage or penetration is reached. In this case, a firm would direct that the transfer prices to the subsidiary be held to a minimum. Transfer pricing may also be used to achieve other objectives, such as shifting revenues from countries with high taxes to those with low taxes. For example, if a parent company in a high-tax country charged low prices on input goods for a subsidiary in a low-tax country, it could realize higher income in the second country and pay less tax, while keeping expenses high in the country with high tax rates. This practice may be illegal in some countries, as in the United States, where suspicion of the use of transfer pricing for tax evasion can lead to the Internal Revenue Service challenging a company's tax returns and determining tax liability using arm's length pricing.

Transfer pricing can also be used to circumvent restrictions by foreign governments on the repatriation of profits to the multinational parent or on the convertibility of currencies into the currency of the home country. In these situations, the parent artificially hikes the prices of transferred goods for the subsidiaries and their payment of these "costs" are happily received by a third arm of the company in a different location. Similarly, transfer pricing can be used to lower profits to avoid government pressure to reduce prices. Profits can be lowered to avoid concessions to the demands of labor to share in company profits.

International pricing is also affected by other factors in world markets. One major force is that of governmental power overpricing that is exercised in order to achieve national or economic objectives. To achieve goals such as economic or production growth, nations sometimes intervene in the pricing process by levying duties or tariffs on goods and services entering their country and, in turn, raising their cost to importers. For example, in Canada, tobacco products are heavily taxed in an effort to curb consumption. Canadian government estimates conclude that 70% of the price of a carton of cigarettes in Canada is due to the taxation of the product. The Tobacco Act of 1997 mandates that wherever cigarettes are sold, there must be information on the packaging that clearly describes the hazards associated with the use and the emissions from the product. This is typically done via graphic pictures on the package and the store displays.

Producers of goods within countries also might face government intervention in pricing through the establishment of price freezes, price subsidies, floors or ceilings on prices, or artificial limits for goods considered as satisfying basic or fundamental needs of the populace.

A second problem encountered by firms that vary their pricing procedures according to prices set by differing markets is that of **gray market exports**, which are situations where individuals or entities take advantage of a firm's pricing policies that account for market variations in demand and acceptable prices. With gray market exports, goods are legally imported from the producing country into another country, and then are **re-exported** to a third country where higher prices are charged for the same goods. Thus, because of pricing differences by the original firm, the exporters of the second country can compete successfully with the MNC in selling its own goods in foreign markets. These gray markets exist in many industrialized countries where currencies are strong and markets for goods are large. In the United States, for example, gray markets flourish in foreign-made consumer goods, such as watches or cameras.

Setting prices can also be affected by legal constraints in individual countries. In the United States, under the terms of antitrust laws, price-fixing or the administration of prices is illegal, but legal restrictions in other nations may differ on prices administered nationally or internationally.

Placement decisions: distribution of products

The importance of placement

The marketing function of distribution involves the critical process of ensuring that the products of a firm reach the proper location for sale at the proper time and in proper quantity. Breaks in the distribution flow can have critical ramifications, in the form of disgruntled customers, spoiled or damaged goods, excessive costs, and lost sales.

Thus, the type of product being transported determines the appropriate method of distribution and choice of channel. For example, one of the companies of United Technologies manufactures refrigerated transportation containers for fresh produce in which temperatures must remain constant, or importers are faced with receiving, say, instead of bananas, a shipment of imported brown mush.

Distribution decisions are also of critical importance because they are often long-term in nature, involving the signing of contracts with transporters or equipment leasers or the development of expensive capital equipment or infrastructures, such as rail lines, wharfs, ports, docks, and loading facilities.

This process, difficult in domestic markets, grows more complicated in international environments because it has two stages. First, the international exporter must transport goods from the domestic production site to the foreign market, then they must establish methods of distribution for the goods within the foreign country.

Numerous players within distribution systems are required to get goods to market. The **distribution chain** begins with the producer of the goods and then generally flows through an intermediary in the form of a wholesaler or distributor, who in turn provides the retailer with his goods for sale. Other services provided in the distribution of goods are storage facilities, transportation

34 International marketing

to markets via rail, truck, barge, or plane, and insurance services for those goods being carried between nations.

This relatively simple scenario becomes much more complicated with the addition of the international component, at which point other people enter the act to facilitate these exchanges. There are **freight forwarders**, who see to the details of international transportation, and exporters and importers, who conduct their international trading as either agents or brokers. Sometimes these individuals take title to the goods and trade them on their own behalf (**merchant middlemen**); alternatively, they represent the firm's interests and arrange for the distribution of goods for a fee (**agent middlemen**). Other players in the distribution game are **resident buyers** who work in foreign markets to acquire goods, and **foreign sales agents** who sell a product line in international markets. These classifications are augmented by such entrants in the process as **export management companies**, which provide distribution services for firms under contract; buyers for exports, who actively seek merchandise for purchase by the principals they represent; and selling groups, such as those established in the United States under the terms of the **Webb-Pomerane Act** to promote trade. Some agents specialize and focus primarily on barter or counter-trade agreements with non-market economy countries. Further down the chain, key players are those who deal directly with customers, such as a sales force, door-to-door salespersons, individual merchants, and the customers themselves.

Factors involved in distribution decisions

Distribution choices depend on several factors. One is the nature of the product. Is it perishable or fragile or a product that will require after-sales service? Might it be better distributed by an authorized company dealer? Another consideration is the degree of control over distribution. Greater control over the distribution process requires greater involvement by a firm in terms of time, money, and energy.

Another factor is costs. Whatever mix a firm wishes to employ may be constrained by the availability of middlemen or channels of distribution, by physical limitations imposed by the characteristics of the country, or by infrastructural deficiencies in the country, which limit types and methods of usable distribution modes. In some countries foreign firms do not have access to all distribution modes, as in Japan, where the distribution system is controlled predominantly by **sogo shosha**, enormous general trading companies that control much of the import and export trade (e.g. Sumitomo, Mitsubishi, Toyota Tsusho, and Mitsui).

The choice of a distribution program is also constrained or defined by the nature of the outlets for goods or services, and nations differ quite extensively in these frameworks. While some countries, such as the United States, have a variety of small and large retail outlets, other countries, such as Japan, have an enormous number of mom-and-pop retail outlets, which provide Japanese customers with individualized service. In France, a U.S. cosmetics company made a strategic mistake by assuming that its products would be appropriately distributed through a chain store's sole rights to distributorship. Its assumption was wrong, because in France cosmetics are traditionally distributed by perfumers, small retailers who specialize in cosmetics and are considered the ultimate arbiters of fashion.

The developmental level of a nation also affects its distribution resources and networks. A lack of refrigerated methods of transportation will limit the marketing for frozen goods or fresh produce. Similarly, income levels might support the air-freight delivery of live lobsters in rich countries, while poorer countries rely on slow delivery by boat of less-exotic foodstuffs.

Distribution decisions can be even more complex in less-developed countries where distribution channels are dominated by specific ethnic groups within the country. This control, called **ethno-domination**, means that a multinational firm must be aware of and gain access to the members of the distribution channel in order to get its goods to retail outlets. Examples of ethno-domination are the Chinese ethnic groups who control the wholesale trade of vanilla and cloves in Madagascar, rice distribution and milling in Vietnam, retail trade in the Philippines and Cambodia, and poultry and pineapple production in Malaya.

The standardization debate on international marketing strategies was raised in the 1960s among members of the marketing community who put forth that the world was developing into an enormous global market where few differences existed between consumers from various countries in their tastes, standards of living, and buying behavior. Others discovered, however, that crucial differences between countries militated against such globalization of markets and the standardization of the marketing function. Exhibit 2.1 outlines obstacles to standardization in global markets.

Indeed, many have found that standardization efforts are foiled primarily by the vast diversities among consumers in world markets. Indeed, there may be a class of world consumers that consists of well-traveled and sophisticated people who are receptive to universal advertising and global themes. Still, this group of consumers is very small and the majority of consumers, internationally, varies enormously in their national identities, tastes, preferences, languages, and cultural environments. Thus, all facets of the marketing function are susceptible to failure because of improper attention to the differences between markets that are caused by differences between cultures.

Obstacles to standardization in international marketing strategies

	Elements of marketing program	
Factors limiting standardization	*Product design*	*Pricing*
Market characteristics		
Physical environment	Climate Product use conditions	
Stage of economic and industrial development	Income levels Labor costs in relation to capital costs	Income levels
Cultural factors	"Customs and tradition" Attitudes toward foreign goods	Attitudes toward bargaining
Industry conditions		
Stage of product life cycle	Extent of product in each market	Elasticity of demand
Competition	Quality levels	Local costs Prices of substitutes
Marketing institutions		
Distributive system Advertising media and agencies	Availability of outlets	Prevailing margins
Legal restrictions	Product standards Patent laws Tariffs and taxes	Tariffs and taxes Antitrust laws Resale price Maintenance
Elements of marketing program		
Distribution	*Sales force*	*Ads & promotion* *Brand & Packaging*
Customer Mobility	Dispersion of customers	Access to media Climate
Consumer shopping patterns	Wage levels, availability of manpower Attitudes toward selling	Need for convenience rather than economy Purchase quantities Language, literacy Symbolism
Availability of outlets	Need for missionary sales effort	Awareness, experience with products
Competitors' control of outlets	Competitors' sales forces	Competitive expenditure messages
Number and variety	Number, size,	Extent of self-service
Ability to "force" distribution	Effectiveness of advertising, need for substitutes	Media availability, costs, overlaps
Restrictions on product lines	General employment restrictions	Specific restrictions on messages, costs
Resale price maintenance	Specific restrictions on selling	Trademark laws

Exhibit 2.1 Obstacles to standardization in global markets

Summary

The basic marketing functions of the four P's: product, pricing, promotion, and place (distribution), are similar for both domestic and international marketing. Because of the complexities and differences of cultural, legal, and political environments, international marketing becomes much more complex. Two crucial decisions facing the international marketer are the extent to which products are standardized or adapted to meet the needs and wants of the local consumer, and whether international marketing programs should be centralized or decentralized. Industrial products are more easily standardized, while consumer products generally require adaptation to meet local preferences. Management of international marketing programs tend to rely on corporate headquarters for overall strategy, research and development, brand names, and packaging, with the foreign subsidiary developing locally sensitive pricing, promotion, and distribution strategies. Extensive ongoing communication between headquarters and the foreign subsidiary, however, is crucial to effective coordination of the marketing program.

Five product-promotion strategies can be adopted to market the same product, an adapted product, or a totally new product using the same message or an adapted message specially designed for the foreign market.

While advertising methods are relatively similar throughout the world, actual promotional campaigns must be adapted to meet the product characteristics, cultural environment, and media availability in foreign markets. Personal selling programs may be standardized, however, while other promotion tools, such as sales promotion and publicity, require adaptation to the local environment and must be responsive to legal constraints.

Various pricing methods, such as cost-plus and target-return can be used, but consideration of long-term strategic objectives of MNCs and applicable governmental regulations should also be included in the development of an international pricing strategy. Distribution channels, their availability and limitations in different locations, and the extent to which the marketed product requires follow up servicing and support can create a wide degree of variability when developing an international distribution policy.

Discussion questions

1 What are the four Ps of marketing?
2 How does international marketing differ from solely domestic marketing?
3 What are the advantages of a standardized marketing strategy? What are the disadvantages?
4 What types of products are best suited to standardization?
5 How does the total product differ from the physical product?
6 Discuss the basic strategies through which multinationals introduce and promote products in a foreign market.

38   *International marketing*

7 Discuss the four major tools used in promotion. What are the types of concerns of an advertising manager in the MNC home office when developing a promotion strategy?
8 What is cost-plus pricing? Average cost-pricing?
9 How can transfer-pricing costs be assessed within a multinational corporation?
10 What factors should be considered when making distribution decisions?

Bibliography

Buzzell, Robert D. 1968. "Can You Standardize Multinational Marketing?" *Harvard Business Review* (November/December): 74.

Darlin, Damon. 1980. "Japanese Ads Take Earthiness to Levels Out of This World." *Wall Street Journal* (August 30): 11.

Douglas, Susan P., and Yoram Wind. 1987. The Myth of Globalization. *Columbia Journal of World Business* (Winter): 19–29.

Essential Action, http://www.essentialaction.org/tobacco/intro/funny.html, accessed April 3, 2017.

Flynn, Brian H. 1987. The Challenges of Multinational Sales Training. *Training and Development Journal* (November): 54–5.

Foxman, Ellen R., Patriya S. Tansuhaj, and John K. Wong. 1988. Evaluating Cross-National Sales Promotion Strategy An Audit App, well. *International Marketing Review* (Winter): 7–15.

Health Canada, https://www.canada.ca/en/health-canada/services/health-concerns/tobacco.html, accessed July 18, 2017.

Green, Robert T., William H. Cunningham, and Isabella C. Cunningham. 1975. The Effectiveness of Standerdized Global Advertising. *Journal of Advertising* 4: 25–30.

Jain, Subhash C. 1989. Standardization of International Marketing Strategy: Some Research Hypotheses. *Journal of Marketing* (January): 70–79.

Jain, Subhash C. 1990. *International Marketing Management*, 3rd ed., Boston: Kent.

Jain, Subhash C., and Lewis R. Tucker Jr. 1986. *International Marketing: Managerial Perspectives*, 2nd ed. Boston: Kent.

Kahler, Ruel. 1983. *International Marketing*, 5th ed. Cincinnati: South-Western.

Keegan, Warren J. 1969. Multinational Product Planning: Strategic Alternatives. *Journal of Marketing* (January): 58–62.

Leavitt, Theodore. 1983. The Globalization of Markets. *Harvard Business Review* (May/June): 92–102.

Muskie, Edmund S., and Daniel J. Greenwood III. 1988. The Nestle Infant Formula Audit Commission as a Model. *Journal of Business Strategy* (Spring): 19–23.

Nagashima, Akira. 1970. A Comparison of Japanese and U.S. Attitudes Toward Foreign Products. *Journal of Marketing* (January): 68–74.

Nagashima, Akira. 1977. A Comparative "Made in" Product Image Survey among Japanese Businessmen. *Journal of Marketing* (July): 95–100.

Peebles, Dean M., and John K. Ryans. 1984. *Management of International Advertising: A Marketing Approach*. Newton, MA: Allyn & Bacon.

Quelch, John A., and Edward J. Hoff. 1986. Customizing Global Marketing. *Harvard Business Review* (May/June): 59–68.

Reierson, Curtis. 1967. Attitude Changes Toward Foreign Products. *Journal of Marketing Research* (November): 385–387.

Ricks, David A. 1983. *Big Business Blunders: Mistakes in Multinational Marketing.* Homewood, IL: Dow Jones-Irwin.

Ryans, John K. Jr. 1969. Is It Too Soon to Put a Tiger in Every Tank? *Columbia Journal of World Business* (March/April): 69–75.

Samiee, Saeed. 1987. Pricing in Market Strategies of U.S. and Foreign-Based Companies. *Journal of Business Research* (February): 17–30.

Simmonds, Kenneth. 1985. Global Strategy. Achieving the Geocentric Ideal. *International Marketing Review* (Spring): 8–17.

Simon-Miller, Francoise. 1986. World Marketing: Going Global or Acting Local? Five Expert Viewpoints. *Journal of Consumer Marketing* 3(2): 5–7.

Terpstra, Vern. 1985. *International Dimensions of Marketing*, 2nd ed. Boston: Kent.

Appendix
A Checklist for export marketing

In this appendix, a classic example of questions to consider when developing an export marketing program is presented. While the original intended user of this checklist was American businesses, the questions are applicable in most situations today.

Market potential

Segmentation
- Are the ultimate consumers American tourists or foreign citizens?
- Are we tapping the burgeoning middle class in industrialized nations?
- Are our customers the wealthy elite in the underdeveloped countries?
- Are our buyers affiliates of our company?

Size of market
- How long is the sales potential?
- What volume could be sold at higher/lower prices?
- What sales potential do we estimate for the next few years?

Special opportunities
- Would differential pricing be noticed, and be objectionable?
- Do prices abroad fluctuate seasonally?
- Could some particular price policy foster trust and long-term relations?
- How does the delivered price relate to other elements of the marketing mix?

Marketing mix

Individualizing and adaption
- Should our product be modified (simplified or embellished) to increase its suitability for foreign markets?

International marketing 41

- How should we position our product to gain for it the appropriate level of price perception?
- Could special packing or packaging enhance the value of our product?
- Would freight, customs duty, and so on be substantially lower for separate components to be assembled abroad?
- Is assembly abroad less expensive than in the United States?

Reducing the buyer's risk
- Does our price include warranty service?
- How quickly and assuredly are spare parts available?
- Might feasibility studies cause our product to be specified?
- In the country of destination, at what stage of the product life cycle is our offering?

Buyer-Seller relationship
- How closely can we estimate what the buyer is willing to pay?
- What is our reputation for quality and commercial integrity
- Have we avoided misunderstandings about measurement units such as "ton" and commercial terms such as "CIF" (cost, insurance and freight)?
- Should our quotation include a cushion for later price concessions?

Channel
- At what point in the distribution process is our price compared with those of competitors?
- How many middle agents are in the distribution chain, and what functions do they perform?
- Can we reduce the cost of distribution?

Foreign market environment

Degree of market control
- Is the price of our commodity determined through market institutions?
- How closely do we control the availabilities and prices of our line at the point of final sale?

Foreign attitudes
- How important is price in the purchasing decision?
- Is the prevalent business philosophy "low turnover–big markup"?
- Are high-priced goods subject to special tariff surcharges?

42   *International marketing*

- What is the business culture with respect to haggling, price-fixing, and boycotting the price-cutters?
- Are price deals effective?
- In what ways are we affected by any foreign laws in margins, prices, price changes, inter-company pricing, and the "most favored customer clause"?

Competition

- In our line, how active is worldwide competition?
- Are the competitor's quotations valid?
- Is our price level encouraging foreign imitators?

Some alternatives

- What do we learn from foreign competitor's prices about manufacturing opportunities abroad?
- Have we considered licensing as an alternative to selling?
- Could multilateral transactions in foreign exchange of foreign merchandise make our product's final price more attractive?

Cost considerations

Commercial risks

- What are the costs and risks of submitting a foreign quotation?
- Could our exported merchandise be shipped back to the United States and interfere with our domestic marketing?

Incremental costs

- Are foreign orders absorbing idle capacity?
- Are we disposing of excess inventory?
- Does potential foreign business warrant expansion that captures economies of scale?
- Are we pricing a product line, a single product, or a one-time opportunity?
- Have we separated our variable and fixed costs?
- Do foreign orders require special production changes, extra shifts, or other costly adjustments?
- What are the differential marketing & administrative costs of selling abroad?
- What is the total impact of export sales on our costs?
- How closely does the country of destination enforce its antidumping laws?

Special risks and opportunities

- Have we costed out all possible modes of transportation?
- Do our costs include insurance on our goods until we receive payment, even if the purchaser insists on insurance coverage?
- Do our credit terms reflect various risks: (a) commercial, (b) inflation, (c) currency exchange rate, (d) blocking of remittances, (e) expropriation, (f) interest rate fluctuations?
- Do export sales offer any tax advantages?
- What is our profitability mix between original equipment and spare parts, initial order and reorder?

Administrative considerations

Internal organization

- What are our objectives in international business?
- What are our specific goals with respect to the present quotation?
- Who (title and location) is authorized to quote a binding price?
- What intra-firm conflicting interests regarding international marketing must be resolved?
- Do our affiliates in different countries compete against each other?

Price policy

- What is our basic price policy (such as same FOB factory price to everyone)?
- What is our stance toward competition: price higher, same, lower, ignored?
- How flexible are we: to accommodate good customers, meet competition, offset new duties or changes in currency values?
- How important is foreign business for us?
- Could our foreign involvement harm our image domestically?

Procedures

- Have we ensured compliance with applicable U.S. laws?
- Do we use standard forms for preparing quotations?
- Do our quotations have a time limit?
- Do we formally review quotations accepted and rejected?

44   International marketing

Intra-company policy

- Is pricing a legal means of repatriating earnings?
- Are we permitted to avoid foreign customs duties through high prices on raw materials and low prices on finished goods?
- What is the influence of our intra-company pricing on income taxes in the United States and in the country of destination?
- Are we quoting "arm's length" prices to our affiliates?

Source: S.C. Jain, International Marketing Management, 3rd. ed., Boston: Plus-Kent © 1990. Reprinted by permission.

3 International finance

To abjure money is to abjure life.

(George Orwell)

Chapter objectives

This chapter will:

- Emphasize the importance of managing working capital within the multinational corporation.
- Outline the development of the international capital markets, Euromarkets, and the international equities markets.
- Describe techniques for dealing with inflation, taxes, and blocked funds.
- Present sources of capital for financing MNC operations.

Financing international business

The financing of international business operations is a far more complex, tricky, and challenging task than managing the finances of a domestic business. Several additional considerations and factors that affect finances come into play when a business goes international. Many of these factors are positive ones, for example, newer, larger, and more flexible sources of financing and access to a greater variety of financial instruments for more efficient use of financial resources. On the other hand, financial operations become subject to a variety of new constraints and risks. The task of financial managers in international business, therefore, becomes a twofold operation: minimizing the risks to the finances of a company, and maximizing the utilization of the new opportunities presented by the international environment.

Working capital management

In an international business, the management of working capital has several imperatives in addition to the traditional requirements. In domestic selling

46 *International finance*

optimal working capital management requires the following: the availability of liquid resources in adequate amounts to meet due obligations; management of the timing of the flow of financial resources, accelerating the inflow of receivables and lagging the outflow of payables; and maintaining an optimum level of liquid cash in order to minimize the occurrence of idle balances.

Maintaining an effective amount of working capital is essential for companies of all sizes, but may be even more important for small, growing companies participating in the international arena. Exhibit 3.1 illustrates the effects that management of the trade accounts (accounts receivable, accounts payable, and inventory) can have on the working capital needs of a hypothetical small business.

As you can see from Exhibit 3.1, the hypothetical example maintains the same levels of annual revenues and annual cost of goods sold, so that the effect of the cash conversion cycle can be illustrated. The **cash conversion cycle**

Paradorn, LLC	Year 1	Year 2	Year 3	Year 4	Year 5
Cash Conversion Cycle (Days)	**37**	**72**	**145**	**13**	**6**
		All Rise	Stale Inventory	Lead A/R	Lag A/P
YE Sales	$1,500,000	$1,500,000	$1,500,000	$1,500,000	$1,500,000
Daily Sales	$4,167	$4,167	$4,167	$4,167	$4,167
YE COGS	$750,000	$750,000	$750,000	$750,000	$750,000
Daily COGS	$2,083	$2,083	$2,083	$2,083	$2,083
Inventory	$125,000	**$200,000**	**$350,000**	$125,000	$125,000
YE Accounts Receivables	$175,000	**$250,000**	$175,000	**$75,000**	$175,000
YE Accounts Payables	$135,000	**$175,000**	$135,000	$135,000	**$200,000**
Inventory Days (COGS)	60	**96**	**168**	60	60
Accounts Receivable Days (Sales)	42	**60**	42	**18**	42
Accounts Payable Days (COGS)	65	**84**	65	65	**96**
Required Working Capital	**$77,500**	**$150,000**	**$302,500**	**$27,500**	**$12,500**

Exhibit 3.1 Effect of trade account movements on working capital needs for a small business

International finance   47

for a business is the length of time (usually expressed in days) between the purchasing of raw materials until the receipt of cash after the finished goods have been sold. The length of days in the cash conversion cycle is calculated as follows: *inventory days on hand + accounts receivable days on hand − accounts payable days on hand*. The shorter the length of the cash conversion cycle, the less working capital needs to be financed from outside of the company's operations (and the more working capital can be generated internally). In the example above, the required working capital for each year is determined by multiplying the daily amount of cost of goods sold by the number of days in the cash cycle. So, the required working capital for year one is calculated as: $2,083 ⋆ 37 = $77,071 (which is rounded up to $77,500). In the second year, the required working capital almost doubles when the cash conversion cycle moves from 37 days to 72 days. The required working capital more than doubles from year two to year three, as the cash conversion cycle moves from an average of 72 days to an average of 145 days. Year 4 is an example of how accelerating the inflow of accounts receivable can significantly reduce the required working capital borrowing need, while year 5 is an example of how lagging the outflow of payables can achieve similar benefits in terms of the amount of working capital that is required to be financed outside the operations of the business (this of course assumes that the creditors of Paradorn, LLC do not sever their business relationship with this small company!).

In addition to these basic factors, several other considerations come into play when working capital requirements of an MNC spread across several countries. The first factor is the availability of the appropriate currency. Unlike a purely domestic business, an MNC can have short-term financial obligations falling due in several currencies at its different locations around the globe. The financial manager, therefore, must decide between maintaining liquid reserves of the needed foreign currencies or moving the currencies in the spot exchange market, or, if it is available, making necessary arrangements through the forward exchange market.

The requirements of financing in different currencies to meet short-term obligations can also be met by borrowing locally in the different money and financial markets. These options generate the consideration of whether the option of borrowing locally is better than taking a covered position in the forward exchange market. In other words, a choice has to be made between a money market hedge and an exchange market hedge. The decision will depend on several factors, primarily the expected level of exchange rate fluctuation and the interest rate differentials and their expected reliability.

The presence of exchange risk and the risk tolerance of the international corporation are other crucial variables that impact on the management of working capital across national boundaries. **Exchange risk** will depend on the foreign currency liabilities created by a firm that are not matched by offsetting transactions. How a firm chooses to determine its level of tolerable exposure and how it deals with it depends largely on the internal policy of the firm. Attitudes vary considerably in this respect. Several firms will spend considerable

48 *International finance*

time, effort, and money at minimizing their exposure to currency fluctuations. On the other hand, many firms prefer to take the risk exposure and hope to profit from favorable currency movements. This latter approach is more speculative.

The necessity to manage working capital over a wide geographical base is another major challenge faced by international financial managers. In a multifaceted organization with financial centers located in different cities, there is a need to coordinate the financial position of different offices, which is vital to secure the optimum utilization of company funds and avoid unnecessary costs because of idle funds or short-term borrowing.

Management of working capital in different countries also implies the necessity of ensuring a relatively smooth transfer of funds, both within and outside the corporation. There are distinct possibilities that unexpected hurdles may arise because of government restrictions, exchange controls, or other political risk-related factors that may prevent funds from reaching their destination on time. Moreover, these considerations also influence fundamental financing decisions, such as whether to bring funds from the home country, a third country, or to raise resources locally. Although modern technology has made almost instantaneous transfer of funds around the world fairly easy, there are still the possibilities of problems, because of inaccurate messages, incorrect codes, and transit system failures. It is clearly more difficult to ensure the reliability of international financial technology in a wide range of countries, some of which are not advanced technologically.

Another challenge that confronts international managers is taxation. Taxation laws vary between countries and are often fairly complex. Moreover, in several countries there are frequent major changes in tax laws that could adversely affect the management of working capital, which is run on a fairly tight basis and which has little room for maneuvering. Moreover, different tax laws often require that transactions be structured in such a way as to minimize tax liability and achieve the lowest possible post-tax financing costs.

Intra-company pooling

Intra-company pooling is a financing technique that seeks to optimize the total availability of resources on a worldwide or area-group basis. A multinational corporation is likely to have several offices, each of which generates income and incurs expenditures and, therefore, has either operational surpluses or shortages of financial resources at any given time. The advantages of this technique are obvious. The surplus funds held with one office or subsidiary of a company would essentially be idle, because they are not utilized in production. If intra-company pooling is effective, the corporate financial headquarters or regional control centers will know the exact locations of surpluses and shortages. With this knowledge available at a centralized point, instructions can be sent to move funds from the surplus to the deficit locations, which evens out the imbalances. Considerable cost savings are achieved

International finance 49

because the idling of funds is avoided and the need to borrow funds at interest is obviated. Consider an example of a company with one branch in Manila, the Philippines, and other in Cairo, Egypt. The corporate headquarters of the company, located in Phoenix, Arizona, keeps a constant eye on the funds position of the overseas offices. In the course of business, it is possible that one of the branches, say Manila, is saddled with surplus funds of $300,000, while the Cairo branch finds itself confronted with a short-term deficit of $250,000. In the absence of intra-company pooling, the Manila funds would be idle for perhaps a month, while the Cairo branch would have to borrow $250,000 for a month, which could be at a rate of 10% per annum, or as much as $2,083 in interest charges monthly. If, however, the Phoenix headquarters can monitor this situation, they can arrange for the Manila branch to remit $250,000 to the Cairo branch, reducing the former's idle funds and saving the interest charges of the Cairo branch.

Another strategy that corporate headquarters can devise, at their level or at that of a regional center especially designated for this purpose, is a policy that requires all surplus balances of the different branches and offices of a company to be maintained at a particular central place. Several benefits accrue from such a strategy. First, the different locations minimize the size of their resources and are in fact saved from the effort involved in utilizing them productively. Moreover, adequate opportunities for remunerative investments of short-term funds may not be available in many branch locations.

Centralized pooling of additional resources, therefore, can be located at centers where there are wide opportunities for short-term investments at competitive terms. Such centers would have the necessary liquidity for absorbing sizable investments without any significant effect on market conditions. Pooling of surplus balances at one location also creates personnel economies because this task is consolidated at one point and can be managed more efficiently with fewer staff than if it was managed at several locations. Further, expertise in funds management can be concentrated at one point and used effectively, and funds from many branches would contribute toward sizable volume at the central location, reducing transaction costs and increasing the possibility of securing better returns on short-term investments.

Centralizing the management of funds reduces to some extent the political risk associated with assets held in overseas locations. The MNC is able to move funds to a safe location before a restriction comes into effect. As a result, the total volume of funds exposed to an impending or even possible government restriction on repatriation is substantially reduced. The centralized management of funds makes it possible for the corporation to devise and implement a global financial strategy that ties into the overall strategy for achieving the global corporate objectives.

Global coordination and pooling of intra-company transactions is, however, not free from problems. Transferring funds out of certain countries is subject to exchange and capital controls and may, therefore, not be possible at all. Moreover, many countries have differing laws that could levy a tax on even the

50 *International finance*

temporary repatriation of funds from the country. Also, devising and installing an efficient and versatile global electronic communication and funds transfer system, generally through a multinational financial institution, is quite expensive, both in terms of initial and recurring costs (service, rental, and maintenance). A corporation has to clearly weigh the expenses against the potential benefits of such an arrangement. Usually only large companies with locations in different parts of the world find it economically viable to establish intra-company funds transfer and management systems.

Even those companies that find the establishment of an intra-company funds transfer system viable must take several other measures to make the system cost effective. Costs involved in intra-company transactions can be considerable, and reducing them can add significantly to the company's bottom line. Minimizing transaction costs can be achieved by reducing the number of individual transactions through the consolidation of small transactions. Alternatively, offsetting arrangements can be made for different branches of the company, and only the residual balances need to be actually transferred through the system. Transaction costs can also be reduced by using more efficient and cost-effective means of funds transfer, such as online transfers through major banks.

Hedging against inflation

Dealing with inflation in different countries calls for active working capital management policies. High inflation tends to erode the value of receivables, but also lessens the burden of payables in real terms. When inflation is expected to rise, plans are made for local receivables to be delivered at the earliest possible date. **Leading** is the technical term for the early receipt of goods. Conversely, an MNC would tend to delay its payables. The policy of creating deliberate delays with respect of outflows or inflows is called **lagging**. Centralized cash management systems also help in the corporate efforts to minimize the inflationary erosion of liquid assets by permitting their transfer to locations where there are lower inflation rates and expectations.

Managing blocked funds

Blocked funds are generally those resources of overseas entities that are not allowed to be repatriated, at least temporarily, by national governments. Blocking of funds can take place for a number of reasons. A government may face difficulties in its balance of payments, which would bring down the available resources of foreign exchange. In order to optimize the use of limited resources, a government may block repatriable funds of overseas entities and limit foreign exchange to financing essential imports and other payments. Occasionally a change of government can lead to an across-the-board blocking of funds usually repatriable by overseas entities, which could be motivated by political considerations of discrediting the former government

International finance 51

or overturning its policies. In specific cases blocking may occur if a particular overseas corporation fails to comply with certain local regulations or requirements or is considered politically to be working against the best interests of the host nation.

Blocking can take various forms. At one end the host currency is deemed nonconvertible and repatriation of any funds is ruled out. Other forms of blocking would involve repatriation of only a portion of the funds, repatriation only after a certain time lag, a combination of restrictions on the percentage of assets to be repatriated and the time constraints, absolute ceilings on the total quantum of funds that can be repatriated over a certain time period, pre-approval requirements for repatriation of funds, and special conditions placed on companies seeking repatriation.

Techniques for dealing with blocked funds

EXPORT ORIENTATION FOR MULTINATIONALS

Because the basic rationale for nearly all decisions and regulations that block funds is the shortage of foreign exchange, many MNCs seek to address host country concerns by developing an export orientation that would create foreign exchange inflows that offset the outflows because of the repatriation of assets. Thus, many MNCs whose primary business is production, sales, or services for the domestic market tend to divert some of their production to other foreign markets, thereby earning foreign exchange for the host country. In some instances, MNCs who do not produce exportable goods in the host country use their international marketing prowess, through their branches and affiliates abroad, to market goods produced by other manufacturers in the host country. Some MNCs, in fact, go so far as to start new export-oriented product lines either through their existing company or through another local subsidiary. The export earnings achieved are surrendered to the national authorities, who, in turn, unblock MNC funds, which can be repatriated.

SUBSTITUTION OF FRESH INVESTMENTS

Many MNCs substitute blocked funds for fresh investments from abroad. If funds are not allowed to be repatriated, a company often uses them to meet local expenses connected with fresh investments, either in new projects or the expansion of existing ones. These funds are used in some instances to defray the ongoing expenses that arise in the course of day-to-day operations. This utilization is tantamount to repatriation, in as much as funds would not be required to be remitted from the head office. In some countries, such adjustments are prohibited and firms must bring in additional resources of foreign exchange from abroad if they wish to make new investments in startups or expansions. In the case of investments where the company is bringing advanced and new technology to the country, however, authorities tend to

52 International finance

take a more lenient view and permit such arrangements. Such companies usually face fewer restrictions on repatriation of their funds.

NON-FORMAL TECHNIQUES

MNCs very often use informal means to secure repatriation of blocked funds. One important way is the exertion of pressure on the host government through diplomatic channels. At other times pressure is exerted through the home government of the parent company on the host government. Occasionally, MNCs seek to influence host governments through their own governments at a time of negotiations for aid programs or other economic agreements from which the host country is expected to benefit substantially.

Direct attempts to influence government decisions are not uncommon. The frequency of such attempts and the degree of their success varies from country to country. In some countries attempts to bribe government officials are taken as almost routine, and several instances have been reported in the international press where multinationals have sought to directly influence government officials in order to obtain repatriation approvals. In some situations, however, such attempts rebound. For example, an MNC may become extremely influential with a particular host government and secure favorable terms. In the event this particular government is removed from office, the ties with the ousted government can be held against the MNC, and it may face an extremely hostile attitude from the new government, including placing the repatriation of its funds in jeopardy.

FINANCIAL TECHNIQUES

Blocked funds take the form of idle balances when they cannot be repatriated, invested in new projects or expansions, or be used to meet the operating expenses of the company. In this eventuality, MNCs attempt to seek direct answers in the local financial markets and indirectly in the international financial markets. In the local financial markets, corporations attempt to invest the blocked funds in instruments whose maturities are similar to the expected duration of blocking. Of course, an ideal match is not always available because of the relatively undeveloped financial markets of many countries and the fact that the exact duration the funds will remain blocked is rarely known.

Accessing the international markets for utilizing blocked funds is, however, not straightforward and involves, in most cases, either circumvention of host country regulations or, at a minimum, exploitation of certain loopholes. One way this is done is to place the blocked funds as security or collateral with multinational banks located in the host country for loans taken abroad by branches in other countries. It is extremely difficult for authorities in the host countries to monitor all such deals and prove the precise links between a particular deposit locally and a loan extended overseas.

International finance 53

Parallel or **back-to-back loans** are another technique employed by MNCs to use blocked funds productively through the international markets. Under this arrangement, blocked funds are lent out to a local company, who arranges an equivalent loan to the parent company overseas.

Transfer pricing

Transfer pricing is one of the most controversial issues surrounding the operation of MNCs in different countries. The term itself refers to the pricing arrangements made between different units of a multinational corporation. Transfer pricing is discussed in the context of international marketing in Chapter 2; the discussion in this chapter focuses on the financial implications of this technique. In any MNC, affiliates receive from one another a wide array of raw materials, intermediate products, semi-finished goods, services, technical know-how, patents, and so on, which must be paid for. Because both parties in these transactions belong to the same organization, the main determinant of prices will be the policy of the headquarters. Actually, the pricing decision in this instance would not be derived so much economically as administratively or strategically. It is inherently difficult in this situation to ensure a fair price. First, the definition of what is fair will vary from the perspective of the host government, that of an MNC, and often even from the perspective of an MNC's home government. Second, given this leverage, an MNC is bound to use it to offset constraints in other areas of its operation. It is treated, in fact, more as a fund management technique by MNCs, because it offers considerable maneuverability in moving funds from one subsidiary to another, avoiding taxes, dodging tariffs, and financing imbalances in different operational locations.

Capital budgeting and financial structure of an MNC

The financial analysis needed to make decisions about investments in different countries must go beyond the exercise for domestic investments and incorporate several additional factors and variables that influence project performance and returns.

Exchange control restrictions on remittances

A project may be financially stable in terms of the revenue it generates in the country where it is located, but government restrictions may not allow the profits to be either partially or fully repatriated or may place time constraints on the repatriation. From the point of view of the parent company, this would not be a financially viable project because the actual returns on investment would not meet acceptable standards.

54   *International finance*

Political risks

Political risks are connected to the issue of government restrictions of remittances. Such risks arise from the possibility of new or more stringent regulations being imposed by the host government. Such regulations could be imposed not only on the remittance of profits, but also on the type of activities an MNC can perform or on the manner in which it conducts its business. Political risk also incorporates the possibility of **expropriation** of assets, and the risk becomes an important factor in new investment decisions, because it raises the kind of uncertainty that would affect future returns on investments. Although it is difficult to quantify political risk because of several subjective considerations, methods have been devised to provide a numerical grading of the different levels of political risk attached by overseas investors with respect to different countries. The basis of most of these methods is a relative weighting scale of comparative risks in different countries. There is some justification to this approach, because in many instances the investment decision for an MNC involves a choice of locating the investment in several countries.

Tax considerations

Tax regimes vary greatly in different countries, both with respect to the statutes and implementation procedures and practices. A financial analyst of an MNC evaluating an investment decision in an overseas location must factor in the implications of the host country's tax regulations. In most countries income on investments by overseas entities is taxed at special or different rates, which may be higher in cases of repatriation of funds.

Sources of funds

Sources of funds for financing investments overseas are important considerations that enter into any financial analysis preceding the investment decision. A corporation may have access to cheaper local financing or in greater volume because of its credit rating in the overseas market. It may be able to raise funds in third-country markets. At the same time, it may face funding constraints because local regulations prohibit overseas borrowings for projects located in a host country. Local financing may be accompanied by special disclosure, operating, and reporting requirements. There also may be certain local restrictions placed on overseas entities receiving funds from particular sources.

Credit ratings are helpful for large, publicly traded companies, in terms of accessing equity markets. But not all of the participants in the international business arena are sufficiently large enough to obtain a credit rating from a reputable credit agency such as Moody's or Standard & Poor's. These smaller, often private, companies must find additional methods of accessing capital.

Some local governments provide assistance to smaller companies that are attempting to enter the exporting market. In the United States, for example, the Export-Import Bank of the United States provides working capital financing that enables U.S. exporters to obtain loans to produce or buy goods or services for export. These working capital loans are made by commercial banks, but are backed with the guarantee of the Ex-Im Bank. For eligible exporters, the Ex-Im Bank has assumed up to 90% of the bank loan, which means that if the exporter fails to pay back the commercial lender, the Ex-Im Bank will cover up to this amount of the outstanding principal and interest at the time the borrower defaults on the loan. Ex-Im Bank requirements include that the company be located in the United States, have at least one year of operating history, and have a positive company net worth. An additional program to the benefit of small exporting companies in the United States is currently available via the Small Business Administration (SBA). The SBA Export Express program, as well as its Export Working Capital, and International Trade Loan program, are examples of government sponsored assistance programs to aid small businesses in entering the export market. Many of the SBA programs do not necessarily require an extensive amount of exporting experience. But these programs do have requirements for successful domestic operation over a reasonable period of time. As with the Ex-Im Bank guarantee program, obtaining an SBA loan also involves getting credit approval from a commercial bank.

Currency of borrowing investments

In overseas investments the commitment of an MNC's own or borrowed resources has to be made in a particular foreign currency. The investment decision must be aware of the different options available with regard to the choice of currency. The wrong choice of currency for borrowing could lead to substantial financial losses because of adverse fluctuations in exchange rates over the life of the loan.

Different inflation rates

Different inflation rates are an extremely important consideration in evaluating investment decisions because the entire profitability of a project could be eliminated by inflation losses. Inflation rates became particularly important in the 1980s because many developing countries where MNCs of industrialized countries have substantial investments experienced hyper-inflationary rates. When making a decision to invest in a country where inflation rates are expected to be high, the financial manager has to realistically assess the impact of inflation on net returns to the parent company and devise inflation-adjusting mechanisms in the financing strategy, so that the returns can be made to the greatest extent possible, immune from inflationary conditions in the host country.

56 *International finance*

Letters of credit in international trade

Another important aspect of international finance is how an international transaction takes place between the seller of a good (the exporter) and the buyer of a good (the importer). Sometimes firms enter into agreements with their local banks to provide assistance in facilitating an international trade. One example of such an agreement is a draft. A **draft** is a demand for payment from the buyer at a specified time. Two primary types of drafts are sight drafts and time drafts. The **sight draft** requires payment when the importer receives the goods, while a **time draft** extends credit to an importer for a specified period of time. When the bank is involved in the processing and acceptance of a time draft, the collection process is simplified for the exporter. The bank would agree to accept the time draft for a fee, and the exporter would hold the **banker's acceptance** until it comes due. Once the time draft is accepted, it is referred to as a trade acceptance, which is legally enforceable once the word "accepted" is written on the draft. Sometimes, problems can arise with this form of payment. If an importer refuses shipment for some reason (could have found a better deal for example), the exporter will incur legal fees in an attempt to receive payment. The exporter might also incur **demurrage fees**, which are fees for storage of the exporter's goods at the foreign loading dock.

In order to remove the concern of an importer refusing to pay for the shipment of goods, a more effective process is the letter of credit. A **letter of credit** is a written commitment by a bank, made at the request of a customer (the buyer), to effect payment or honor drafts of the seller, if the seller complies with certain specific conditions. Thus a letter of credit can be issued by a bank that promises to pay an exporter once the exporter has fulfilled their part of the bargain. The letter of credit details conditions where an importer shall pay the exporter for goods. Some letters of credit are **clean letters of credit**. These do not require the presentation of any documentation, other than the bill of exchange, to obtain payment. Most letters of credit are **documentary letters of credit**. In this form of letter of credit, the bank will require the presentation of documentation in order to obtain payment such as the invoice, customs documents, proof of insurance, a packing list, an export license (from the exporter's home country), the certification of product origin (in order to assess tariffs and quotas), an inspection certificate (to see if the goods meet quality standards), and a bill of lading. A **bill of lading** is a receipt given by the carrier to the shipper acknowledging receipt of the goods being shipped, and specifying the terms of the delivery. The bill of lading is the most important document in a letter of credit, and it is also the document that has historically raised the most controversies during international transactions. The bill of lading is a receipt for the goods being shipped, a document of title for the property included in the shipment, an evidence of the contract of carriage, and it is a negotiable document.

There are many different forms of letters of credit. A **revocable letter of credit** can be modified or revoked by the issuing bank without notice or consent from the beneficiary (seller/exporter). An **irrevocable letter of**

credit can only be modified or revoked with the consent of the beneficiary. Similarly, letters of credit can be either confirmed or unconfirmed. A **confirmed letter of credit** is where the **advising bank** is committed to honor the payment of the credit, *provided that the beneficiary meets the terms and conditions of the credit*. Having a confirmed letter of credit is particularly important when an exporter is dealing with a buyer from a country that is politically or economically unstable. The safest form of letter of credit for an exporter is a confirmed, irrevocable letter of credit.

Sometimes, an exporter may want to have a **transferable letter of credit**. The beneficiary (exporter) can request that the letter of credit be transferred to another beneficiary for execution. If multiple transactions are being undertaken by the same parties, a **revolving letter of credit** can be established. This establishes a credit exactly the same as the original letter of credit but with shorter periods for shipment, and the ability to substitute documents specific to the current transaction.

The final form of letter of credit that we will discuss is the **Stand-by letter of credit**. This form of letter of credit is a bank guarantee, where the beneficiary (seller/exporter) can claim payment if the principal (buyer/importer) does not fulfill their obligations. The bank will require proof of default, and the only time that the beneficiary obtains payment from the bank is when the principal fails to pay for the shipment of goods. The bank charges associated with this form of letter of credit are less than for the other types, as the utilization of the stand-by letter of credit is the exception rather than the rule. Thus, there are many different forms of letters of credit, and this section has only highlighted some of the more typical forms. The utilization of a letter of credit can reduce the risk of non-payment for the exporter, and can facilitate trade in some areas of the world that otherwise would be too risky to sell goods without this form of protection.

International capital markets

International capital markets have become increasingly important as a source for financing the operations of MNCs, not only because of the decline in bank financing, but also largely because of several developments that have increased the competitiveness, size, and sophistication of the financial markets themselves. International capital markets or international financial markets are terms used to describe the three basic types of markets where MNCs can raise money: national financial markets, Eurocurrency markets, and national stock markets.

It should be noted, however, that both national financial markets and national stock markets are international in the sense that, although they are located in a particular country and are subject to that country's laws and regulations, they are open to foreign borrowers and investors. The degree to which they are internationalized varies, of course, but in general the financial and equity markets of nearly all the industrialized countries are open to foreign borrowers.

58   *International finance*

An essential difference between borrowing funds from a bank and raising funds from a financial market is that when a corporation borrows from a bank, the bank takes on the risk, and the depositors who place funds with the bank are not in any way responsible. Because the bank is taking the risk and going through the effort of pooling the funds of depositors, it receives certain remuneration, which can be quite high. On the other hand, borrowing in a financial market implies that a corporation is reaching the investing public directly, without using the intermediary services provided by the bank. The corporation has to make the necessary arrangements on its own to inform the investors that it is in the market to raise funds and to convince them of its credit-worthiness. Some banks, especially investment banks, do play a role in such transactions, but it is marginal in the sense that they provide only certain types of services, which are paid for by fees. Generally, therefore, corporations find it cheaper to raise funds through the international capital markets because they are able to save the intermediation costs involved in bank financing.

Another important reason why MNCs would use this option is the sheer size of the resources that can be raised in these markets. There are limits on which banks can lend funds because they do not have such large resources at their disposal and are not willing to take excessive risks.

Financial markets provide a wide variety of financial instruments that can be combined and tailored to serve individual financing needs. Almost every aspect of a financing transaction can be custom designed to serve the purpose of an MNC. For example: the maturity, currency, dates of transaction, repayment schedule, and types of interest rate arrangement.

The emergence of international capital markets

Bank lending dominated the international financial arena through the 1970s, although signs of strains had become evident toward the end of the decade. The international debt crisis, which became publicly known in 1982, signaled a formal end to the domination of bank lending as the main source of international finance.

Through the 1970s and the 1980s, several developments had prepared the financial markets of the world to literally take off. One important step in this direction was financial deregulation in many industrialized countries. The United States, Great Britain, France, and Japan introduced, at different stages, legislation that eliminated, to a significant extent, restrictions on the free flow of funds across their countries. The deregulation measures also improved the access of borrowers from these and other countries to overseas markets. Unfortunately, the improvement in the movement of capital was not accompanied with the improvement of the ability of many commercial lenders to adequately quantify the risk in their loan portfolios. The Asian Financial Crisis in the late 1990s brought this need to the forefront. While commercial banks are currently in the process of developing similar risk rating systems for their credit portfolios via the **Basel Accords**, there remains the need for enhanced control on the movement of currencies in some parts of the world.

Dramatic improvements in information and telecommunication technology enabled the transfer of funds and market information around the world almost instantaneously, which gave the financial community the power to deal in several markets simultaneously. Effectively, the communications and information revolution integrated the international markets to a much higher degree. The widespread use and application of computer technology enabled financial managers to create a wide array of highly complex financial instruments that could be fine-tuned to client requirements.

The distinction between domestic and international markets has become blurred with the rapid mobility of capital and almost instantaneous communication. What has emerged is a truly international market that offers a wide range of financing options to MNCs.

National financial markets

The major national financial markets that serve as international financial centers are New York City, Tokyo, and London. Other important national markets that are open to foreign borrowers as well as investors are Geneva, Hong Kong, Paris, Frankfurt, and Singapore.

These markets are generally free from government control as far as day-to-day operations are concerned. There are few, if any, restrictions on the inflow and outflow of funds from these markets to and from other financial centers. All of these markets have excellent communications and other infrastructural facilities necessary for the smooth operation and execution of a very large volume of transactions on a daily basis. As can be expected, most of the major international financial players – commercial banks, investment banks, and securities and brokerage houses – have a presence in nearly all of these markets. Most of the borrowing in national markets by foreign borrowers is done in the form of bond issues and commercial paper. Bonds are fixed-term promissory notes, usually issued at a discount from face value, which is equal to the rate of interest received by the investor of the bond until maturity. A corporation that wants to raise funds through a bond issue usually hires an investment bank or securities brokerage house to underwrite and actually make the transaction. The lead underwriter or lead manager generally organizes a syndicate of other similar financial institutions that agree to underwrite some part of the issue for a share in the fees. The actual arrangements can vary considerably, depending upon the kind of services to be performed by the underwriter or lead manager. Often the underwriter or lead manager, along with the syndicate, buys the entire issue of bonds from the borrowers and then sells or places them with investors. The difference between the price at which the lead manager and syndicate buy the bonds and the price at which they sell them constitutes their spread or profit margin. In addition, the lead manager gets a separate fee for bringing together the syndicate and arranging the various services required for

60   *International finance*

a bond issue. Alternatively, the bonds can be sold directly to investors with the underwriters agreeing, for a certain fee, to buy on their own account any bonds that are not sold.

Bonds issued by a foreign party in a national market require the services of a local underwriter or lead manager familiar with local regulations and market conditions and with the necessary connections in the financial and investment community who can successfully launch and sell the bonds. Because the bonds represent an unsecured loan to a particular company that is not located within the sovereign jurisdiction of the country, investors have to be absolutely certain of the credit-worthiness of the foreign issuer. Moreover, the regulatory authorities of certain countries, especially the United States, impose stringent disclosure requirements on foreign issuers before they can float their bonds. In addition to disclosure, in most instances a foreign issuer must obtain a report on its credit-worthiness from a leading rating agency. The two leading agencies are Moody's Investor Service and Standard & Poor's, both located in New York City. The rating given a particular corporation or other borrower not only determines whether it will be able to issue bonds in a particular market, but also decides the rate of interest it will have to pay on the bonds. A company that receives a better credit rating will be able to borrow at a lower interest rate because investors will be willing to accept a lower return in exchange for a better risk.

Despite their openness, national bond markets are somewhat restricted for overseas borrowers with respect to taxes and the amounts that can be issued.

Foreign bond issues in different markets are known by individual market names. Those issued in the United States are known as **yankee bonds**, in Japan as **samurai bonds**, in Great Britain as **bulldog bonds**.

Match the home country currency with the foreign bond name....

Bond Name:	*Denominated in:*
1. Yankee bond	A. Chinese Yuan
2. Samurai bond	B. New Zealand dollars
3. Bulldog bond	C. Japanese Yen
4. Uridashi bond	D. UK Pound
5. Dim sum bond	E. US dollars
6. Kiwi bond	F. Aussie dollars
7. Kangaroo bond	G. Russian ruble bonds sold in Japan
8. Dragon bond	H. Bond issued in Asia (ex-Japan) in US dollars
9. Shogun bond	I. Foreign denominated bonds issued in Japan
10. Maple Bond	J. Canadian dollars
11. Matador Bond	K. Issued in Spain by non-Spanish firms
12. Sushi Bond	L. Issued by Japanese firms outside of Japan

Exhibit 3.2 Name that Eurobond!★
★To test your knowledge, refer to the answer key on page 71.

The Euromarkets

Euromarkets refer to three main types of financial markets that emerged in the 1970s and 1980s and how they dominate the financial arena. They are Eurocurrency markets, Eurobond markets, and Euro-equities markets. The prefix Euro does not imply that the currency, bond, or a particular equity is that of a European country (or the European Union). A **Eurocurrency**, in effect, is any freely convertible currency (including the U.S. dollar) that is held in a bank outside the country of its origin. For example, if U.S. dollars are deposited with Natwest Bank London, these dollars would be termed Eurodollars. It is not necessary that the bank may be a foreign one. The important factor here is that it be located outside the country of the relevant currency. If U.S. dollars were held in the Paris branch of Citibank, they would still be Eurodollars. The crucial feature in the creation of Eurocurrency is the shifting of their ownership outside the country of their origin. The dollars deposited with Citibank Paris or Natwest London will be credited to the bank's account in dollars, which will be maintained in the United States. Thus, there would be no outflow of actual dollars from the United States, but from the U.S. standpoint, these funds would become deposits held by overseas entities. Eurodollar deposits can be created in a number of ways. For example, an Austrian company sells chemicals to a U.S. importer and receives payments in U.S. dollars and wants to reclaim its earnings in dollars. It can either deposit these dollars with a bank in the U.S. or a bank elsewhere. If it takes the latter option and deposits the dollars with a bank in, say Frankfurt, it would create a Eurodollar deposit. The Frankfurt bank, which now holds the funds, can lend them to another bank or borrower, and then lend the funds to additional banks. Borrowers using the funds to finance purchases can lead to the creation of further Eurodollar deposits, because their suppliers could again redeposit the funds with a bank outside the United States. Thus, the Eurodollar volume can increase in multiples of the original through this sequence of deposits and loans. In fact, the Euromarkets have grown tremendously over the years, especially during the 1980s and 1990s. This growth was not only because of the process of multiple deposit-loan creations. Several additional factors were responsible for its explosive increase in size, activity and depth.

Origins and development of the Euromarkets

Although as far back as the 1920s, European banks took deposits in the currencies of countries other than the ones in which they were located, Euromarkets as they exist today began to emerge only after World War II.

Postwar tension between the United States and the Soviet bloc countries generated the fear of a general freeze on the latter's dollar assets held in the United States. To preempt such an eventuality, these countries moved their dollar assets from banks in the United States to banks in Europe. A large proportion of these dollar funds were deposited with two Western Europe

62   *International finance*

branches of two Russian-owned banks: the Banque Commerciale pour l'Europe du Nord in Paris, and the London branch of Moscow Nardony Bank. The funds were channeled into other European-based banks, primarily in London.

This initial impetus to holding U.S. dollars outside the United States was encouraged by a series of U.S. government regulations that made holding Eurodollars a profitable proposition. Interest rate ceilings were imposed by the U.S. government under **Regulation Q** in 1966, which led U.S. depositors to place their funds with European banks in order to take advantage of the prevailing higher interest rates. The demand for U.S. dollars based outside the country also arose simultaneously, because heavy taxes were levied on foreign borrowers raising funds in U.S. markets. Dollar funds could be raised at lower costs in Europe, where the European banks could lend their dollar assets without borrowers having to pay high U.S. taxes. The difficulties of the U.S. dollar in the Bretton Woods system had become quite apparent by the late 1960s. In 1968 the U.S. government, keen to slow down the building up of external obligations in U.S. dollars, restricted U.S. corporations from exporting domestic capital (that is, dollars) to finance their overseas expansion. This move created an enormous demand for non-U.S.-based dollar funding, which was met to a great extent by the Euromarkets.

Apart from U.S. government restrictions, the international monetary developments under the Bretton Woods arrangements also helped create the Eurodollar market. Under the Bretton Woods arrangements, the U.S. dollar became, in addition to gold, one of the major forms of holding international reserves by the world's central banks, which led to an accumulation of dollar assets held outside the United States, in effect creating a huge supply of Eurodollars. Added to this basic accumulation were the commercial banks and other financial institutions in Europe who had dollar balances to their credit. They found that holding dollars outside the United States gave them greater operational flexibility and, for the most part, offered a better return than dollars held in the United States.

The increase in supply of U.S. dollars was matched by an increase in demand for non-U.S. based dollar loans. The imposition of exchange controls on the lending of pound sterling funds to nonresidents of the United Kingdom also stimulated the demand for the lending of U.S. dollars by London banks, who now could not make loans in their own currency.

Apart from these historical factors, there are some general factors that attracted both borrowers and investors to the Euromarkets. For one, the markets are decidedly more efficient than the traditional banking markets. This efficiency translates into a lower spread or interest differential between the borrowing and lending rates. The lower spread implies that intermediation costs are lower, and both the borrowers and investors benefit. The borrowers can raise funds at a lower interest rate, while the investors get a higher rate of return.

There are several reasons why interest rate spreads are lower in the Euromarkets. For one, the banks do not have to maintain any specified reserves of Eurocurrencies and are not subject to central bank regulatory requirements, which lowers the costs for the bankers because a greater proportion of the funds can be now utilized for lending and do not have to be blocked up as required reserves.

Funds held by banks outside the country of their origin are also cheaper to hold, because they are not covered under any federal deposit insurance scheme and no premium has to be paid for the purpose. The savings can be passed on, in part, to the depositors by allowing them a higher rate of interest on deposits of the same maturity in the domestic market.

Transactions in the Euromarkets are usually for very large amounts. Moreover, there is acute competition for business among major international banks. The huge size of the transactions brings in economies of scale, thereby reducing costs. Costs are pared still further by competition, because banks try to under-price competitive offers in an effort to obtain huge volumes of business, which is very profitable because of the overall turnover. Transactions in the international capital markets generally involve a direct deal between a corporation (issuer) and the investing public, and therefore only companies with excellent credit ratings can expect to access these markets for any sizable amounts. Therefore, nearly all participants in the Euromarkets are entities with high credit ratings and are generally known internationally. Such companies usually demand and receive the best rates for their transactions, which reduces the overall average cost of funds raised in the Euromarkets.

The Euromarket, in effect, is a wholesale market where transactions generally range in multiples of millions of dollars and the smallest deals are about $500,000. The large size of transactions introduces economies of scale because the overhead costs incurred by financial institutions (which are primarily fixed costs) can be spread over the transaction.

There are, however, certain risks attached to Euromarket operations. Deposits and investments are not guaranteed by any central bank, and if one party reneges on a contract, there is no recourse available with the monetary authorities of the reneging party's country. Also, because the market consists of funds held in countries other than those from which they originate, there is no lender of last resort, which means that in the event of a financial panic, such as a market crash, there is no safety net that can prevent the bottom of the market from falling out. Thus, if a crash occurs, instability and chaos can be expected, because there is no authority, such as a central bank, in charge of restoring orderly conditions.

Another danger that has emerged from the rapid development of Euromarkets is the possibility of taking high and unwarranted risks. These markets are free from regulatory controls, which leave the participants free to determine their own degree of risk exposure. In the absence of regulatory control and in the face of the possibility of extremely high profits, it is quite possible that many participants might be tempted to take unwarranted risks and destabilize the entire market, or at least parts of it if they find their gambles failing. The lack of disclosure requirements in the markets, as well as the fact that many

64 *International finance*

Euromarket accounts do not show up on the balance sheets of financial institutions, increases the possibility of a buildup of hidden risks that could overwhelm participating institutions without a warning. The absence of such activities from balance sheets also prevents regulators in the home countries of Euromarket participants from monitoring and supervising their activities effectively.

International equities markets

Raising funds by listing and selling corporate stocks on exchanges outside a home country has become an important source of financing for corporations involved in international business. During the 1990s many stock markets of the world showed impressive performances and registered substantial gains. Many investors and multinational corporations realized that listing in different stock exchanges worldwide could lead to a better diversification of risks because many stock markets do not move in tandem. Thus, losses in one market can be offset by gains in another, which would add to the financial stability of an overall portfolio.

Many of the world's stock markets also grew considerably in size and depth over this period, as more and more companies listed their shares and there was an increase in trading volume. An important factor that encouraged this trend was the deregulation of some of the major stock exchanges, which widened the scope for international participation. The major world stock markets are located in Tokyo, New York, London, Taiwan, Hong Kong, Frankfurt, and Paris.

Many companies are finding overseas listings attractive because it increases the overall demand for their shares, which pushes up their values. The international character of a company is also firmly established with an internationally listed equity. In addition, a company is able to lower the cost of the capital, because it is able to raise equity instead of going in for high-cost debt financing. In addition, the option of listing internationally opens up a whole new avenue of raising capital.

Listing on international stock exchanges can be done by either a Euroequity issue or a dual equity issue. In a **Euroequity issue**, shares are sold solely outside the country of the issuer. On the other hand, a **dual equity issue** is split up into two parts, one sold domestically and the other overseas.

Usually, the markets of the industrialized countries permit the listing of foreign stocks and their purchase and that of local stocks by foreign Investors. Some newly industrialized countries permit overseas listings, while others permit limited investment by overseas investors.

New York

New York is the world's largest securities market. Generally, the shares of larger and well-established companies are listed on the New York exchange. There are various types of memberships in the stock exchange, which provide the right to perform different types of stock market activities. For example, commission brokers execute orders on behalf of customers and convey them to floor brokers who do the actual trading on the floor of the exchange. The New York Stock Exchange, like all other exchanges in the United States, is controlled by a federal authority, the Securities and Exchange Commission. The SEC guidelines and supervisory activities are intended to ensure smooth operation of stock market activities and prevent any fraudulent or unethical trading practices or transactions. The main indicator of the overall price movements on the New York Stock Exchange is the Dow Jones Industrial Average. The Standard & Poor's 500 Index is another widely published and accepted index. As of December 31, 2015, the total market capitalization of the NYSE stood at $18 trillion. Exhibit 3.3 itemizes the calendar year end market capitalization of select world stock exchanges for the years 2005, 2010, and 2015.

Tokyo

The Tokyo stock exchange is one of the largest in the world in terms of **market capitalization** (the value of total stocks outstanding at a particular point of time). The market is extremely active and has generally been characterized by upward movements, so that it has an extremely high price–earnings ratio – the ratio of the prices of shares of listed companies to their earnings. Nominal prices are kept extremely low and tradable amounts are denominated in units of 1,000 shares. The NIKKEI 225 is now one of the leading performance indicators in international economics, and the market is still essentially dominated by three major securities houses: Nomura, Nikko, and Daiwa. Market capitalization of the Tokyo stock exchange as of December 31, 2015, stood at $4.9 trillion.

London

London is a truly international stock exchange, with more than three hundred overseas companies listed, representing more than fifty countries. Two main types of stocks are available: ordinary and preferred. Ordinary shares confer voting rights, while preferred shares give the first right to holders on the assets of the company. The most commonly quoted index is the Financial Times (FT) Index. After 1986, many regulations that limited activity on the London Stock Exchange were removed, and banks were permitted to undertake securities transactions by acquiring securities houses. This reform also removed the distinction between different types of stock market functionaries: brokers and jobbers. Since the 1986 reforms, which were known as the "big bang", London has grown to be a major center for the listing and trading of international stocks. In 2001, the 200th anniversary of the modern stock exchange was celebrated. In 2017, a proposed merger of the London Stock Exchange Group, LLC with the Deutsche Börse was rejected by the European Union owing to anti-trust concerns, although this decision came just prior the start of official

66 International finance

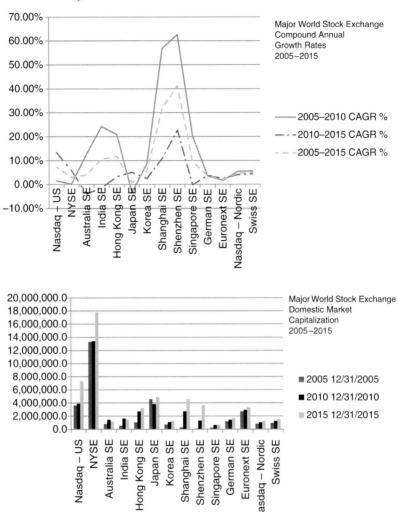

Exhibit 3.3 Market capitalization of select world stock exchanges 2005–2015

Source: World Federation of Exchanges members

discussions for the United Kingdom leaving the EU, which is known as **Brexit**. While there is some concern about London's continued prominence as a financial center after the Brexit decision, it is hard to envision material change in London's historical position.

Euronext: Paris, Amsterdam, Brussels, etc.

The Paris stock market has been liberalized considerably in recent years and a large number of international stocks are listed there. Although in absolute size

International finance   67

the Paris market is considerable, it is relatively small in relation to the industrial size of France because of several historical reasons, chiefly the tendency of French companies to rely on debt rather than equity financing to meet their needs. The market has historically been organized in two sections: spot and forward. Special procedures apply in the Paris market for the trading of stocks. Prices are set at periodic fixings, usually twice a day. The price established at the fixing is the official price, although other market-determined prices can prevail with respect to the orders executed in between the fixings. The forward market operates on the basis of a call-over method, where stocks are traded as they are called up. Securities of small companies are traded on an over-the-counter market located within the exchange and operated by stockbrokers who are members of the exchange.

Given the increasing financial integration in the continent of Europe, the Paris stock market merged with the exchanges of Amsterdam and Brussels in September 2000 to create the Euronext. In 2002, the Euronext merged with the Portuguese exchange, and also acquired London's Futures and Options market. Over the last few years, steps have been undertaken to merge these formerly separate exchanges into one large continental market. Thus, investors located in these countries of the European Union have the ability to invest in securities in multiple countries. The NYSE and Euronext merged in April 2007, to form NYSE Euronext. Currently, 1,300 companies are listed on the Euronext, including Euronext, Alternext, and Free Market. The latter two markets are for small to medium sized companies. As of December 31, 2015, the Euronext had market capitalization of $3.3 trillion.

NASDAQ Nordics

In 1998, the Copenhagen stock exchange and the Stockholm stock exchange established the NOREX alliance. Since that time the stock exchanges of Norway, Iceland, Finland, Estonia, and Latvia have also joined the alliance. This was the first stock exchange in the world to implement a common system for share trading, and to harmonize the trading and membership rules and regulations for exchanges in different countries. Nasdaq merged with OMX, a leading exchange operator in the Scandinavia, in 2007. As yet another example of the increasing integration of global financial markets, the Nasdaq Nordics exchange includes the shares of approximately 850 companies, and had a total market capitalization of $1.2 trillion as of December 15, 2015.

Frankfurt

Frankfurt is another major European stock market, which had a market capitalization of $1.7 trillion as of December 31, 2015. Regulation of the Frankfurt Stock Exchange is somewhat more stringent than the exchanges of other industrialized countries. Trading is limited on the Frankfurt exchange because many Germany companies are closely held. In addition, German

68 International finance

shareholders tend to take a long-term view of their equity investments and to hold on to shares even if the companies are not performing up to the expected level at a particular point in time. Moreover, high listing costs and availability of other financing services have discouraged several German companies from using the stock exchange to mobilize resources. Shares are usually not registered and there are no limits placed on foreign ownership of equity in German companies. The Frankfurt Stock Exchange uses the trading post system, where transactions in specified securities are conducted at a particular place on the trading floor. Frankfurt is the main stock exchange of Germany. *Open market operations* of the European Central Bank (ECB) are also conducted through Frankfurt.

Hong Kong

Hong Kong is one of the most important stock exchanges in the Far East. It has extremely active primary and secondary markets. A large percentage of companies on the Hong Kong exchange are real estate firms, reflecting the importance of this business for Hong Kong. The Hong Kong exchange is under the supervision of the China Securities Regulatory Commission for general regulatory purposes. Day-to-day transactions are, however, unfettered by government regulations. Trading volume generally tends to be very high and the market offers excellent liquidity. The total market capitalization as of December 31, 2015 was U.S. $3.2 trillion.

Emerging markets

In the late 1970s and 1980s, several newly industrialized countries (NICs) and the stock markets of developing countries were opened to foreign investors to varying degrees. The most important of these were Taiwan, Malaysia, and South Korea. The Taiwanese market is one of the very large ones, with a market capitalization of $745 billion as of December 31, 2015. The market is dominated by a few very large companies whose individual market capitalizations are in excess of $1 billion. In 2003, the requirements for foreign institutional investors were deregulated somewhat to allow for an increase in foreign investment. Mainland China has also seen a rapid increase in the performance of its stock markets. Since their inception three decades ago, the Shenzhen and Shanghai stock markets have grown to include over 1,250 listed companies, and over 60 million investor accounts. The mainland continues its integration with Hong Kong, as each year hundreds of "**red chip**" stocks are issued on the Hong Kong stock exchange, but are controlled by the mainland.

The Malaysian stock markets are also considerably well-developed, especially by developing-country standards. As of December 31, 2015, the market capitalization of the Kuala Lumpur market was $383 billion. A number of Singapore and British stocks are listed on the Kuala Lumpur exchange, which has had considerable activity ever since its inauguration in 1973, which is attributed largely to greater demand from the investing public. Several public brokerage firms perform brokerage services. Stocks on the Kuala Lumpur exchange also can be bought through the Singapore exchange. To list its shares on the Kuala Lumpur stock exchange, a company has to meet certain requirements set by the Malaysian authorities. The Singapore exchange is another increasingly important stock market in the Asia-Pacific region. The country, which has benefited by having free trade agreements with many countries in the world, has seen rapid growth in its economy and stock market over the last few years. The Singapore exchange has also teamed up recently with the American stock exchange (AMEX), the Australian stock exchange (ASX), and others in an effort to provide investment alternatives to their investors.

The South Korean equity market grew rapidly over the last three decades. As of December 31, 2015, its market capitalization was $1.2 trillion. There are certain restrictions on foreign ownership of Korean stocks, but there are special channels, such as country funds, through which overseas investors can participate in the Korean stock market. Other stock markets, such as the National Stock Exchange of India, have seen large increases in market capitalization following the reduction of regulation in the financial sector.

It is expected that along with the general economic development, newly industrializing countries and other more advanced developing countries will witness an increase in the size, sophistication, and activity of their capital markets. These markets are expected to open up in a phased manner, first to overseas investors and then to borrowers. Once this occurs, it will be possible for multinational corporations to raise equity capital in local markets and diversify the composition of their international asset holdings by including in them stocks listed on the exchanges of various developing countries.

Summary

In addition to the needs of maintaining liquid resources, managing the timing of cash flows, and minimizing idle cash balances required by domestic finance operations, international finance requires the management of currency exchange risks, the transfer of funds between countries, and international tax issues. Intra-company pooling optimizes the total availability of capital resources on a global basis; surplus funds from operations in one location are used to offset shortages in another location. International financial managers must consider host country foreign exchange and capital repatriation controls, as well as taxation laws, in determining whether to centralize or decentralize working capital funds.

Leading and lagging techniques in receivables and payables serve to offset the effects of high inflation in the host country. To deal with blocked funds, MNCs may develop various strategies: develop an export orientation, use the blocked funds for investments in the host country, exert pressure on the host government through diplomatic channels, or invest in financial instruments in the local

70 International finance

financial market. Transfer pricing is a technique that MNCs use to avoid taxation and tariffs and improve their competitive positions.

MNCs must constantly manage foreign exchange and transaction exposure. Parallel loans, timing of funds transfers, centers for fund transfers, and credit and currency swaps are useful techniques. Debt-equity decisions, local ownership laws, and host government attitudes affect the financial structure of MNC subsidiaries and affiliates. External sources of funds for investments are the large commercial banks and international capital markets, such as the Eurocurrency markets and national capital and stock markets. Eurocurrency markets offer a variety of financial instruments in hard currencies held outside the national borders of the currency, including Eurocredits, certificates of deposit, Eurobonds, swaps, note issuance facilities, and Euro-commercial paper. In addition, to the Tokyo, New York, and London stock exchanges, other stock markets, such as Paris, Frankfurt, Hong Kong, Taiwan, Malaysia, and South Korea, are playing increasingly important roles as external sources of capital.

Discussion questions

1 What are the two major tasks of the international financial manager?
2 What is intra-company pooling?
3 What is leading and lagging? How can these techniques benefit the MNC?
4 How can a multinational utilize funds in a foreign subsidiary that have been blocked by the host government?
5 What are some of the additional factors that must be included in a financial analysis when making an international rather than a domestic investment decision?
6 What are the advantages of raising capital in the financial markets rather than through a bank? What are the disadvantages?
7 Discuss the services investment banks provide. What is a lead underwriter? What is a syndicate?
8 What are Euromarkets? Where are they located?
9 Where are the primary international equity markets located?

Bibliography

Argy, Victor E. 1982. *Exchange Rate Management in Theory and Practice.* Princeton, NJ: International Finance Section, Department of Economics, Princeton University.

Babbel, David F. 1983. Determining the Optimum Strategy for Hedging Currency Exposure. *Journal of International Business Studies* (Spring/Summer): 133–139.

Cha, Laura M. 2001. The Future of China's Capital Markets and the Role of Corporate Governance. *China Securities Regulatory Commission*, www.csrc.gov.cn, accessed July 17, 2017.

Griffith, V., and H. Southworth. 1990. Chaos Theory. *Banker* (January): 51, 54.

Herring, Richard J., ed. 1983. *Managing Foreign Exchange Risk: Essays Commissioned in Honor of the Centenary of the Wharton School, University of Pennsylvania.* New York: Cambridge University Press.

Kenyon, Alfred. 1981. *Currency Risk Management*. New York: John Wiley & Sons.

Kettell, Brian. 1981. *The Finance of International Business*. Westport, CT: Quorum Books.

Madura, Jeff. 1985. Development and Evaluation of International Financing Models. *Management International Review* (Fourth Quarter): 17–27.

Madura, Jeff. 1989. *International Financial Management*, 2nd edn. St Paul, MN: West Publishing.

Meek, G. K., and S. J. Gray. 1989. Globalization of Stock Markets and Foreign Listing Requirements: Voluntary Disclosures by Continental European Companies Listed on the London Stock Exchange. *Journal of International Business Studies* (Summer): 315–336.

Parrott, M., S. Kanji, D. Lane, and E. Cohen. 1988. European Stock Markets: A Bad Hangover. *Banker* (January): 25–32.

Rodriquez, Rita M. 1980. *Foreign Exchange Management in U S. Multinationals*. Lexington, MA: Lexington Books.

Tyan, Salim V. 2005, T&D Mideast Ltd. corporate website, http://www.dsuper.net/~styan/rice.htm.

Vinson, Joseph D. 1952. Financial Planning for the Multinational Corporation with Multiple Goals. *Journal of International Business Studies* (Winter): 43–58.

Warren, Geoffrey. 1987. Latest in Currency Hedging Methods. *Euromoney* (May): 245–264.

⋆Match that Eurobond! Answer key:

1) E   2) C   3) D   4) G   5) A   6) B   7) F   8) H   9) I   10) J   11) K   12) L

4 International accounting

> You would rather consider yourself an unpaid creditor in this world than cancel it.
>
> (Soren Kierkegaard)

Chapter objectives

This chapter will:

- Present the role and importance of accounting information to internal and external users.
- Describe the differences in accounting conventions and disclosure requirements as practiced around the world.
- Discuss the current efforts toward harmonization of accounting standards in the United States and the rest of the world.
- Identify special accounting problems affecting multinational corporations.
- Examine the accounting functions of planning, control, and auditing within a multinational context.

What is accounting?

Accounting is essentially the recording and interpretation of financial information related to the functioning of a business. Accounting systems provide valuable information about the financial activity and position of a firm, which is interpreted for different users. Information users can be divided into two categories: external and internal. Information users in each category require different types of accounting information, and their needs are met by two different types of accounting functions: managerial and financial accounting.

Managerial accounting is concerned with the information needs of the internal users of an enterprise who require detailed information on all of its business activities.

Financial accounting is oriented toward external users and is concerned with providing relevant information about the activities of the enterprise.

External users can be classified according to their use of financial information. Potential investors want detailed information on past sales, earnings performance, and present strength. With such information, they can formulate expectations of future performance and potential returns of a firm and make appropriate decisions.

Creditors are also interested in the future performance of a firm but more so in relation to evaluating its creditworthiness. Thus, banks making loans or suppliers providing credit need to determine the ability of a business to meet its obligations.

Government representatives also use financial information, not only as potential creditors or customers of the firm, but also as regulators that monitor the activities of an enterprise to ensure that they are within the bounds of law. Customers and employees require information about a firm in order to make decisions about what products to buy, who to do business with, and where to seek employment.

In order to meet the financial information needs of all interested parties, business enterprises must maintain and provide data on its activities from a number of perspectives and in a number of forms.

The task of meeting the financial information needs of internal and external users becomes extremely complex when an enterprise takes its business activities across borders. Additional problems arise not only from transactions between countries, such as the buying and selling of goods, but also because multinational operations are conducted in the sovereign jurisdiction of other countries. A firm must first recognize and respond to the accounting practices, conventions, reporting requirements, and currencies of different nations. Then it faces the problem of integrating the accounts of subsidiaries prepared in accordance with local conventions and regulations with the consolidated accounts of the entire corporation.

Differences in accounting practices among countries

Factors affecting accounting systems

Differences in accounting practices, standards, and conventions among different countries exist because of diverse economic, legal, political, and sociocultural environments. The level of development in each country is directly related to the degree of sophistication required by the system. For example, nations with highly developed manufacturing and service sectors and a great deal of international trading activity will require more detailed accounting and recording systems than countries with limited economic activity.

The nature of business activities in each nation also contributes to the molding of accounting systems. Systems are developed to cater to particular types of business activities. For example, countries with a concentration of large corporations and complex business structures are likely to have more advanced accounting systems than countries with simple business organizations.

74   *International accounting*

Accounting systems in different countries are also directly affected by legal considerations. In some countries accounting practices are determined almost entirely by legal constraints. In other countries, such as the United States, accounting practices develop through a mixture of law and standards set by members of the accounting profession.

The accounting system of a nation is also determined, in part, by its political orientation and the level of government involvement in business activity. For example, in a market-based economic system, the financial reporting function is geared toward information disclosure for several interested parties: investors, creditors, regulators, employees, and customers. Thus, the reports are varied in their form and content. In contrast, in a non-market economy, where the government owns and runs large portions of business operations, accounting systems are oriented not to external users but to the internal users, that is, the government. Thus, the emphasis of such systems would be on standardization and uniformity of information in order to facilitate centralized, state control. Between these two extremes are nations that have mixed political systems and correspondingly hybrid accounting systems.

The development and nature of accounting systems in different countries are also affected by **sociocultural factors**. For example, in a country where the virtues of trust and honor are highly prized, such as Japan, it would be considered offensive to ask for proof or documentation of business activities in an audit. Similarly, other attributes, such as conservatism and fatalism, affect the nature and development of accounting conventions. Conservatism might evidence itself in larger estimates of bad debt reserves or smaller projections for sales estimates. Planning and budgeting for the future are likely to hold little importance or credence among members of a fatalistic society.

Notions of time affect not only the frequency of reporting, but also the long-term and short-term views. What might be considered short-term or current in one accounting system might be considered long-term in another.

The educational, training, and learning characteristics of a nation also affect the type and level of accounting systems used, because relative levels of literacy and sophistication of the work force affect the applicability or utility of information.

An accounting system is also affected by attitudes commonly held within a country regarding business operations and the nature of the accounting profession. If business is considered as a force that is to be mistrusted, then pressure would be expected upon an enterprise to have larger and fuller disclosure of operations. Similarly, if business is esteemed and trusted, one would expect to see less public scrutiny of operations. In countries where the accounting system is not well-developed, there is less interest and credence placed in accounting practices.

What type of differences emerge?

The practice of holding reserves is one of the most important differences encountered in the accounting practices of different countries. In general, reserves are held by firms to protect against special situations, such as expectations that all the debts of a firm will not be repaid. In some countries, however, reserves are used much more extensively for situations that some consider the normal ups and downs of business operations. In these cases, reserves are used to smooth incomes and taxes from year to year. In profitable years, funds are moved to reserve accounts and thus escape taxation; in less profitable years, the firm can draw upon this cushion to boost flagging income. Reserves have been used to stabilize income by a majority of firms in Switzerland, about half of Italian companies, and in at least a dozen other countries. This practice, however, has the effect of reducing the significance of a firm's income statements to such users as investors or creditors.

Other differences are found in definitions, terminology, and formats. For example, in the United States, long-term investments, assets, and liabilities are defined as those held for more than one year. In other countries, this definition may provide for longer holding periods, such as three years or more. The meaning of **turnover** varies even in English-speaking countries. In the United Kingdom turnover is another term for sales, while in the United States, it refers to the renewal or replenishment of inventory stock.

Differences in valuation

Differences also emerge in the way firms measure the value of assets and the way they determine income. These differences become apparent in a number of procedural areas, such as accounting for leases, carrying long-term debt, assigning value to shares held of a company's own stock, research and development expenses, depreciation, and inventory valuing techniques. For example, in the United States depreciation is calculated according to the normal life of an asset. The value of the asset, however, is adjusted for the amount of money expected to be gained when that asset is ultimately sold. This eventual sales price is referred to as the salvage value. While U.S. firms are only allowed to depreciate assets minus salvage value, in other countries the final asset is depreciated according to its full purchase price.

Other valuation and income differences emerge when countries do not agree on the use of the matching concept of accounting, a term that refers to the cash method of accounting, in which a business attempts to match expenses to the revenues associated with the incurring of those expenses, despite any differences in timing. Still more differences occur when it is accepted practice to keep certain business items off the balance sheet and out of the public or regulatory eye. In recent years, there has been some debate in accounting circles about how to account for stock options on a company's financial statements.

Occasionally off-the-balance-sheet items derive from the pursuit of illegal activities (for example, illegal payments or bribery) by businesses in countries with little regulatory supervision. The United States, for example, imposes strict requirements on accounting for legal facilitative payments made to

76 *International accounting*

low-level foreign officials to smooth the progress of business in foreign countries. Payments or gifts made to high-level government officials are outlawed. In other countries, these practices are considered to be ordinary expenses of doing business abroad and are deductible for tax purposes.

The impact of accounting differences

The existence of accounting differences creates difficulties for financial analysts to compare the financial information of companies around the world. For example, ratios customarily used to evaluate performance, such as return on income or equity, are not comparable. Thus, statements from foreign firms and the financial data they contain must be evaluated in light of relevant differences, and the analyst of an international firm must be aware of likely differences and make necessary adjustments.

The main differences in accounting practices and conventions can be summarized as follows:

- The availability and the reliability of financial information varies from country to country.
- Financial statements and reports differ in language and terminology.
- Financial statements from different countries may include the same information but present it in different formats.
- Currencies used in the statements will generally differ.
- The amounts and types of information disclosed on financial statements are different from country to country.

All of these differences must be considered by any financial analyst before making judgments about the strength or prospects of a firm. Foreign firms should be evaluated in the perspective of their own country and industry, not according to a home-country reference point.

Differences in disclosure

Information disclosure varies considerably across different countries. Disclosure requirements are a measure of public scrutiny of business enterprises within a country. Greater disclosure implies that the internal strengths and weaknesses of a company are made known to the general public. The differences lie not only in the level of detail, but in the types of disclosed business activities. The amounts and types of disclosure required are determined by several factors: social pressures, legal requirements, and the forces of industry competitors and external users of accounting information.

In the United States, for example, all firms that issue securities (publicly held companies) must file regular, detailed, and extensive reports with the Securities and Exchange Commission (SEC) regarding their business activities. Access to these reports is available to anyone who visits the SEC's public information office in Washington, D.C., or subscribes to an information service that, for a fee, will provide copies of corporate filings. There is also the ability to download company annual filings with the SEC via internet sites such as Edgarscan.

Pressure for extensive disclosure is sometimes encouraged by private interests, such as consumer groups. Corporations, on the other hand, tend to minimize the extent of information they must distribute. The reluctance of corporations to part with information can be attributed to a desire to protect their strategic advantages over competitors.

The type of disclosure required in the United States contrasts with other countries, such as Switzerland, where secrecy is the norm. In Switzerland, which is known for supremely confidential bank accounts, little if any financial information is provided in annual reports, and no information is provided on the derivation of that information. The United States, on the other hand, has increased the standards that are now deemed acceptable in financial reporting. The Sarbanes-Oxley Act of 2002 requires that the board members of corporations be "financially literate", and that at least two of the board members hold the CPA designation (or have held it in the past). Additionally, the CEO and CFO are required to certify the financial results for each reporting year. The penalties for corporate fraud were also increased in the wake of the various corporate reporting scandals in recent times. Patterns of disclosure therefore vary around the nations of the world, with some countries requiring even greater disclosure than the United States and others requiring very little.

Segmentation of accounting

In the United States, firms are required to report their results according to segments of business activities, that is, they are required to disclose in their public reports where large percentages of their business are concentrated (for example, in industry lines, foreign operations, export sales, or to single customers, such as governments). Segments that comprise more than 10% of world revenues, total profits or losses, or total assets of a company must be reported separately.

Once these individual segments are identified, the firm must disclose revenues, operating results, and identifiable assets associated with each segment. The company, however, does have discretion in its segmentation criteria for sales abroad. While many companies segment foreign sales separately as a whole, others segment according to geographic operating areas, such as Europe and North America. The choice of definitional criteria can disguise critical information from the eyes of competitors. For example, a firm might hide its enormous sales in a central African country by treating sales for the entire continent as one segment.

The latest annual reports of Sony Corporation segment sales by area and product group. The areas used are Japan, the United States, Europe, and "other areas," even though sales to other areas in 2015 represented more than 11% of the firm's total sales. Product groups were divided into nine areas: mobile

78 *International accounting*

communications, game and network services, imaging products and services, home entertainment and sound, devices, pictures, music, financial services, and other products (see Exhibit 4.1).

The segmentation at Nestle is also extensive. The company's annual report for 2015 shows sales in millions of Swiss francs, and as percentages for Europe, the Americas, Asia, Africa, and Oceania, as well as sales in main country markets for that year. The report also provides prior-year information regarding sales in those segment areas. The Swiss firm also segments sales according to all main product groups, from beverages, comprising 22%, to water, providing 8% of sales for the year (see Exhibits 4.2 and 4.3).

Research conducted by Frederick D. S. Choi and V B. Bavishi on comparative requirements across countries of geographic disclosure by multinational firms in Europe, North America, and Japan show that nearly all

Yen in Millions						
Year End March 31						
Sales by Area	*2013*	*%*	*2014*	*%*	*2015*	*%*
Japan	2,197,881	32.3%	2,199,099	28.3%	2,233,776	27.2%
USA	1,064,765	15.7%	1,302,052	16.8%	1,528,097	18.6%
Europe	1,362,488	20.0%	1,753,526	22.6%	1,932,941	23.5%
China	464,784	6.8%	520,539	6.7%	546,697	6.7%
Asia–Pacific	806,205	11.9%	1,013,635	13.1%	1,052,453	12.8%
Other	899,381	13.2%	978,415	12.6%	921,916	11.2%
Total	**6,795,504**	100.0%	**7,767,266**	100.0%	**8,215,880**	100.0%
Sales by Product Group	*2013*	*%*	*2014*	*%*	*2015*	*%*
Mobile Communications	733,622	10.8%	1,191,787	15.3%	1,323,205	16.1%
Game & Network Services	646,421	9.5%	946,479	12.2%	1,292,146	15.7%
Imaging Products & Solutions	752,603	11.1%	737,474	9.5%	716,258	8.7%
Home Entertainment & Sound	993,822	14.6%	1,166,007	15.0%	1,204,922	14.7%
Devices	558,027	8.2%	583,089	7.5%	756,724	9.2%
Pictures	732,127	10.8%	828,668	10.7%	876,314	10.7%
Music	431,719	6.4%	492,058	6.3%	533,986	6.5%
Financial Services	999,276	14.7%	988,944	12.7%	1,077,604	13.1%
Other	947,887	13.9%	832,760	10.7%	434,721	5.3%
Total	**6,795,504**	100.0%	**7,767,266**	100.0%	**8,215,880**	100.0%

Exhibit 4.1 Sony's sales by area and product group

Source: 2015 Sony Corporation Annual Report

(In millions of CHF)						
Product	2013	%	2014	%	2015	%
Powdered & Liquid Beverages	20,495	22.2%	20,302	22.2%	19,245	21.7%
Water	6,773	7.3%	6,875	7.5%	7,112	8.0%
Milk products and Ice Cream	17,357	18.8%	16,743	18.3%	14,637	16.5%
Nutrition and Health Science	11,840	12.8%	13,046	14.2%	14,854	16.7%
Prepared Dishes and Cooking Aids	14,171	15.4%	13,538	14.8%	12,579	14.2%
Confectionary	10,283	11.2%	9,769	10.7%	8,870	10.0%
Pet Care	11,239	12.2%	11,339	12.4%	11,488	12.9%
Total Sales	**92,158**	100.0%	**91,612**	100.0%	**88,785**	100.0%

Exhibit 4.2 Nestle sales by product group

Source: 2015 Nestle Annual Report

(In millions of CHF)						
Classification	2013	%	2014	%	2015	%
Zone Americas	28,358	30.8%	27,277	29.8%	25,844	29.1%
Zone Europe	15,567	16.9%	15,175	16.6%	16,403	18.5%
Zone Asia, Oceania, & Africa	18,851	20.5%	18,272	19.9%	14,338	16.1%
Nestle Waters	7,257	7.9%	7,390	8.1%	7,625	8.6%
Nestle Nutrition	9,826	10.7%	9,614	10.5%	10,461	11.8%
Other Activities	12,299	13.3%	13,884	15.2%	14,114	15.9%
Total Sales	**92,158**	100.0%	**91,612**	100.0%	**88,785**	100.0%

Exhibit 4.3 Nestle sales by region

Source: 2015 Nestle Annual Report

firms report foreign sales in general and by geographic area. Disclosure falls off, however, in reporting more sensitive data, such as that on income generated by foreign operations, assets held in foreign geographic areas and exports and capital expenditures by foreign sources and geographic areas.

Social reporting

One area in which reporting requirements for firms operating in different environments differ substantially is in the area of social reporting in financial reports, which goes far beyond the disclosure of such items on a balance sheet and income statement as assets, sales, earnings per share, and taxes. Social reports answer questions raised about the socioeconomic effects of a firm's operations on the quality of life or economic status of a nation. According to one classification, these special impact reports take three forms: environmental

80 *International accounting*

quality, the effect a company has on its employees and the community, and national income accounting. However, some specialists feel that social accounting steps beyond the typical bounds of accounting, stretching into areas better explored in other venues.

The topics covered by special reports include controlling or correcting environmental pollution and ensuring product safety; assuring employee welfare in terms of equal opportunity, safe working conditions, and personnel practices; community involvement and contributions; and corporate morals, as embodied in codes of conduct and ethical guidelines. In some countries firms must attempt to identify the extent of their contribution to the national economic situation, both directly, as a result of investment and operations, and indirectly, by way of its contribution to increased employment. Historically in France, any firm with three hundred or more employees has had to prepare a bilan social, or social balance sheet. A similar kind of report, the *Social Jaareslag*, has been required in the Netherlands, as has a *Sozialbilanz* in Germany.

The trend toward requiring firms to be accountable for the social effects of their operations is growing worldwide. An MNC must take this aspect into consideration when devising accounting procedures and practices for an overseas subsidiary. Necessary expertise must be created to generate such reports, and the company's operations must he sensitive to these concerns. The result is that accountants in these nations and those responsible for reporting from a multinational perspective must enlarge their views and take these reporting requirements into consideration and develop expertise in new areas.

Policy formation and harmonization

Determining policy

The determination of accounting policy – the setting of objectives, standards, and practices used by accounting professionals in each nation of the world – derives from two sources. Policy emanates either from national laws and the codification of practices, or it has developed by members of the accounting profession itself, who represent their entire national membership and agree upon standards to be observed by practitioners.

The legal requirements of, or restrictions upon, accounting practices come either from regulations imposed by government users of accounting information, such as tax authorities, or from planning agencies or national legislators. The relative importance of the roles played by these entities in the determination of accounting policy depends on two major determinants: the status and size of the accounting profession in each nation and the degree to which each government seeks to control or monitor business activity. Thus, it is not surprising that government forces are exceedingly strong in setting accounting policy in nations with planned economic systems, and that they are far weaker and less intrusive in market economies.

International accounting 81

Policymaking in the United States

Accounting policy in the United States is determined primarily by members of its highly sophisticated and well-regulated accounting profession. These members create policy by working together to develop a set of generally accepted accounting principles. The main policy-setting body in the United States is the Financial Accounting Standards Board (FASB), which determines accounting policy and promulgates such determinations through its publication of statements on issues of concern. The policies and statements are accepted by the American Institute of Certified Public Accountants (AICPA), another independent body of professionals, which sets auditing standards for external accounting requirements. Accounting practices are also delineated by law in the United States and are primarily requirements established by the SEC for all companies that issue securities to the public and by federal tax law, as set forth in the federal tax code.

Policymaking in other countries

Policymaking in other countries varies along a continuum, because all countries include some combination of accounting policy set by legislation and by professional practice. The differences in policy come from differences in political orientation, levels of professionalism, the development of the accounting profession in each country, and from the nature and depth of business within each country.

Some countries that rely more on legislation than on practice are those with strong governmental intervention in economic activity, such as France, Germany, Egypt, and Brazil. Other nations, such as England, have a greater combination of law and professional involvement in standard-setting, while others, such as the Netherlands and Switzerland, experience minimal influence from legislative efforts.

Some nations, such as Japan, have only relatively recently developed accounting standards and have patterned their systems on those of other nations; in Japan's case, on the United States and Germany. Some countries, particularly less-developed nations, have adopted the principles of their former colonial governments and rely on legislation to set standards, because the membership of the accounting profession is small and not well regarded.

Harmonization

Divergences have always existed among accounting systems around the world. These differences lead to complications that are intensified with the increase in international business activity. To combat these problems, efforts have been mounted to standardize accounting functions to some degree on a regional and international basis. Such efforts are generally known as harmonization among accounting executives, practices, and standards.

82 *International accounting*

Three different methods of attempting to establish harmony among accounting methods that differ according to the requirements of users or circumstances have been identified: absolute uniformity, circumstantial uniformity, and purposive uniformity.

Absolute uniformity proposes that accounting methods be standardized regardless of the different circumstances of different users. This model has been criticized as being too inflexible and too radical, although it would, theoretically, be easier to administer than other models.

Circumstantial uniformity would use different practices according to the variations in the circumstances of economic facts and conditions. Once these circumstances are identified, accounting practices can be put into place to deal with them on a consistent basis.

Purposive uniformity would vary the determination of accounting practices and standards according to both diversity of users and circumstances. This model has the advantage of providing flexibility for differing environmental situations and purposes and is embodied in U.S. regulatory practices.

The greatest effort to bring the postulates and practices of accounting into harmony in the international accounting arena is the International Accounting Standards Board (IASB), which was formed in April 2001 and in 2016 consisted of accounting professionals representing one hundred twenty countries and a similar number of accounting organizations, under the larger banner of the International Financial Reporting Standards Board. The purpose of the IASB is to provide a forum through which members of professional accounting groups can attempt to develop international standards that can be used in domestic operations. The representatives of the IASB are hampered, however, in that they have no authority to enforce any decisions and can only promise to promote such standards in the publication of financial statements, with policy-setting organizations, and with government or regulatory officials. The hope is that each nation will adopt their standards and resolutions, either as professional standards or as national law.

Another international organization is the International Federation of Accountants (IFAC), which was formed in 1977 to succeed the International Coordination Committee for the Accounting Profession. The objective of the IFAC is to provide a forum through which members of the world's accounting profession can meet to establish international standards and principles for auditing practices, as well as standards for the training, education, and codes of ethics of accountants. The IFAC consists of members from more than 130 countries and a similar number of professional accounting groups.

Regional harmonization efforts

Regional efforts at harmonization often fall in line with historical economic or political groupings of nations. Some of the regional national accounting associations are the Inter-American Accounting Association (IAA) and the Association of Accountants and Auditors in Europe (AAAE). The problem with these groups is that although they can meet and attempt to harmonize standards, they are generally comprised of practitioners who have no authority behind their decision-making to promote standardization. They can, however, use their influence to affect policy-setting in individual countries and among their own national professional associations.

One regional grouping where the force of law is brought to bear on the practice of accounting, however, is the European Union (EU). In the EU, accounting standards are developed through the issuance of directives developed by its Council of Ministers. The EU's progress toward harmonization of accounting practices has led to mandates for member countries to bring their laws into harmonization on selected topics.

Special accounting problems

Despite efforts to harmonize accounting practices and standards around the world, the managers of enterprises with operations in multiple foreign settings face formidable difficulties. Four specific problems faced by multinational firms are accounting for differences in gains and losses because of differences in currency exchange rates, the question of consolidating returns, accounting under conditions of inflation, and the problems faced in attempting to establish appropriate prices and costs for a multinational's products around the world and between units.

Differences in currency exchange rates

One of the most crucial problems that international firms face is accounting for a transaction that is conducted in a different currency. How is such a transaction to be recorded on the books or reported to management in a consistent manner?

Differences in exchange rates between currencies lead to two separate problems for the international business firm. The first is that of accounting for business transactions and gains and losses from currency rate differentials that arise during such business activity. The second problem is interpreting financial results of transactions conducted in different currencies or devising translations of currencies to yield comparable and measurable results.

Accounting procedures designed to treat these transactions follow either the one-step transaction or the two-step transaction approaches, both of which provide methods for recording business transactions in a home currency.

The **one-step method** records the transaction using the spot rate for the foreign currency in effect on that day. Assume, for example, that Bob of Bob's Lawn and Garden Store wants to acquire lawn ornaments from a German supplier to round out his inventory in anticipation of heavy summer sales. Thus, on January 1, Bob buys 10,000 gross of pink flamingos for 60,000 euros payable by February 1. On the first of January the euro is trading for $0.50 (that is, each dollar is worth 2 euros). Consequently, under the one-step method Bob's ledger entries would be as follows:

84   International accounting

| Purchases: Pink Flamingos | $30,000 |
| Accounts Payable | $30,000 (€ @ $0.50) |

If, however, exchange rates change between the time Bob places his order, records it in his books, and pays his account with the German flamingo maker, he will need to change his records to record the facts and the rate of exchange when the transaction is completed or actually settled. For example, if the value of the dollar falls and it takes $0.75 to buy a euro, Bob's costs for his pink flamingos will rise and must be accounted for as an adjustment to the original cost of the flamingos. The entries he must make will be:

Purchases	$30,000
Accounts Payable	$15,000
Cash	$45,000 (€ @ $0.75)

The **two-step method** of accounting for gains or losses in transactions separates the activities of business activity and currency exchanges. The key difference from the one-step method is that gains or losses from the transaction do not affect the value of the asset acquired but are treated separately, as a result of assuming risk in engaging in the activity and opening the firm to fluctuations in exchange rates. Consequently, under this method our transaction above would be noted as follows:

Accounts Payable	$30,000
Exchange Adjustment: Loss	$15,000
Cash	$45,000 (€ @ $0.75)

In this method, the pink flamingos retain their value of $30,000 on Bob's books, and the difference between the agreed-upon price or costs and the actual amount paid is noted in an exchange adjustment account that is eventually netted and applied as an adjustment to shareholder equity.

Some countries require the use of the one-step method, while others employ the two-step method. The United States has historically employed the two-step method and has required the immediate recognition of gains or losses from foreign currency transactions. In other countries it is common accounting practice to defer gains and losses from accounts payable and receivable until the transactions are completed, and these results are not taken to the income statement.

These accounting steps become far more involved when firms engage in hedging to protect themselves from fluctuations in rates of exchanges between countries. It must be remembered, however, that such complications arise only when the transaction is denominated in a foreign currency. Bob could have asked to pay his bill in dollars, in which case he would have no risk because of changes in the rate of exchange between euros and dollars. Instead, the German manufacturer would take the currency risk and account for any changes in the dollar's value.

Problems arise for multinational firms with business operations that are carried out in different locales and reported in different currencies. When MNCs are required to translate local currency accounts into home currency at the close of the financial year, what criteria does an MNC use to report and compare its operations in different environments? These problems are not ones of valuation (determining appropriate values for assets in terms of other currencies) or of converting currencies from foreign to a uniform home currency, but are those involved in restating operational results. The objective is for results to be integrated so that they can be analyzed by management and reported to regulatory authorities. The process of restating financial statements into a uniform currency is called **translation.** When the financial statements from all operating units of an MNC are combined, they are said to be consolidated.

Foreign statement translation is a two-step process for the controller of an MNC. First, the accounts must be brought into consistency by being restated according to the same accounting principles, such as those for valuing inventories and assets and determining depreciation. After the basis of the accounts has been adjusted to provide for consistency, the foreign currency amounts represented in the results can be translated into the reporting or home currency. Translation must not be confused with conversion. Translating is merely the restating of currencies, while conversion refers to the actual physical trade or exchange of units of one currency for another.

Accountants use four different methods of translating statements from local currencies to the reporting or home currency: the current-rate method, the temporal method, the monetary/non-monetary method, and the current/non-current method (see Exhibit 4.4).

Statement number 52 of the Financial Accounting Standards Board (FASB) introduced some new definitional concepts to the translation of foreign exchange accounts. The first is the use of a **functional currency,** which is defined as the "currency of the primary economic environment in which the entity operates." It is differentiated from the **reporting currency**, which is the reporting currency of the parent. The determination of a functional currency is tricky for some subsidiaries. It could be the local currency if most of the subsidiary's business of buying, selling, or manufacturing is conducted using the local currency. The parent company's reporting currency could also be the functional currency, if the subsidiary's operations consist mostly of selling goods to the parent, or could even be the currency of a third country, if the bulk of the entity's business is conducted in a third country.

The responsibility for choosing the functional currency rests with each firm, based on operational criteria regarding currencies involved in cash flows, prices, sales market, expenses, financing, and inter-company indicators. Functional currencies can change, but only if there is a change in the initial underlying operational criteria, a stipulation imposed by the FASB to prevent arbitrary changes in functional currencies that aggressive accountants might make to put financial statements in the best possible light.

86 *International accounting*

Once the functional currency is determined, a firm can begin its process of translating statements under FASB #52 and consolidating, or combining, the results of disparate operations. The use of either the current or the temporal rate is determined by the location of operations and resulting functional currency. If the books and records are kept in the currency of the parent, no restatement is necessary. If, however, the books and records are kept in a local currency, the subsidiary has three different translation routes, depending on the functional currency.

If the functional currency is the local currency of the subsidiary, the parent merely translates the statements into U.S. dollars using the current-rate method. This situation holds unless the functional currency is a local currency in a high-inflation country, in which case the firm must use the temporal method of translation. High-inflation countries are defined as those as with inflation rates greater than 100% for three consecutive years.

If the functional currency is the parent's home currency, even if the books are kept in the local currency, the firm uses the temporal method to re-measure results. If the functional currency is a third currency, the firm re-measures from the local to the functional currency using the temporal method and then translates the result into the home currency using the current-rate method. Exhibit 4.5 provides a clearer description of this process.

	Current	*Current-Noncurrent*	*Monetary-Nonmonetary*	*Temporal*
Cash	C	C	C	C
Accounts Receivable	C	C	C	C
Inventories				
Cost	C	C	H	H
Market	C	C	H	C
Investments				
Cost	C	H	H	H
Market	C	H	H	C
Fixed Assets	C	H	H	H
Other Assets	C	H	H	H
Accounts Payable	C	C	C	C
Long-term Debt	C	H	C	C
Common Stock	H	H	H	H
Retaining Earnings	★	★	★	★

Exhibit 4.4 Exchange rates employed in different translation methods for specific balance sheet items

Note: C = current rate; H = historical rate; and ★ = residual, balancing figure representing a composite of successive current rates

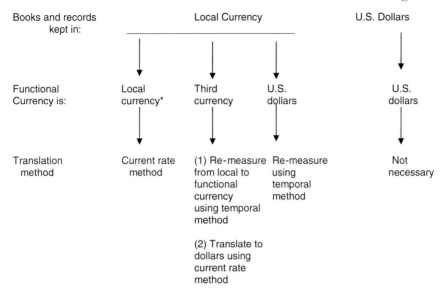

Exhibit 4.5 Translating a firm's functional currency into a reporting currency

Consolidation problems

The results of these financial machinations are then integrated into a firm's comprehensive reckoning of operations and results. This consolidation process raises some special considerations for a MNC and questions about a firm's organizational and investment decisions. For example, what operations should be consolidated into the firms overall operations? Some countries require only that the parent report the results of its operations and do not require the integration of the results of subsidiary or affiliated arms. In the United States, for example, tax laws require that firms consolidate their operations globally, because firms are taxed on worldwide income (although they are given credit for taxes paid to other governments). Some other issues raised are: What if a parent corporation owns only part interest in a subsidiary? What level of investment determines ownership or determines control? What distinction is made between having an investment in another concern or that concern's being an integral part of the parent corporation's network?

Consolidation rules in the United States

In the United States the questions about whether or not a parent consolidates the results of subsidiary operations into its own depends on the level and type of involvement of the parent in the activities of the subsidiary. There are three different ways an investment in another enterprise can be handled under

88 International accounting

accounting rules: the **cost method**, the equity method, or consolidation. The **cost method** is employed when the parent firm holds an unsubstantial investment in the subsidiary. Under this method, the parent carries the investment as such and only reports income from the subsidiary when the subsidiary declares a dividend to the parent. Typically, the cost method is used in the United States when the parent owns less than 20% of the voting stock of the affiliate and was acquired initially through purchasing. Monies flowing back to the parent are treated as dividends and do not change the level of the investment account of the parent.

If the parent owns a substantial portion of the stock of the subsidiary, from 20% to 50%, it reports income from the subsidiary as it is earned, not as it is received. The investment is carried on the parent's books at original cost and is adjusted according to earnings or dividends received from the subsidiary. Income from the foreign subsidiary increases the value of the parent's investment (whether it is received or not), and thus the value of the holding is adjusted upward to reflect an increase in the share of profits. Any dividends received by the parent from its holdings in the subsidiary have the effect of reducing the investment's book value, because it is considered to have the effect of lowering the profits of the subsidiary.

If the parent owns more than 50% of the subsidiary, it has a controlling interest in the foreign affiliate and must consolidate the results of the affiliate into its own reports. The consolidation process is carried out line by line to agree with the financial statements of the parent. Thus, before the two sets of figures are aggregated, they must be adjusted to agree according to the accounting principles used, and foreign currencies must be translated into the reporting currency. The parent and the affiliate must also adjust their books to correct for their inter-corporate transactions and profits that have resulted from business dealings between the two entities.

Inflation

Companies doing business in high-inflation countries must develop special procedures for dealing with the effects of inflation on the valuation of assets. Inflation also raises problems for MNCs in their attempts to evaluate and predict purchasing power for foreign operations and in evaluating their financial reports. As long as there are few changes in prices in a country, MNCs attempting to value their assets can use historical costs for those assets as appropriate measures. When inflation is significant, however, the value of those assets stated in historical terms inaccurately represents the wealth of the firm.

There are basically two responses when dealing with inflation. One can either reestablish a new basis for historical values that reflects the effects of inflation, or one can put into place a system that constantly corrects for changes in prices. In practice, under the first model, all financial statements are adjusted at a single point in time, and these adjusted costs become the new historical basis; under the second model, values are indexed on a continual basis according to changes in prices.

In accounting practice the use of models depends on the objectives of the financial reports. The two methods of handling inflation in terms of accounting methods are constant dollar (or general purchasing power) accounting and current cost accounting.

The goal of **constant dollar accounting** is to report assets, liabilities, expenses, and revenues in terms of the same purchasing power. The original basis of the valuations, the historical costs, does not change under this accounting method. Instead, non-financial items are restated to reflect the purchasing power in effect on the date of the balance sheet. Financial items on the statements, such as cash, receivables, and payables, would not be restated because their monetary valuation would already reflect the purchasing power of the currency on the date of the report.

In **current cost accounting** the emphasis is not on the loss of purchasing power associated with a specific currency, but the amount of money it would take to replace assets because of price increases. Thus, under current cost accounting, historical costs are supplanted by new, adjusted costs, such as replacement costs. Its objective is to account for the effects of inflation as it relates to the increases in the costs of specific assets and not overall prices.

The treatment of inflation in the presentation of accounting records differs around the world. In the United States, firms are required to continue to use the historical cost standard as their basis for reporting financial results, but they are also required to disclose supplementary information regarding both price level and current cost accounting (also known as fair value accounting). Fair value is used for derivatives and stock options, for example. Other countries have different requirements. In Great Britain, current cost balance sheets and income statements must be presented, and such financial statements may be presented as supplements to or in place of historical costs financial statements. Some high-inflation countries require that firms adjust their statements to reflect the enormous rates of inflation, and require the use of an inflation index and a monetary correction system, respectively.

The result of these different methods of accounting for inflation is that the MNC operating in a multitude of foreign environments must often keep multiple sets of books in order to adhere to the reporting requirements of each jurisdiction and the parent firm's home authorities.

Transfer pricing and costing

The international nature of the business of MNCs introduces a number of factors that have to be accounted for in determining the costs of their products around the world. Although multinational firms use the same methods for determining costs as domestic enterprises, their efforts are greatly complicated by the nature of operations in a global environment. For example, products and raw materials are not only affected by domestic forces, such as inflation and availability, but are

90   *International accounting*

also affected by such international forces as changes in exchange rates, transportation fees, insurance costs, customs duties, and facilitating payments. Similarly, costs involved in conducting international trade are often influenced by government subsidies that are intended to promote export sales.

Such costing and pricing problems are significant for exported products manufactured domestically; they are even worse for firms that have raw material and parts sourced in several parts of the world. The complications become enormous, as cost accountants attempt to allocate costs to different products and operating units within different countries.

Transfers within the various affiliated arms of an MNC, especially for transfer pricing for goods and services between different parts of the company, create complex accounting issues. MNCs can use transfer pricing to achieve a variety of corporate objectives, such as reducing overall tax burden, avoiding restrictions on repatriation of earnings, or the exchange of local for home country currencies. Thus, transfer prices set by MNCs not only concern the strategic decision-makers in the company, but they also often come under scrutiny of external government officials. An MNC can deal with this problem to some extent by adjusting its performance measures for the subsidiary to focus on different criteria, such as achieving production efficiencies and maintaining low costs.

Companies have three ways of valuing goods and services that pass between arms or branches of the same corporation. They can use a **cost–plus method**, where they take actual costs of production and add a fixed monetary amount or percentage. Alternately, they can use the market price, less a certain percentage discount. Under **arm's length pricing** they can charge the same price for affiliates or parents as they do for third-party buyers. While cost-based transfer pricing has the advantage of providing the firm with flexibility, most governments prefer the easily determined and monitored use of market-based pricing systems by MNCs. The United States requires that firms use arm's-length prices, unless they can justify why different prices based on costs are more reasonable than those based on market prices.

Other international accounting issues

Accounting for expropriation

One potential problem for any firm conducting business in a foreign environment is the political risk that its assets will be taken over by the government through expropriation or nationalization. When a firm is remunerated by a country for expropriated assets, many questions arise about determining the appropriate value of those assets in relation to the monies received. Book or historical values are not usually representative of true, current value, because they may not reflect what it would cost to replace the assets or what monies would actually be received if those assets were sold on the open market. The determination of value is generally arbitrary, not market-oriented, because expropriation usually results from political action. Similarly, there are seldom comparable sales of similar assets or replacement assets in the country on which to base an estimation of value for the expropriated assets.

Consequently, in order to determine its position regarding gain or loss on the disposition of the assets, MNCs in such situations must use an adjusted asset book value that accounts for increases in economic value over time. Thus, values placed on expropriated property are highly subjective. Once these values are estimated and compared to payments made by the expropriating government, the firm must deal with its gain or loss on the property. Such gains and losses shown as operating items do not affect the financial results of the firm in the United States, where losses because of expropriation are reported net of tax effects and are classified as extraordinary items. Most other countries allow such losses to be taken as direct write-offs against owners' equity or equity reserve accounts.

Planning and control

One of the biggest problems faced by MNCs in the implementation of international accounting methods and systems is the sheer multitude and variety of players, reporting sites, requirements, and forms. Thus, it is crucial that the international firm have a well-organized and comprehensive system of financial reporting and control in place to generate accurate, timely, and usable information. Many firms often take their existing domestic systems abroad, but these systems may need to be adjusted for local needs and different accounting requirements and conventions. For example, employees at a foreign site may find systems designed for the home environment too sophisticated for their levels of expertise, training, or abilities.

Ideally, MNCs should develop reporting functions and formats that can be used by all members of the network. Information supplied by all parts of the operating system must be uniform. Therefore, an MNC must decide beforehand on common formats, language, and currencies, as well as a set of procedures to be followed. Similarly, care must be taken in the development of budgets, goals, and objectives for MNC subsidiaries and affiliates. An MNC must take into account different operating environments in setting goals and in evaluating relative performance.

Auditing

Once an accounting system is in place and operational, its efficiency must be continually monitored by auditing. There are two types of auditing in a corporation. Internal audits assess whether or not the firm has proper operational and financial controls to assure the security of its assets and the compliance of individual employees in the operation of the system. External audits look objectively at the ledgers of a firm and provide an opinion as to whether or not the information recorded is valid, reliable, and accurate. This is the attestation function of accounting. External auditors base their judgments on standards

92   *International accounting*

developed by the accounting profession; they are accounting professionals who have no affiliation with the corporation. Conducting external, independent audits provides a large portion of the business of the major accounting firms in the United States.

For internal audits conducted at a foreign subsidiary level, a firm has the choice of using local auditors or bringing in personnel from headquarters. The use of both types of auditors presents problems. Local auditors might facilitate the auditing process in keeping expenses down and avoiding language and cultural differences. Problems might arise, however, in terms of the rigorousness of corporate standards applied by local personnel because of their potential lack of familiarity with corporate requirements. Whereas auditors from headquarters could better examine subsidiary procedural lapses, they would run up against problems of their being unfamiliar with the language, the people, and the business practices accepted in the foreign environment.

Summary

International business transactions present several accounting problems and raise many accounting issues because they encompass different environments, currencies, reporting requirements, and forms. The challenge of satisfying these financial and managerial accounting information needs must be met with an eye to developing uniform systems of reporting information in a manner that provides for its efficient integration and utilization by all users. Effective and accurate reporting of business transactions is required in order to present an accurate picture of the economic situation of the firm to both internal and external users.

Discussion questions

1   Who are the users of accounting information?
2   What factors influence the development of international accounting systems?
3   What is financial disclosure? Can this vary between countries? Explain.
4   What are the main differences in accounting conventions?
5   What is social reporting?
6   What role does the FASB have in setting accounting policy? Explain in terms of its domestic and international roles?
7   What regional international accounting organizations are trying to harmonize accounting practices? Discuss.
8   What is the difference between functional currency and reporting currency?
9   What are the four main accounting problems faced by multinationals?
10   How do multinationals account for losses due to expropriation?
11   Why are planning, control, and auditing important accounting functions?

Bibliography

AICPA website, "The Enron Crisis: The AICPA, The Profession, and the Public Interest: Summary of Sarbanes-Oxley Act of 2002", http://www.aicpa.org/Pages/default.aspx, accessed July 17, 2017.

Arpan, Jeffrey S., and Dhia D. Al-Hashim. 1984. *International Dimensions of Accounting*. Boston: Kent Publishing.

Arpan, Jeffrey S., and Lee H. Radebaugh. 1985. *International Accounting and Multinational Enterprises*, 2nd ed. New York: John Wiley & Sons.

Buckley, Adrian. 1987. Does FX Exposure Matter? *Accountancy* (March): 116–118.

Cairns, David. 1989. IASC's Blueprint for the Future. *Accountancy* (December): 80–82.

Carsberg, B. 1983. FASB #52: Measuring the Performance of Foreign Operations. *Midland Corporate Finance Journal* 1: 47–55.

Choi, Frederick D. S. 1975. Multinational Challenges for Managerial Accountants. *Journal of Contemporary Business* (Autumn): 51–68.

Choi, Frederick D. S. 1982. Diversity in Multinational Accounting. *Financial Executive* (August): 45–49.

Choi, Frederick D. S., and Vinod B. Bavishi. 1981. A Cross-National Assessment of Management's Geographic Disclosure. Paper presented at the Fourth Annual Meeting of the European Accounting Association, Barcelona.

Choi, Frederick D. S., and Gerhard G. Mueller. 1987. *An Introduction to Multinational Accounting*. Englewood Cliffs, N.J.: Prentice-Hall.

Economist, The. "Bean-counting Goes Global." Joanne Ramos, The World in 2005, print edition. http://www.economist.com/node/3373334, accessed July 17, 2017.

Financial Accounting Standards Board. 1977. *Statement of Financial Accounting Standards. No. 52: Foreign Currency Translation*. Stamford, CT: Financial Accounting Standards Board.

Nestle Corporation. 2015. Annual Report, http://www.nestle.com/asset-library/documents/library/documents/annual_reports/2015-annual-review-en.pdf, accessed July 17, 2017.

Sony Corporation. 2015. Annual Report, https://www.sony.net/SonyInfo/IR/library/sec.html, accessed July 17, 2017.

Taylor, Thomas C. 1976. The Illusions of Social Accounting. *The CPA Journal* (January): 24–28.

5 International taxation

Taxes are what we pay for a civilized society.

(Oliver Wendell Holmes)

Chapter objectives

This chapter will:

- Present a rationale for the role and purpose of tax policy in modern society.
- Discuss the major forms of taxation employed by governments, including income, transaction, excise, severance, and tariff taxes, and the differences in compliance and enforcement of tax laws between countries.
- Describe special tax problems, treaties, and credits that may influence site selection for multinational operations.
- Review the advantages offered by international tax havens.
- Examine the types of incentives governments offer to corporations and to foreign nationals to promote international business.

Why taxes?

Taxes paid to governing bodies represent the contributions that all individual citizens and businesses make to public coffers. These funds finance most public services, including public education, state and federal government systems, local police and national defense forces, highway and waterway systems, protection of the environment, maintenance of state and federal parks and wilderness areas, and social programs that provide for the less fortunate by establishing housing, education, health care, and nutritional services.

The societal expectation underlying the principle that all wage earners should make a contribution to society is that it be a fair or equitable share. Every corporation or citizen in the same economic or business situation should thus be required to pay the same level of taxes. While the notion of equity underlies most national tax systems, it is not "fair" because every citizen does not pay the same proportion of wages in taxes. Therefore, most tax systems are **progressive**, and the more a person or corporation earns, the higher their tax bill because they are considered to be better able to pay a larger share.

In addition to the fairness or equity principle, tax systems are frequently based on the notion of neutrality, which means that business decisions and economic activities should not be prejudiced or directed by the consequences of tax policy. The rationale is that economic efficiency dictates that funds or capital should flow to the most efficient use. In practice, however, nations use tax policy to achieve other objectives, often at the expense of reducing economic efficiency of capital resources.

Governments may, for example, assess taxes to discourage consumption of scarce or unhealthy goods, such as alcohol and tobacco. Taxes may be applied to imports to raise their prices, discourage their purchase, and increase the relative attractiveness of domestic goods. Similarly, tax breaks may be instituted to encourage investment in specific industries, such as developing new sources of energy.

Policy objectives differ around the world, as do systems of taxation. These differences create problems for MNCs, which seek to minimize their multinational tax burden while optimizing the use of their financial and other resources in several countries. Unfortunately, taxes often have a major impact on operational decisions. What international activities should be pursued? In which countries should they be pursued? How should activities be financed? Tax considerations are also involved in decisions concerning the form taken by different subsidiaries of an MNC and how prices will be determined between various segments and corporate headquarters.

Tax law is generally complex. In recent years, the US tax code has consisted of 17,000 pages of tax regulations, and some estimates put the total number of pages of the current tax code at 75,000 (up from only 400 pages in 1913). Further explanations of the law and accompanying regulations constitute many thousands more pages of text. However, the Internal Revenue Service found that the tasks of record-keeping, learning about the law, and filing the basic 1040 tax return took longer than an average day's work (nine hours and five minutes). The addition of other schedules, such as Schedule A for itemized deductions, or Schedule B for interest and dividend income, were estimated to require an additional 4.5 and 1.5 hours, respectively.

Multiply such complexity by the addition of business technicalities and information, as well as by the number of international environments in which modern MNCs operate, and you have an idea of the difficulties involved in managing the tax function of a multinational enterprise. These complications also increase the difficulty for managers to factor all relevant tax consequences into business decision-making.

96 *International taxation*

Types of taxes

Income taxes

There are many different types of taxes levied throughout the world. Income taxes are those levied by nation-states on the earnings or other inflows of money of individuals and businesses. Such taxes are generally levied in a progressive manner; the more one earns, the higher a person is taxed. Income taxes are determined according to a person or firm's taxable income, that is, income that has been adjusted or reduced by deductions allowed by law.

Tax deductions account for expenses incurred by businesses or individuals and are subtracted from the taxpayer's total income. Tax deductions for individuals may be itemized or a standardized allowable sum. The standard deduction may be subtracted from income. For individuals, such items as medical expenses, charitable contributions, mortgage interest, and losses from disaster or theft can be itemized and deducted from income before taxes are levied. Alternatively, individuals can take standard deductions, which, under the 2016 U.S. law, range from $6,300 for individuals to $12,600 for married couples filing together or spouses surviving widowhood. In addition, income is adjusted for family size and special circumstances through the allowance of exemptions, each worth $4,050 in deductions from income. Deductions from income yield savings in taxes at the applicable tax rate, not in a dollar-for-dollar manner, because they reduce the income upon which taxes are levied. Thus, if the tax rate applied to one's income is 33%, each dollar's worth of tax deductions yields a saving of $0.33.

Once taxable income is determined, taxes are calculated according to that amount. Adjustments to (reductions in) the amount of taxes due are characterized as tax credits. Because these credits reduce the actual tax liability, they yield tax savings on a dollar-per-dollar basis. Credits are allowed for individuals in the United States for such items as care for children, dependents, or disabled people; for contributions to political parties; taxes paid to foreign governments; and general business credits.

Companies are allowed such credits against their tax bills as expenses for general business; taxes paid to U.S. possessions or foreign governments; and the production of orphan drugs or energy from non-conventional sources. These credits show some of the social considerations taken into account in the development of tax policy. Orphan drugs for example, are those produced in very small quantities and are used by very small groups of consumers. Consequently, they may be economically inefficient to produce by large drug manufacturing concerns. To compensate drug companies for providing this service, a tax credit gives companies an incentive to provide for the medical needs of these citizens. Similarly, a credit for the production of energy from non-conventional sources (such as hydrogen, wind, or solar power) provides incentives for citizens to look to new energy sources and to reduce reliance on fossil fuels.

Transaction taxes

Another method of assessing taxes is that applied to transactions. Transaction taxes are levied at the time a transaction occurs or an exchange takes place. The most common transaction taxes encountered by citizens of the United States are state and local sales taxes, which are paid when items are purchased. Sales or transaction taxes are not progressive and do not discriminate in their application. All people are taxed at the same rate on their purchases, regardless of their individual wealth.

Value-added taxes

One variation of the transaction tax that is widely used in European countries is the **value-added tax** or **VAT**. The VAT was first put into effect in France in 1954 and takes the place of income taxes in some countries. It is a tax that is assessed only upon the value added to products at each level of production. Take for example, a French boutique that sells high-fashion retail clothing. The VAT tax in France is assumed to be 10%. The first stage in the process of producing these items comes with the purchase of material to make the garments; thus, €200 million worth of fabric is bought from suppliers. The VAT tax on the purchase is 20 million francs (10% × €200 million).

At the next stage, the garment pieces are cut and assembled. This production work doubles their value, thus they sell at the wholesale level for €400 million and the VAT connected with the sale is €20 million (10% × (€400 - €200 million)). Finally, the suits sell to the boutique owner for €500 million, and the VAT generated at this stage is €10 million (10% × the value added of €100 million). Thus, the total VAT collected is €50 million on the total value of €500 (see Exhibit 5.1).

In practice, at each stage the buyer pays the VAT on the entire amount, and the seller forwards the tax to the country's treasury department. In our example, the first buyer is the manufacturer (M) who buys fabric for €200 million plus €20 million in VAT. The manufacturer's supplier (S) remits the tax to the appropriate tax authorities. M then sells the fabric as garments to the retailer (R) for €400 million plus €40 million in VAT. M sends the VAT to the government, but applies for a refund of the VAT withheld by the original supplier (S). In this way M is assessed only on the value it added to the raw

Production Value Stage of Product	Value Added		VAT Generated
Raw Material	200		20
Manufacturing	400	200	20
Retail	500	100	10
TOTAL VAT			50

Exhibit 5.1 Example of the application of VAT (in millions of euros).

98   *International taxation*

materials through production efforts of cutting and assembly (400 − 200 × 10% = 20 million).

The VAT is generally passed through to the consumers as an indirect tax; it can, however, be absorbed by the producer. If the product is taken out of the country as an export, the VAT is not applied and is rebated entirely to the exporter. Such rebates create incentives to export because prices for export goods are cheaper than for domestic goods. These rebates on goods exported from European countries have created controversy among members of the international community, who claim that rebating VAT for exports yields incentives that are unfair under the terms of the World Trade Organization (WTO).

In general, VAT taxes have the advantage of being easily administered; they can be raised or lowered easily. They have the disadvantage of not being progressive in that rich and poor people alike make the same contribution to taxes by the purchase of goods, regardless of the type of goods.

Excise taxes

Another type of taxes, **excise taxes** are imposed upon the manufacture, sale, or use of goods or on an activity or occupation. They are frequently levied on luxury commodities, such as tobacco or liquor products (in which case they are often referred to as **sin taxes**); on such basic commodities as gasoline, or on services, such as entertainment. Excise taxes have the advantage of being applicable in specific situations for specific products in order to achieve policy objectives. Some of these objectives may be to limit the use of unhealthy or socially undesirable products, to ration scarce resources, or to regulate the use of specific products. In Canada, for example, a pack of cigarettes now costs CDN$12.00 per pack, and a carton now costs CDN$90.00. A large portion of this price is based on the amount of taxes associated with the purchase of cigarettes. This example of an excise tax is based on the desires of the Health Ministry of Canada to curb the consumption of this harmful product. As is typical when there are arbitrary differences in the price of a product in one country relative to another, the Canadian government makes sure that both visitors and citizens of Canada are not bringing in cigarettes for resale in Canada from countries such as the United States, where the price of cigarettes is not nearly as high!

Extraction taxes

Another type of selective and special tax is a **severance** or **extraction tax**. This type of tax is levied upon producers of mined, extracted, or harvested resources, such as minerals, ores, timber, and fuel products. The severance tax serves to reimburse the local or national community for the depletion of its natural resources. It may be assessed on a per-ton basis for ores or as a stumpage fee for timber depletion.

International taxation 99

Tariffs (border taxes)

Taxes imposed at the borders of a country are generally characterized as **tariffs**. These border taxes not only allow governments to derive revenue from the entry of goods into the country, but serve to discourage the sale of imports by raising prices in the home market. Tariffs, therefore, encourage or support internal domestic production and the entry of foreign producers to build production facilities in the host country. Thus, tariffs are used by countries to achieve economic objectives of growth and domestic production. Tariffs are not done in a vacuum, so any tax increase at the border will result in a tax increase elsewhere. This generally leads to price increases.

Tax compliance and tax enforcement

In addition to this formidable array of tax types, national governments impose many other types of taxes. Some are taxes upon personal property, gifts received by individuals, estates of those who die, and employment taxes to fund various types of social programs. The relative frequency of use of these taxes in different nations is determined by the objectives of the government. In less-developed countries, for example, it is difficult to impose an income tax because income levels are low, and it is difficult to enforce tax compliance. Therefore, in LDCs it would make sense to impose excise taxes upon luxury goods (paid by those who can most afford them) and severance taxes upon extraction activities to fund the operation of government and government programs.

If the types of taxes imposed vary among countries, so does the level of compliance by corporate and individual citizens and the level of enforcement by national officials. Some nations, such as Italy, have historically been considered to be lax; while others, such as Germany and the United States have been considered strict. U.S. tax law makes extensive provisions for the assessment of penalties, fines, and interest payments for failure to file, for a substantial understatement of tax liability and income, for failure to pay taxes due, and for failure to pay estimated taxes. Nevertheless, many Americans continue to engage in tax evasion by attempting to hide income or by conducting business covertly and using cash transactions. Failure to comply with tax laws, however, may include criminal penalties, if the taxpayer intends to defraud the government. Thus, tax laws have been successfully used to prosecute criminals who profit from illegal activities, such as selling drugs or illegal gambling.

Some believe that the level of tax compliance in a country depends not as much on enforcement as on whether or not the public perceives the tax system to be fair. These perceptions explain the foundations of the massive reform effort mounted in the mid-1980s to change U.S. tax law. The belief among some policymakers was that making the law more equitable would induce Americans to pay their fair share. There has been much discussion more recently of increasing the tax liability for upper income citizens, and others

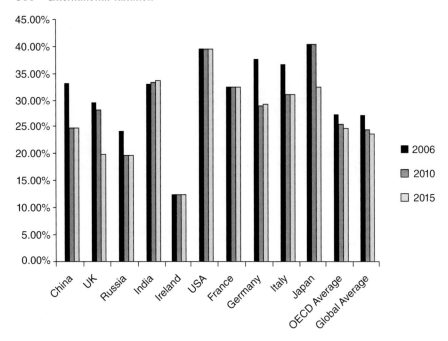

Exhibit 5.2 Corporate tax rate table

have advocated moving to a flat tax. Corporate tax rates affect the location and operating decisions of MNCs. Higher tax rates domestically can lead to **corporate inversions**, where an MNC relocates their legal domicile to a lower tax nation, usually while retaining its material operations in its higher tax country of origin. Exhibit 5.2 provides a chart of comparative corporate tax rates.

International taxation

Taxes: MNCs

Multinational corporations begin to encounter serious tax problems when they establish operations overseas because they must operate under a new tax code, with its own provisions and compliance procedures. Sales of goods through exports do not affect significantly the tax management of an MNC. Sales made from domestic shores are simply included in total domestic sales. Thus, the source of taxable income is unchanged as is the taxation jurisdiction of the company. Once an MNC establishes operations abroad, however, issues arise over the tax treatment of earnings made overseas by the tax authorities of the parent country. In its tax treatment of arms of parent corporations, the United States differentiates tax treatment by the form of the overseas affiliate, that is, between a branch and a subsidiary.

International taxation 101

Foreign branches are integral parts of MNCs and treated as if they were merely domestic branches. Thus, income from overseas branches is added to the parent's domestic income, and taxes are assessed on that amount. As with domestic branches of a parent corporation, income from a foreign branch is taxed as it is earned, not as it is received. The advantage to an MNC of forming a branch overseas is that any losses in operations from that branch can immediately be offset against domestic earnings. The disadvantage is that taxes are immediately payable and cannot be deferred (postponed) because they are applied to income earned by the branch, not as profits are received.

Foreign affiliates of parent corporations formed as subsidiaries receive different tax treatment because they are incorporated within the borders of a different nation, and thus operate under the principle of **juridic domicile** of the country where they are located and which has taxing jurisdiction. Subsidiaries are liable for taxes paid to the foreign (host) government. Income sent to the parent is considered taxable when actually remitted as dividends, not when earned. Thus, through the reinvestment of profits or holding off on declared dividends, the parent is able to defer home country taxes on certain portions of the income from the subsidiary.

Besides deferral of taxes, subsidiaries have other advantages, such as avoiding border taxes or import duties by manufacturing or producing within the country. They sometimes enjoy lower tax rates in the country of incorporation (host country) than in their home country. From a tax perspective, the drawbacks of using a subsidiary form of organization are that losses cannot be used against parental income and the foreign government may impose withholding taxes on the remittance of dividend income to the parent. In some overseas locations, local taxes may be higher than the home country, and the tax procedures could be more cumbersome.

Taxes: U.S. controlled foreign corporations

Because income generated from the operation of subsidiaries can enjoy deferral of taxes by being reinvested, U.S. tax authorities were faced with the problems created by the establishment of paper corporations abroad by U.S. taxpayers to shelter earnings from taxation. Thus, tax law was amended to provide for taxation of income earned overseas but not remitted to owners.

Under amendments to tax law enacted in 1975, limits were set upon the deferral of income for U.S. controlled foreign corporations (CFCs). Controlled foreign corporations are defined as those in which more than 50% of the voting stock, or more than 50% of the value of the outstanding stock of the foreign corporation is owned by U.S. shareholders of any type: individual citizens, partnerships, trusts, or corporations. Therefore, a foreign corporation would be a CFC if five or more entities hold at least 10% ownership each, but not if twenty shareholders each own a 3% interest.

If the corporation is defined as a CFC, the owners cannot defer taxes on income, which is defined as Subpart F. Subpart F is a section of the 1962

102 *International taxation*

Revenue Act that contains provisions for taxation of income accruing to U.S. shareholders in foreign incorporated affiliates of U.S. companies, provided such affiliates are deemed to be controlled foreign corporations. Specifically, income arising out of intra-corporate deals, known as Subpart F income, is subject to tax under this provision.

Classification of Subpart F income of a U.S. affiliate that is also a CFC is a complex process because there are several exceptions and connected regulations that must be considered. Once income is classified as belonging to Subpart F, however, it becomes taxable by U.S. authorities at the time it is earned, regardless of whether it is remitted or not from the overseas affiliate to the U.S. shareholders. Typically, income that is taxable under Subpart F arises out of investment returns by way of dividends, royalties, interest, and so on.

Double taxation

A major problem that occurs for an MNC with overseas operations is that its existence in a multitude of environments subjects it to the jurisdiction of different taxing authorities and to double taxation on the same income. Thus, income earned by an MNC may be taxed when it is earned in the foreign location and again when it is remitted to and realized by the parent corporation. This situation also exists for individuals who earn income abroad. They are taxed on the income earned within the foreign country and by the U.S. government on their worldwide income.

Such double taxation is a clear violation of the U.S. tax principles of equity and fairness. Thus, in order to provide fair treatment of such income, U.S. law provides for a credit against U.S. tax liabilities that can be taken by both corporations and individuals for taxes paid on income to a foreign taxing authority.

Tax treaties

Bilateral and multilateral tax treaties provide a basis for reciprocal recognition of taxes paid to other nations and the allowance of credits for taxes paid in each other's jurisdiction. These treaties also often include provisions for reciprocal reductions in foreign withholding taxes on income earned on licenses, stocks, interest, royalties, and copyrights. They also establish the allocation of certain types of income to certain countries and allow tax audits to take place between countries. Tax treaties frequently also provide for the reciprocal exchange of tax information between nations, which is very important for enforcement of tax laws.

At present, the U.S. is signatory to more than fifty tax treaties with foreign nations, many of which are intricate and complicated. For example, the tax treaty with Canada is more than 11,000 pages long.

Foreign tax credits for U.S. corporations

Foreign tax credits accorded to U.S. taxpayers are based on income taxes paid by a U.S. taxpaying entity to another country's treasury department or revenue service, which means that U.S. taxpayers are not given credits for the payment of value-added, sales, excise, or any other taxes paid to foreign concerns.

The purpose of foreign tax credits is to ensure that taxpayers are not penalized for engaging in foreign operations and that their tax bills abroad do not exceed domestic liabilities. Thus, if the rate paid on income abroad is less than the home or U.S. rate, taxpayers will be liable to the U.S. Treasury Department for the difference. In this way, they take care of their liability and pay their due share, but they are not unduly taxed on the same income.

For example, assume that a U.S. firm has a majority ownership in a subsidiary in Zimbabwe, where the tax rate is appreciably higher at 60% than the U.S. tax rate of 34%. If the subsidiary declares earnings of $100 million in Zimbabwe, it is assessed, and must pay (in Zimbabwean dollars) $60 million in taxes. If that income is also declared in the United States, the parent is liable for $34 million. The payment of $60 million to Zimbabwe, however, not only satisfies that liability but generates an additional foreign tax credit of $26 million ($60 million minus $34 million), which the firm can apply against its total U.S. income tax bill. These examples ignore exchange rate effects, as they are only for illustrative purposes.

If Zimbabwe's tax rate is lower than that of the United States, say 20%, the parent corporation is given credit for $20 million paid to tax authorities in Zimbabwe, but must pay $14 million to satisfy the domestic tax bill of $34 million on the same $100 million of income taxed at a rate of 34%.

The key to determining whether or not U.S. firms can use foreign tax credits on taxes paid to foreign governments depends on whether or not an MNC declares the same income that was taxed abroad on its U.S. tax return. Thus, in order to take the credit for taxes paid abroad, the firm must recognize the income at home.

Foreign tax credits for corporations can be either direct or indirect, depending on the tax imposed by the foreign government. Direct taxes are those that are charged directly to the taxpayer, and, in this instance, would consist of foreign taxes on an MNC's branch income or foreign withholding taxes on remittances to a parent or U.S. investors. Under U.S. tax law, credits against U.S. tax liability may be taken in the amount of these paid taxes.

The code also provides a tax credit for indirect taxes paid by different segments of an MNC. These taxes come about when a subsidiary is taxed on its income earned in the foreign site and then the parent is taxed again on dividends it receives from the subsidiary. Thus, the code provides for an indirect foreign tax credit that can be taken in addition to the direct foreign tax credit. Parent corporations are allowed to make use of the indirect foreign tax credit when they own 10% or more of the voting stock of the foreign subsidiary. This credit is called a deemed paid credit and is based on the

104 *International taxation*

dividends paid by the subsidiary and the amount of foreign income taxes paid. The formula for determining the deemed paid credit is:

$$\frac{\text{dividend (including withholding tax)}}{\text{earnings net of (minus) foreign income taxes}} \times \text{foreign tax} = \text{deemed paid credit}$$

Thus, many international corporations are not penalized for doing business in different international operating environments because they receive credit for direct and indirect income taxes paid to foreign governments. The use of foreign tax credits is, however, subject to limits and does raise some issues in taxation.

Limits and issues in allocation of foreign tax credit

The use of the foreign tax credit is subject to two major limitations. The first is that credit can only be taken against income taxes paid to foreign tax authorities, not on sales, value-added, or excise taxes. This limitation is a special concern for subsidiaries operating in countries where the government relies more on the use of a VAT or other transaction than on income tax.

The second major limitation is that foreign tax credits can only be used to offset taxes to the full extent of a person's or a company's U.S. tax liability. (Exceeding such liability would give the taxpayer a negative tax bill and entitle him to a rebate from the government.) Thus, a situation can arise for multinational firms where they develop credits for foreign taxes paid in excess of domestic liabilities. U.S. law provides relief for these individuals and allows tax credits to be carried back and forward by the taxpayer. The carry-back is allowed for one year and is utilized by filing amended tax returns for prior years. Excess tax credits can be carried forward for ten years. If the taxpayer does not have enough tax liability to use these credits within the carry-back and carry-forward periods, they are lost.

Beyond these limitations, concerns also arise in relation to issues regarding the administration and determination of foreign tax credits used against U.S. liabilities. Two such issues are the determination of taxable income and the allocation of deductions according to foreign-based and home-based income. Because taxable income (not gross income or sales) determines the amount of foreign taxes paid and resultant foreign tax credits, differences in accounting and tax practices between countries can lead to controversy in the determination of taxes and tax credits. Remember, gross income figures are reduced by deductions for the costs and expenses of doing business to arrive at an adjusted figure representing taxable income.

What may be considered an allowable deduction under the accounting practices of one country may not suffice under the tax law of another. Such differences often lead to disputes between MNCs and the tax authorities of the countries involved over what expenses are allowable in the conduct of business. Frequently, even if the corporations and the tax authorities agree about the method used to determine the firm's expenses and income, they may disagree on the allocation of that income to the expenses incurred in its generation among worldwide locations.

U.S. accounting conventions hold that expenses are matched to income for appropriate characterization of financial flows. In the operation of a global company, the question arises as to how to allocate deductible expenses. For example, what if a multinational firm is organized so that all international functions and operations are coordinated from a central headquarters? What portion of the company's general and administrative expenses for operating their headquarters should be applied to foreign income earned? The same problem arises in the allocation of research and development expenses for products marketed in a multitude of locations. To satisfy these questions, the Internal Revenue Service issued stricter regulations in 1977 regarding the allocation of administrative and research expenses of multinationals to foreign-source income.

A problem remained, however, in that the resultant allocation of expenses is not always reciprocally recognized by foreign tax officials and does not always lead to a reduction of the related foreign-source taxable income. Foreign governments could tax the MNC on an amount that the U.S. government considers to be expenses (and, therefore, nontaxable). Thus, the MNC could wind up paying more in foreign taxes than they are required to pay by U.S. authorities, which creates a foreign tax credit. The solution pursued by multinationals is to create additional Subpart F income, from which they can generate and use more foreign tax credits.

Special issues and problems in international taxation tax havens

Despite extensive nets cast by U.S. tax authorities to capture taxes owed, many individuals and corporations attempt to avoid being taxed on their income earned abroad. Although this activity has been limited by the imposition of regulations and taxes on unremitted earnings, crafty financiers continue to attempt to shelter income. One method of accomplishing that objective is to keep income overseas (and, thus, off domestic books) in countries without tax treaties with the MNC's home government. These countries provide sanctuary for foreign-earned income and impose few or no taxes at all and are termed tax havens. Monies deposited in these nations are safe from taxation until the subsidiary declares a dividend to the parent, at which time the remittance becomes taxable by the home tax authority.

In order to be efficient sanctuaries for a corporation's worldwide income, tax havens must satisfy several criteria:

- They must not have a tax treaty with the corporation's domestic government that allows for the reciprocal tax treatment of income. Such a treaty would entail the sharing of earnings information and data.

106 *International taxation*

- These nations must have low or no taxes on foreign-source funds. (Some tax haven countries do not provide equivalent tax amnesty for earnings within their own countries.)
- The countries must provide stable political and economic environments, so that funds deposited there will remain safe.
- The nations must allow for the free convertibility of currencies and have few if any restrictions on the inflow and outflow of currencies.
- The policies of the nations must be centered on a positive attitude toward businesses and their activities and, thus, have liberal incorporation laws.
- To accommodate financial flows, the countries must have well-developed banking systems with some degree of banking secrecy.
- The countries must also have infrastructures that support and facilitate general business operations, including such amenities as dependable telecommunications and transportation systems. A tax haven's close physical proximity to the home country makes it easier for depositors, who may then use the same lines or systems of communication and be in the same time zones.

Tax havens vary in their structure. Some countries, such as Caribbean tax havens, have very low or zero taxes on foreign or domestic income. These tax haven countries include the Bahamas, the Cayman Islands, Bermuda, the British Virgin Islands, and the Netherlands Antilles and are often used by U.S. nationals and corporations.

Other nations provide sanctuary for foreign sources of funds, but tax domestically produced income. Some such countries are Panama and Liechtenstein. Still other countries provide havens from taxation only for specific purposes or industries. These countries are primarily those that encourage investment within their boundaries by providing for tax exemptions for certain periods of time to promote industrial development. Two such countries that provide tax holidays are Ireland and Singapore, which provide tax incentives or lowered tax rates for the establishment of facilities in specific regions or zones. Exhibit 5.3 lists various traditional tax havens in the world.

Transfer pricing

Multinational firms use the pricing of goods and services between their different operating arms to achieve a number of objectives, such as increasing rates of return in specific operating locations, lowering product prices in specific markets, circumventing restrictions regarding repatriation of parent company profits, and getting around inconvertibility of host country currencies. In addition, the uses of transfer pricing in intra-company transactions can also provide a method for MNCs to manage their international tax liability.

By shifting costs to countries with high tax rates, an MNC can enjoy savings on its tax bills, because by raising the costs of goods sold, a company can lower its taxable income, shifting profits to countries where tax rates on corporate

Caribbean/West Indies	Anguilla, Antigua & Barbuda, Aruba, Bahamas, British Virgin Islands, Cayman Islands Dominica, Grenada, Montserrat, Curacao & St. Maarten, St. Kitts & Nevis, St. Vincent & Grenadines, Turks & Caicos, US Virgin Islands
Central America	Belize, Costa Rica, Panama
Coast of East Asia	Hong Kong, Macau, Singapore
Europe/Mediterranean	Andorra, Channel Islands (Guernsey & Jersey), Cyprus, Gibraltar, Isle of Man Ireland, Lichtenstein, Luxembourg, Malta, Monaco, San Marino, Switzerland
Indian Ocean	Maldives, Mauritius, Seychelles
Middle East	Bahrain, Jordan, Lebanon
North Atlantic	Bermuda
Pacific/South Pacific	Cook Islands, Marshall Islands, Samoa, Nauru, Niue, Tonga, Vanuatu
West Africa	Liberia

Exhibit 5.3 Tax havens of the world

profits are lower. U.S. companies usually attempt to shift deductible costs to themselves or to a parent corporation's accounts from the books of the affiliates. Thus, the costs of such items as intra-company loans, the sale of inventory and machinery, and the transfer of intangible property and their associated deductibility are transferred to high-tax-rate environments.

Such practices have come under intense scrutiny both by host governments and the U.S. Internal Revenue Service, and the IRS can now challenge prices set by MNCs. Under certain circumstances, the IRS has the authority to recalculate those prices and assess tax liabilities according to prices set at arm's length, those prices that would have been reached if two independent parties engaged in the same transaction.

Unitary taxes

A special problem that has emerged in international taxation is the issue of applying **unitary taxes**, taxes imposed by a specific state on the basis of an MNC's multi-state or worldwide profits, not merely those profits generated by operations in that state. This practice, originally developed in California, includes the assessment of a tax upon the firm's total domestic or worldwide earnings based on a specific percentage figure. This percentage is derived from the proportion of the company's in-state sales, property, and personnel payroll in relation to its total national or global figures for sales, property held, and payroll. A rationale for the levying of such taxes by states is that doing so keeps corporations from using transfer pricing within different branches to shift income and tax bills to states that impose lower tax rates.

108 *International taxation*

The use of unitary taxation has come under a great deal of criticism from all sides. U.S. multinational firms and the Treasury Department and foreign MNCs and their governments have protested loudly against the practice of levying unitary taxes and the method of income allocation. In the past, severe criticisms have emerged from U.S. trading partners, such as Great Britain and Japan.

This pressure from foreign multinational corporations has given rise to a solution called **water's edge taxation**, which limits states to taxing only income from operations within the United States, not from global sales. It is more likely that changes in unitary taxation policy by individual states will come from opposition by MNCs and their decisions to disinvest in such states and move to states that do not apply the unitary tax concept. The state of California in the United States began implementing a form of water's edge taxation in 1986. Given the state's fiscal crisis in recent years, there have been calls for further modifying the tax code to allow for more taxation of the foreign activities of multinationals headquartered in California. The US government in recent years has attempted to broaden the methods of taxation of international profits given MNC evasion of U.S. tax laws via changes in the legal domicile or transfer payments within the MNC.

Tax incentives for international business

Governments are not only concerned with garnering tax income from the operations of international firms, but they also use taxation policy as a tool to promote international trade. Countries that impose value-added taxes frequently rebate those taxes on exported goods in order to encourage exports. Similarly, the United States promotes exports of U.S. goods through tax policy. At one time, the United States had six different incentive programs to encourage international trade by U.S. companies. Each involved the formation of special corporate entities for conducting such trade to keep it segregated from normal operations to receive special treatment.

U.S. possessions corporations

If a domestic operation derives at least 80% of its income from a U.S. possession (excluding the Virgin Islands) and generates at least 75% of its gross income from active trade, it may be able to take advantage of tax benefits established for U.S. possessions corporations. If these conditions are met for three years prior to the establishment of the corporation, it has the advantage of limitations on taxation of income from outside the United States, tax-free repatriation of earnings to the United States, liberal interpretation of transfer prices, and possible exemption from Puerto Rican taxation if it operates manufacturing facilities in certain areas of Puerto Rico.

Influence of U.S. tax law on corporate operations

Clearly, managing the international tax function for a major MNC corporation involves many different facets that relate directly to managerial decision-making. The effects of taxation upon the future operations of a corporation play a large role in determining where activities are carried out and in what type of legal form (branch, subsidiary, or export arm). Taxes must be factored into prices set for external and internal intra-company purchases, and must be considered in determining appropriate cash levels, flows, and locations among worldwide operations. The international taxation situation is so complex that many MNCs use complex computer programs that can determine the tax effects of various managerial decisions regarding international financing, cash flows, and operations.

Taxation of individual foreign-source income

The existence of business operations in a multitude of environments and of a far-flung management staff involves the compensation of employees in foreign tax jurisdictions and subsequent taxation complications. In some countries, the principle of **juridic domicile** is strictly applied, that is, the citizen's income is not taxed by his or her home country if it is not earned or received within that country. The United States, however, differs greatly in this approach. Under the Sixteenth Amendment to the U.S. Constitution, U.S. citizens are taxed on all of their income regardless of where it is sourced or earned in the world.

Naturally, the application of this principle could result in problems for U.S. citizens working in and being taxed by a host government, especially the problem of double taxation of the same income. Consequently, tax law provides relief for the U.S. expatriate who is earning income abroad and for the U.S investor receiving income from foreign sources. These situations provide for a distinction in foreign income determination between that which is earned and that which is unearned.

Foreign-earned income consists of all monies employees receive as payment for services rendered and includes wages, salaries, and commissions. Earned income does not include wages or salaries received in return for services rendered by employees of the U.S. government. Foreign unearned income is that which is derived from an individual's overseas investments. These sources of income include interest on investments, dividends, pensions, annuities, and even gambling winnings.

In order to provide for equity or fairness in the tax treatment of U.S. expatriates and to encourage citizens to work abroad, tax law provides for alternate forms of relief from taxes on foreign-earned income and double taxation by both home and host governments. A U.S. citizen qualifies for special treatment if he or she satisfies the requirements of overseas employment by being either a bona fide resident of the foreign country or by being away at least 330 days during any twelve consecutive months.

110 *International taxation*

An employee on foreign soil has two ways to treat foreign-earned income. First, a portion of foreign-earned income can be excluded up to a limit of $100,800 per year (for 2015). If the minimum 330-day residency requirement is met, but was less than a year, the allowance is prorated proportionately to provide for a new maximum exclusion. Married employees may each use the exclusion if they satisfy the other requirements of the relief provision.

The second alternative open to expatriate employees in handling foreign-earned income is to include it in their income basis but claim foreign tax credits on their returns for taxes paid abroad on those earnings or wages. Generally, most expatriates, especially those in low-tax foreign countries, use the income exclusion provisions of tax law. Thus, if the tax abroad is lower than at home, employees pay less tax because they do not have to make up the difference.

Alternatively, individuals use the foreign tax credit when their earnings or wages far exceed the amount of the exclusion and their foreign taxes paid far exceed comparable U.S. tax on the excluded amount. Expatriates also might choose to use the foreign tax credit rather than the exclusions, if the tax rate in the host country is much higher than that of the United States. In such a case, the international employee would use a credit to eliminate U.S. taxes for the existing year and in years ahead under carry-forward provisions. Once, however, an expatriate elects to use the foreign tax credit, it must be applied to all subsequent years unless it is actively revoked. A revocation is then effective not only for the year of change, but also for four subsequent years.

As for corporations, the foreign tax credit of individuals is subject to limitations. For example it can only be calculated according to foreign taxes paid on income and the United States uses its own criteria in determining whether or not the tax paid is an income tax. Consequently, sales, value-added, property, severance, and excise taxes are not included in determining the credit. Some of these, however, may be deductible as a state, local, or personal property tax under Section 164 of the Internal Revenue Code. Also, according to the alternative minimum tax provisions of U.S. tax law, foreign tax credits cannot be used to reduce tax liability by more than 90%.

Expenses of U.S. expatriates

U.S. tax law also takes into account the rigors and additional costs involved in overseas assignments and provides relief for expenses incurred abroad in securing scarce housing or paying a higher cost of living in a more expensive economy. Thus, the law provides relief for the expatriate who receives reimbursement for housing costs, which are deemed to include rent, insurance, and utilities. They do not include interest or taxes paid on housing, because these costs are deductible under other provisions of law. Under the provisions, the employee may exclude from income an amount in addition to basic exclusion to compensate for these additional costs.

Summary

The management of the international tax function for a multinational enterprise is very involved and complicated and can have a profound effect upon the welfare and profitability of a firm. The effects of taxation policies in home and foreign operating environments frequently determine managerial decisions regarding choice of international operations, the legal forms of such operations, price-setting between branches of the enterprise and with the public, and the financing and cash flows of international operations around the world.

Individual nations vary in the types of taxes they levy and in assessment rates. All countries provide relief for taxpayers from being doubly taxed on the same income, and in order to facilitate international trade and investment flows, nations join in agreements regarding taxation of their citizens and reciprocal recognition of taxes paid within their jurisdictions. These tax treaties also frequently provide for the mutual exchange of information regarding business operations of multinational firms and facilitate enforcement of tax laws. Some countries purposefully avoid entering into such agreements in order to provide sanctuaries for foreign-earned income so that it can find a safe haven from the long arms of domestic tax authorities.

Nations of the world use taxation as an arm of policymaking to achieve social, economic, and political objectives, as well as to raise revenues. Most countries have as one such objective the increase of export trade from their borders. Consequently, they use tax incentive programs to promote such trade. Nevertheless, objectives, policies, and tax structures differ widely around the world. Thus, the tax manager of an international concern is faced with the formidable task of managing the multinational tax function in order to provide for the minimization of taxes in the pursuit of maximization of operational efficiencies and worldwide profitability.

Discussion questions

1 Why do governments levy taxes? What services do they fund?
2 What is tax equity?
3 How can taxes encourage or discourage certain activities? Explain.
4 What types of taxes may be levied other than income taxes?
5 What is a VAT?
6 What is double taxation? How can individuals or corporations avoid double taxation?
7 What is a tax haven? Identify five countries that qualify as tax havens.
8 Why must MNCs concern themselves with taxes?
9 Does U.S. tax policy provide any incentives to U.S. citizens to work overseas?

112 *International taxation*

Bibliography

Bische, Jon E. 1985. *Fundamentals of International Taxation*, 2nd ed. New York: Practicing Law Institute.

Bond, Eric W., and Larry Samuelson. 1989. Strategic Behavior and the Rules for International Taxation of Capital. *Economic Journal* (December): 1099–1111.

Borsack, Scott P. 1987. Choosing to Do Business Through a Foreign Branch or a Foreign Subsidiary. A Tax Analysis. *Case Western Reserve Journal of International Law* (Summer): 393–419.

Chambost, Edouard. 1983. *Bank Accounts: A World Guide to Confidentiality*. New York: John Wiley & Sons.

CNN Money website. http://money.cnn.com/2011/01/05/pf/taxes/IRS_tax_study/.

Commerce Clearing House. 1988. *Internal Revenue Code of 1986*. Chicago: Commerce Clearing House, Inc.

Doernberg, Richard L. 1989. *International Taxation in a Nutshell*. St. Paul, MN: West Publishing Company.

Granell, A. W., B. Hirsh, and D. R. Milton. 1986. Worldwide Unitary Tax: Is It Invalid Under Treaties of Friendship, Commerce and Navigation? *Tax & Policy in International Business* 18: 695–758.

Gutfeld, Rose. 1988. It Seems like Days, but IRS Estimates Tax Filing Takes Only About Nine Hours. *Wall Street Journal* (September 1): 23.

Hoffman, William H. Jr., and Eugene Willis. 1988. *West's Federal Taxation: Comprehensive Volume*. St. Paul, MN: West Publishing Company.

IRS website. "What are U.S. Possessions Corporation Returns?" https://www.irs.gov/uac/soi-tax-stats-u-s-possessions-corporation-returns-metadata, accessed July 17, 2017.

Miller, Richard Bradford. 1988. *Tax Haven Investing: A Guide to Offshore Banking and Investment Opportunities*. Chicago: Probus Publishing Company.

Rothschild, Leonard W. Jr. 1986. Worldwide Unitary Taxation: The End is in Sight. *Journal of Accountancy* (December): 178–185.

Shapiro, Alan. 1986. *Multinational Financial Management*. Newton, MA: Allyn and Bacon.

Sinn, Hans-Werner. 1988. U.S. Tax Reform 1981 and 1986: Impact on International Capital Markets and Capital Flows. *National Tax Journal* (September): 71.

Sinning, Kathleen E., ed. 1986. *Comparative International Taxation*. Sarasota, FL: International Accounting Association of the American Accounting Association.

U.S. Department of the Treasury, Internal Revenue Service. 1986. Explanation of Tax Reform Act of 1986 for Individuals, Publication 920.

U.S. Department of the Treasury, Internal Revenue Service. 2004. Tax Guide for U.S. Citizens and Resident Aliens Abroad, Publication 54.

U.S. Department of the Treasury, Internal Revenue Service. 2016. Foreign Tax Credit for Individuals, Publication 514. https://www.irs.gov/pub/irs-pdf/p514.pdf, accessed July 17, 2017.

6 International staffing and labor issues

> The world is a mirror, reflecting his image to the beholder.
>
> (Aldous Huxley)

Chapter objectives

This chapter will:

- Identify common organizational structures used by multinational corporations.
- Discuss how MNCs recruit, select, train, and motivate management staffs.
- Describe the cultural and economic forces that influence the international manager's performance.
- Consider the problems of repatriating international managers and other ethical issues.
- Identify the tradeoffs between localized and centralized management of labor.
- Discuss the major labor issues of wages and benefits, job security, and productivity as they relate to MNC operations.
- Present how international labor movements and codetermination are influencing MNC operations.

Organizing a multinational corporation

International firms can organize their operations in a number of different ways. Four of these organizing strategies are the functional structure, the regional structure, the product structure, and the matrix structure.

Function structure

Under this structure, responsibilities at headquarters are divided according to functions, such as marketing and finance, and the head of each division is responsible for the conduct of that function internationally. This strategy is

114 *International staffing and labor issues*

efficient if there is a standardized product line. It permits coordination of the aspects of a function in one department, but this strategy also encourages a narrow viewpoint, is inflexible, and can be time-consuming. It is hard to adapt this centralized approach to changing local conditions, and the overall integration of the various functions internationally is very difficult to achieve.

Regional structure

In the regional structure of an MNC, the headquarters retains responsibility for overall global strategy and control, but an area manager has responsibility for all the operations and functions of a certain region. The regions should be organized on the basis of similar characteristics with less emphasis on the basis of functional categories. This structure also integrates the separate functions very well throughout each region, but its drawback is that each function must be standardized in order to integrate across all the regions.

Product structure

As with the regional structure, corporate headquarters has control of overall global strategy in a product structure. Within the guidelines set down by headquarters, a manager has international control over all the operations related to a single product. A major advantage of this structure is that all the functions relating to a single product are integrated and perform as a whole internationally. The major drawback is that it is difficult to coordinate policies and strategies across product lines.

Matrix structure

The matrix structure involves dual lines of authority in which managers may report to two or more superiors. For example, they may have to report to the head of the product line and to the chief of a geographical region. This structure provides for coordination of the various departments, while still recognizing differences, and leads to standardization of functions and overall control, and imparts flexibility to respond to environmental differences.

International staffing

International staffing involves the four basic stages of recruitment, selection, training, and motivation of the right person to fill a job available in a foreign setting.

Recruitment

Recruitment is the process of attracting people to apply for job vacancies within a firm. There are two main sources of recruitment for international positions: internal and external. Internal sources consist of promotion from within the company and employee referrals. Promotion from within is a very low-cost method for the firm. It has the added benefit of increasing employee morale because they see an opportunity for advancement. Uncertainty about an applicant and training costs are reduced because employees are already familiar with the objectives and procedures of the firm. Employee referrals involve the recommendation by a present employee of a family member or friend and encouraging them to apply. The benefits of an employee referral are the low cost to the firm and the fact that the referrals will probably be fairly well-informed about the various aspects of the firm.

External sources of recruitment include the internet, newspaper and radio advertising, trade schools, employment agencies, job fairs, and labor unions. There is a difference, however, between recruitment in industrialized countries and in the less-developed countries. In the less-developed countries, there is an overabundance of unskilled workers because of high unemployment and a shortage of skilled workers. Newspapers may not be effective in LDCs because much of the population may be illiterate, and there are usually very few employment agencies. In industrialized countries, the problems are reversed; there are too many skilled workers and too few unskilled workers.

Selection

Employee selection involves choosing from an available pool of applicants that the firm considers best able to meet the requirements of the position. In industrialized countries the firm considers people through standardized procedures, such as application forms, personal interviews, and possibly physical or psychological exams. The selection process in LDCs is less formal and involves less testing. Such considerations as family ties, social status or caste, language, and common origin tend to influence the selection process.

Training

For an MNC training of its overseas employees is an extremely important issue. Employees in overseas locations come from a different society and culture, which means that they have varying attitudes toward work, conduct, and other behavioral aspects that may be quite different from the expectations and standards of an MNC. It is therefore critical for an MNC to train its overseas employees to orient them toward its work ethics, discipline, efficiency standards, operating procedures, and, of course, the necessary operational skills.

One major limitation in many countries is that adequate training resources by way of instructors, experienced personnel, and training facilities may not be available. Generally, MNCs fly in large numbers of key technical personnel to train newly hired employees in foreign locations, who lead training sessions for both theoretical and on-the-job training. Some personnel in charge of sensitive

116 *International staffing and labor issues*

and complex industrial operations have to remain at the overseas locations before the local trainees are considered adequately trained and have enough experience to run the operations themselves.

For lower-level employees, typically factory workers, language is another important barrier to overcome. Companies take different approaches to this problem. Interpreters are used where language is an intractable problem. Often companies train bilingual local employees, who in turn pass on the training to those local employees who do not understand the foreign language. Because most workers at the plant floor level are not involved in significant amounts of theoretical work, this problem is mitigated to a large extent as long as they are able to understand the operating instructions for their specific tasks.

Motivation

Motivating overseas employees also presents complex problems. Employees, especially at the lower levels, are relatively **ethnocentric** in their views, and their priorities and goals often differ from their counterparts in Western countries. While mobility, compensation, challenges in the work environment, and independence in functioning are important motivating factors for employees in Western industrialized countries, workers in LDCs tend to attach greater value to job security, number of holidays, working hours, social benefits, and so on. An MNC, therefore, must judge the local climate and expectations very carefully and come up with an appropriate mix of incentives that would motivate employees without being unduly expensive.

Compare, for example, workers in a developed country and a developing country. The worker in the developed country is consumption-oriented and wants compensation in terms of money. While vacation days are desirable, the employee tends to work more days of the year to increase the compensation package. The employee is interested in moving up the ladder to better jobs, but not necessarily in the same company.

A worker in a developing country, on the other hand, wants job security because industrial jobs are scarce, and if the worker loses his job, there may not be any other means of livelihood, especially because there would ordinarily be no social security or unemployment insurance.

There are a number of religious festivals in societies where the hold of traditional socio-religious practices is still strong, and workers in developing countries would like to be certain that they have those days off. Historically, many workers in developing countries expect their employers to provide them with housing assistance or similar benefits because these are not readily available. Thus, an MNC may have to create a compensation package that relies less on salary and more on other benefits for its workers in developing countries. Salary levels, however, also must be a little higher than the local going rate to guard against allegations that the MNC is exploiting local workers.

Managerial staffing

Value to firm

Choosing a manager for an overseas operation is an important task because this choice can profoundly affect overseas growth and operations. The subsidiary manager will have a great deal of responsibility, more than a counterpart in a home production facility. The overseas manager must be multicultural and sensitive to business practices and customs of the host country, while being responsible for following the global objectives of the MNC and being able to put these objectives ahead of the local operation's well-being.

The success of its overseas managers is particularly important to MNCs for a number of reasons. A failure in the overseas assignment leads to large corporate costs in time and resources in replacing the expatriate, the lost productivity of the manager, and slowdowns in productivity at the overseas plant. Bereft of skillful management, the overseas operation is more likely to experience such problems as increases in labor strikes, employee problems, government relations problems, and legal suits, because backup management resources may not be easily forthcoming.

To motivate their overseas managers, MNCs provide huge employment incentives in the form of large increases in salary and benefits, and most assignments carry the glamour of widening horizons, enriching experiences, and an excitingly different lifestyle. Nevertheless, one out of every three expatriate workers from the United States finds that the assignment has gone wrong. In a classic study by Rosalie Tung, it was found that "incidences where expatriates had to be recalled to corporate headquarters or dismissed from the company because of their inability to perform effectively in a foreign country were numerous." More than half of the eighty companies she surveyed reported failure rates between 10% and 20%. Some estimates hold that failure rates for poorly trained expatriate managers and personnel, based on location, are more in the range of 33% to 66%. More recent studies have indicated that failure rates range from 30% to 50%.

The answer to minimizing failures in deploying personnel abroad lies in planning the management of a global corporation and carefully selecting and training these global managers. Managers with aptitude, ability, and willingness for serving in international assignments must be identified by the corporation and trained extensively. Appropriate financial and career incentives have to be created to attract managers to international assignments and reward those who accept them.

Branch manager versus home office: who is in charge?

Overseas managers of MNCs face several challenges that arise from their unique position between not only two parts of a company (the parent corporation and the subsidiary), but also between two countries and two cultures. In addition,

118 *International staffing and labor issues*

there is always a considerable physical distance between them and the corporate office. Consequently, overseas managers have a much greater degree of autonomy than their peers at the corporate office. As heads of local operations, they are fully responsible for their performance and must make a variety of executive decisions. Greater decision-making authority devolves both by design as well as circumstance. The costs and delays associated with overseas communication encourage the parent corporation to give substantial leeway to the local manager. Even in areas where the decision-making is reserved by the parent office, the local manager may have to exercise discretionary authority in emergency situations, when there is a breakdown in the communication channels, especially when decisions are needed immediately and cannot wait for a response from the head office.

Many parent offices delegate substantial authority to on-the-spot local managers in the belief that they will be able to make better-informed decisions. Generally, day-to-day operational decisions are vested with the local managers, while the overall global strategic decisions are made by the corporate office. Overseas managers have to adjust their decision-making to corporate policy and maintain the fine balance needed for exercising just the right degree of discretionary authority at the local level.

Overseas managers have the effective responsibilities, in many ways, of the CEOs of corporations. Therefore, they must have an overall perspective of their operations, the internal and external environments, the trends in the local political and economic situations, and a clear perception of the opportunities and threats to the local operations. As the head of a local operation, the overseas manager represents the MNC to the local government, other firms, customers, and suppliers. It is essential that the manager deal effectively with each of these entities, all of whom are important for the success of any business operation.

Adaptability is probably one of the most important qualities required of an overseas manager. Managers sent to different countries can land in a completely different professional and cultural environment. In addition, there are the problems of adjustment by spouses and families, which have to be addressed. A large number of expatriate managers have failed in their assignments because their families had difficulty adjusting to the changed environment. Thus, the adaptability of both manager and family is crucial to success in an overseas assignment.

Branch managers: who should firms choose?

A major issue for an MNC in staffing overseas facilities is whether to use a home country national, a host country national, or a third-country national.

Home country nationals are citizens of the country where the headquarters are located. Home country nationals who live and work in foreign countries are called **expatriates**. **Host country nationals** are citizens of the country where the subsidiary exists. They are local employees. **Third-country**

International staffing and labor issues 119

nationals are citizens of neither the country of the subsidiary or the headquarters. For example, a German working in Brazil for a U.S.-based company would be a third-country national.

Home country nationals as overseas managers offer several advantages for managing a foreign subsidiary. Home country managers are well-trained and familiar with the company's operating requirements and practices. Thus, they have a better perception of corporate goals, policies, and strategies and would design their local operations accordingly. Overseas assignments will broaden the perspectives of home country managers, and they will begin to factor in the worldwide implications of decision-making, which is essential for all top executives of the firm. The overseas assignment of home country executives thus provides valuable training for the company's future senior management. A home country national in an overseas location provides headquarters with a presence in the foreign environment and enables the firm to stay abreast of developments first hand. A home country national also can represent the firm's interests with the host government more easily than a host country national, who might encounter a conflict if asked to handle a confrontation with the host government.

Host country nationals also have several advantages as local managers. They know the local language, the culture, and the customs and may have valuable contacts in the local business world. Costs associated with hiring a local manager are usually lower because there are no relocation costs. Training costs can sometimes be higher, because the manager may need to be trained in the home country, but, in the long run, these costs generally are not significant. Hiring a host country national may ease tensions with the host government and may in fact serve to comply with local requirements. The local manager may also be able to deal better with local employees, especially unions.

There are also disadvantages in using host country nationals. These managers may be unfamiliar with home country cultures and the MNC's policies and practices and may have different attitudes and values than those of the people at headquarters. Occasionally, these employees are hired away from the MNC by local competitors after the MNC has spent considerable time and money in training, and local managers may experience conflicts in loyalty between their country and the MNC.

Third-country nationals may be hired for several reasons. They may possess skills lacking in both home and host country nationals. They may be more familiar with the language and culture of the host country than a home country national, and they may appease the host government by being a third-country national. Many times there is the natural progression from one post to another. For example, a French national in charge of a French subsidiary may be relocated to head the Mexican subsidiary.

120 _International staffing and labor issues_

Choosing branch managers: selection criteria

Labor pool

The labor pool has a direct effect on the MNC's choice of a manager. The availability, quality, and technical competence of managers in the host country are important factors in deciding on the overseas assignment. If the local labor pool is unable to provide managers with the required qualifications, a home country national will have to be sent abroad.

Corporate policies

The corporate objectives and policies of a firm will affect its choice of an overseas manager. If the firm wants to maintain a high level of control of the subsidiary operations and ensure that things are done strictly according to the policies of headquarters, it will choose to send home country nationals to overseas posts. Also, the MNC may want to promote management development of headquarters personnel by expanding their perspectives to include global considerations and exposing them to the overall corporate system.

Environmental constraints, the costs involved, and the legal and cultural environments of the host country will also affect the courses of action available to the firm. If the cost of relocating and compensating a headquarters employee is prohibitive, a host country national may be chosen. Similarly, there may be legal restrictions requiring the use of host country nationals or restricting the number of foreign personnel allowed into the country. If foreign personnel are allowed into the country, permission from the government may be slow and difficult to obtain.

Desired local image

The type of local image the firm portrays is very important. Most MNCs want to have a favorable local image in order to attract and retain employees and to smooth governmental relations. Choosing a host country national may reduce tensions with the host government and can result in considerable goodwill that may be of use later. In addition, the image of the firm with the local population may be enhanced and, thus, possibly increase sales and the morale of the employees.

Local employee incentives

If host country nationals are hired for management positions, it may give current local employees an incentive to remain with the firm and to work harder because they can see a possible future with the firm, because there is the possibility of advancement. Therefore, the multinational enterprise will tend to limit the management positions filled by expatriates.

Existing methods of selection

MNCs may find personnel for overseas assignments through a number of methods. If they acquire a local, ongoing business, the personnel resources of that entity become available from which managers can be selected for the local operation. If the local operation is in the form of a joint venture, the partner in the venture may contribute the management expertise and personnel to the project. This may not always be the best alternative, however, because the partner's personnel may lack the necessary technical knowledge, be unfamiliar with the practices of the parent firm, and be difficult to control because of an allegiance to the MNC's partners and not the MNC itself.

Home country records can be used as a tool in selecting management personnel. Personnel records for each employee can include information on technical knowledge, language abilities, willingness to relocate, and the results of any adaptability tests. It is extremely important to consider the spouse of a potential candidate, because it is usually more stressful for the spouse to relocate to a foreign country.

Potential for culture shock

Culture shock can be identified as a pronounced reaction to the psychological disorientation caused by moving to a totally different environment. When a person is relocated to a different country, there is an initial phase of excitement and enchantment with the new culture, then a period of disillusionment and negative feelings sets in toward the culture. This disillusionment may be because of a lack of adaptability or, alternatively, a firm's lack of knowledge of a situation and not fully preparing a person for possible difficulties. Culture shock can result in extreme bitterness toward the foreign country and its culture, and even in physical illness. There may also be **reverse culture shock** when an expatriate is repatriated to the home culture.

Two factors may help to lessen the effects of culture shock: empathy and the avoidance of stereotypes. Empathy is the ability to understand what another person is feeling, in essence, to be able to see the world through their eyes. If the expatriate is able to expand this ability to encompass the whole culture, to achieve cultural empathy, that person will go a long way to understanding the views and actions of the members of the foreign culture. Stereotypes can be avoided by thoroughly researching the foreign country prior to relocating in the area. There are various online sources that help educate future expatriates concerning differences that they might encounter while working abroad. There are also books that help ease the transition, such as the "Culture Shock!" series of books that discuss cultural differences within specific countries such as France, Denmark, New Zealand, Argentina, Morocco, the United States, and many others.

122 *International staffing and labor issues*

Training branch managers

Alternative models

Training is necessary to avoid problems in sending people to work abroad and to ensure project completion. In general, the depth of cross-cultural training for overseas managers ranges from reading up on the assignment locale to ad hoc corporate training and in-depth immersion programs. A variety of resources are available for training. These vary from how-to books for conducting business abroad to videos and orientation programs. The effectiveness of this training correlates with the amount of preparation engaged in prior to a manager's departure for an overseas assignment. The highest degree of expatriate success is experienced by managers who have had individual training tailored to their assignment in a specific country.

One categorization of cross-cultural training programs lists four different training models. The intellectual model consists of readings and lectures about the host culture and assumes that an exchange of information about another culture is effective preparation for living or working in that culture. The area simulation model is a culture-specific training program based on the belief that an individual must be prepared and trained to enter a specific culture. It involves the simulation of future experiences and practice functioning in the new culture.

The self-awareness model is based on the assumption that understanding and accepting oneself is critical to understanding a person from another culture. Sensitivity training is a main component of this method. The cultural awareness model, which is practiced in current progressive training programs, assumes that in order to function successfully in another culture, an individual must learn the principles of behavior that exist across cultures. Understanding intercultural communication from the perspective of recognizing that one's own culture influences personal values, behaviors, and cognitions is expected to result in an enhancement of a person's skill at diagnosing difficulties in intercultural communication.

Business Council for International Understanding

One example of a comprehensive cross-cultural training program for overseas managers and their families is the program given by the Business Council for International Understanding (BCIU). The objective of the BCIU is not just to brief managers and family members, but to provide them with the tools to ensure their ability to adapt to, or cope with, difficulties encountered abroad. The orientation strives to portray the situation as realistically as possible, which means discussing the negative as well as the positive aspects of overseas assignments.

The program at the institute includes five specific components: language studies, intercultural communications, area/country studies, practical training tailored to the specific country and the manager's functional area, and addressing spousal and family needs.

While the global manager learns some of the practicalities of doing business in the assignment country, family members receive concurrent training on problems to be expected and on alternatives to their current lifestyles. For example, spouses of managers going abroad may have to deal with the issue of trying to find employment in the foreign country or coping with a change from working outside to working inside the home. In some Middle Eastern countries, for example, female spouses are not allowed to work officially, but can find jobs through informal channels. Other issues dealt with include managing domestic staff, raising a family abroad, and transferring activities and interests to another environment.

Compensating branch managers

Wages

There are many problems associated with deciding on the amount of compensation to be given to an overseas manager. The local rate may be above or below the person's current salary, thus causing pay differentials between home and host country nationals performing the same job. An expatriate is usually paid an allowance and bonuses above the local rate. Problems arise when a person is transferred to another post or back to headquarters. What salary does the firm pay? Does the firm lower the salary to the old level or keep it elevated? There is also the problem of which currency to use to pay a salary because of fluctuating exchange rates. Compensation is usually paid in some combination of both currencies thereby allowing tax breaks and an ability to save money in the home country.

Allowances are paid to cover the additional costs of living overseas. They are meant to keep the manager's standard of living approximately the same while in the foreign country. Allowances cover the differing costs of housing, food, utilities, transportation, clothing, personal and medical services, and education for any children. In addition, the firm will always cover the cost of additional taxes incurred in a foreign country.

Bonuses are usually paid to compensate an employee for any hardships, sacrifices, and inconveniences incurred as a result of the move. Bonuses are rare, however, and are usually given only if the manager is assigned to a particularly underdeveloped, violent, or dangerous country.

In addition to allowances and bonuses, a firm will usually provide home leaves for expatriates and their families and pay for periodic trips home. Home travel is considered essential for expatriate managers and their families to alleviate the pressures and tensions of overseas assignments.

124 *International staffing and labor issues*

Taxes

Tax laws vary greatly from country to country. In some countries, foreign workers are only taxed on the income they receive in the country. In the United States, 2015 tax law allows a U.S. citizen to exempt the first $100,800 of income earned abroad from U.S. taxes. The rest is taxed at the regular rate. If the United States has a tax treaty with the foreign country in question, the amount of foreign taxes paid on unearned income (interest, dividends) can be credited against the amount of owed U.S. taxes. In order to get a foreign tax credit on the amount of earned income (salaries), expatriates must prove that they have been residents in a foreign country for at least a year and the assignment to a foreign location must be for at least two years.

Repatriating branch managers

Reverse culture shock

There are three problem areas associated with the repatriation of employees: personal finances, readjustment to home country corporate structure, and re-acclimatization to life in the home country. Upon reentry into the home country, an expatriate will lose all the allowances and bonuses that encourage foreign assignments. For many, this means a substantial decrease in salary. Also, they may find that consumer prices and housing costs have greatly increased during the time abroad.

Once back at headquarters, managers may find that peers have been promoted and that they have less autonomy in decision-making and fewer responsibilities. A manager also may feel left out of the corporate information loop. The corporation should make foreign assignments as prestigious and important as possible in the corporate framework in order to attract candidates, which will help to ease the transition back into the corporate scheme by increasing the esteem a manager is given at headquarters by peers.

The family of an expatriate may find that their comparative social status has dropped. In many countries, subsidiary managers are thought of as corporate "big wheels" representing the entire company and, as such, receive club memberships and invitations to important government and social functions. Once at home, however, the situation changes and they are no longer the center of such attention. Children must adjust to new schools and lifestyles, and spouses who have grown accustomed to domestic help may find themselves on their own again.

To help with the problems associated with repatriation, there are several things that can be done while an employee is still at the overseas assignment. The earlier the notification of return, the longer is the time for adjustment. Headquarters can give the maximum amount of information available about the new job to the expatriate to allay fears of a demotion. The firm also should bring the employee back to headquarters periodically so that the employee will not feel isolated and forgotten. A mentor might also be assigned to look out for the interests of the expatriate and to help with readjustment. The firm can also provide housing assistance and an orientation program once the family is back.

Ethical issues

Female managers overseas

There is a definite lack of consideration of women as candidates for expatriate assignments. According to a classic study by Nancy Adler of McGill University, only 3% of expatriate managers from 686 North American firms were women. Adler attributes this scarcity to three beliefs held by MNC executives:

1 Women do not want foreign assignments.
2 Corporations resist sending women abroad.
3 Women would not be effective because of the prejudices of foreigners.

Adler refutes the first point, having found that there is no difference between men and women MBAs in attitudes toward overseas assignments. Rather than differences, she found that males and females showed equal interest in pursuing international careers.

Adler found confirmation of the second belief that corporations are indeed hesitant to assign women overseas. The reasons cited by respondents in her study were the prejudices of foreigners, dual-career marriages, a scarcity of women willing to go abroad, and concerns regarding the possible dangers to personnel based overseas from isolation and hardship. In addressing the third point, that corporations assume that women will have reduced effectiveness overseas because of the prejudice of foreigners against women in the workforce, Adler asserts that while there "are genuine barriers in many Middle Eastern nations, most countries make a distinction between American women professionals and local women." Since this study was first published, there has been progress in the area of gender equality in the workplace, but there is still some room for improvement. In 2005, available studies showed that the female percentage had risen to 23%, and indications are that this trend will continue.

Overseas assignments as dumping grounds

One important issue that an MNC faces in making decisions on selecting personnel for overseas assignments is the possible use of these assignments to remove undesirable or inefficient executives. This is a dangerous trend, however, that could harm the interests of the corporation in the long run. For example, the demands of an overseas assignment are usually much more complex and intense than a domestic assignment, and an executive who is regarded as a failure in a home country could be an even bigger failure overseas.

126 *International staffing and labor issues*

The failure of local operations in one country may not affect the overall bottom line of a large MNC significantly, but it could prove damaging to its global image. Another problem associated with this approach is that the company is not likely to find good personnel in the future willing to take overseas assignments, once it is known within the corporation that they have been used to ease out inefficient or difficult personnel.

International labor issues

International labor issues are important considerations for multinational corporations operating manufacturing or service facilities in different countries. Managing a labor force that comprises different nationalities, has different work ethics and cultures, is governed by a variety of local laws, and has different traditions of union activities is an extremely complex and often a very difficult proposition.

Managing an international workforce

Given the differences in union–management relations around the world and the need to maintain a uniform industrial relations policy throughout a corporation, MNCs are invariably faced with the decision of whom to give the responsibility for handling overall industrial relations. The approach that an MNC takes generally depends on its world view, whether it is **ethnocentric**, **polycentric**, or **geocentric**. Although MNCs are found to be widely different in their overall management policies from these three standpoints, some do take an **ethnocentric** view, where the parent office exercises substantial control over the local subsidiaries. When it comes to dealing with industrial relations in different countries, however, most companies give substantial freedom to their local managers to deal with local industrial relations problems. Exhibit 6.1 highlights the advantages and disadvantages of the various staffing models.

Different social and political structures, different local laws, varying labor psychology, and unique traditions that influence industrial relations are the primary factors that help to justify this policy, which places substantial responsibility on local managers to deal with industrial relations problems as they arise. Moreover, the active and continuous involvement of local managers in handling local issues provides them with the opportunity to develop an ongoing relationship with workers and union representatives, which is essential to the smooth functioning of any operation and for the building of a basic understanding between management and labor.

Most corporations, however, do insist on a certain level of control by the parent company over the industrial relations policies followed by subsidiaries. On most occasions, however, this control simply takes the form of coordination, where the overall policy is decided by the parent office and local issues are left to the subsidiary managers.

Geocentric staffing
Mode: Assign positions to best qualified, regardless of employee's background, culture, or country of origin.
Adv: Flexible, increased culture knowledge
Disadv: Difficult due to immigration, costs of worker relocation, and diversity

Polycentric staffing
Mode: Home country workers get top positions in headquarters, while overseas local workers are assigned abroad.
Adv: Organizational learning in local markets, better advancement for locals, leads to more commitment and being seen as a local firm.
Disadv: Knowledge and performance gaps between overseas managers and home country managers.

Ethnocentric staffing
Mode: home country nationals are designated as top ranking employees in global operations (i.e. US executives in Indonesian branch)
Adv: People in leadership are known and know business, unified corporate culture
Disadv: Local knowledge not fully transferred, locals blocked from promotion, firm may be seen as a foreign firm operating abroad.

Exhibit 6.1 Various staffing models: advantages and disadvantages

Some major corporations have a tendency to create an industrial relations arrangement where unions are not a part of the scene. While this could work in certain countries, it may not in others. It is clear that while coordination is workable, central control is not practical in organizing and managing industrial relations in a multinational corporation. Some multinationals use their multiple sourcing and labor transfer capabilities to exercise leverage against unions in particular countries. For example, if a plant in one country is closed by striking union members, an MNC can shift production to a plant in a different country and maintain its stance against the striking workers in the first country.

Wages and benefits

Wages and benefits vary around the world. The differences in the levels of wages and benefits workers enjoy are particularly pronounced when compared between industrialized and developing countries. There are also substantial differences within the industrial countries and developing countries themselves.

There are several reasons why such important differences exist. First, wages are determined by the local cost of living, which may be determined by a comparative index. This general determination is influenced by the existing wages in some industries or comparative industry sectors for comparative jobs. Government legislation or intervention is also a determinant. Many countries have minimum wage legislation, and some have legislation on maximum wages that can be paid. Tax issues also influence wage levels, because in high-tax countries companies must pay higher wages or provide additional benefits to offset the impact of higher taxation levels. The level and militancy of union

128 *International staffing and labor issues*

organizations in different countries and the capacity for collective bargaining is often an important determinant of wage levels.

Patterns of fringe benefits also differ widely. In countries with a strong welfare or socialist sociopolitical orientation, greater emphasis is placed on fringe benefits as a part of the overall compensation package, unlike some industrial nations where compensation is almost entirely in the form of monetary income. In many countries, certain fringe benefits are required by government legislation to be paid by companies. Thus, the percentage of fringe benefits in the total compensation package varies considerably in different countries.

Workers in Europe have historically received additional compensation according to the number of family members they support, or if they work in unpleasant conditions. In Belgium and the Netherlands, commuting costs have also been reimbursed to workers. One of the most comprehensive fringe benefits systems has been found in Japan, where Japanese workers have received a family allowance, housing subsidies, free lunches, free education for their children, and subsidized vacations.

Procedures for increasing levels of compensation also vary considerably. In the United States, there has been a precipitous drop in the number of union workers over the last few decades. Where unions exist, wages are governed usually by labor-management contracts that have a particular life span, usually three years, after which they have to be renegotiated. Increases are often determined on the basis of a mutually agreed formula that links wage increases to some cost-of-living index. There is room within the general formula for individual wage increases on the basis of performance during a particular time period, typically a year. In Japan a certain group of unions, which are seen as role models for a particular industry, lead the way for wage negotiation, which, among other things, takes into account the increases in the cost of living since the last wage settlement.

Once agreements have been reached with the leading unions in a particular industry, other unions in the same industry come to an agreement with their management, more or less on the same basis. Wage increases in Great Britain are somewhat less stable and can be demanded by individual groups of workers within a particular company, and the demands often may not be related to the compensation being paid to workers in different companies in the same industry, or, for that matter, other groups of workers within the same company. Industry-wide wages are generally standard in Germany, however, and strikes that demand wage increases outside the scope of industry-wide agreements are not typically recognized. In most developing countries, **collective bargaining** by unions and intervention by the government are the main determinants of wage increases.

Usually MNCs have to pay a relatively higher wage to their employees in developing countries, in comparison to wages being paid for similar work in the industry by domestic companies. This differential wage policy is necessitated by the need for an MNC to counter and prevent criticism from the government,

International staffing and labor issues 129

local politicians, the media, and trade union organizations that it is an agent of foreign exploitation of the country. Foreign exploitation is a particularly sensitive issue in most developing countries, given the colonial legacy in which these countries were subjected to substantial economic exploitation by their rulers and by companies from the ruling countries.

Job security and layoffs

Emphasis on job security varies widely from country to country, and MNCs must take into consideration local laws, practices, and socioeconomic conditions while formulating policies and procedures for layoffs, suspensions, and termination of employee services. The emphasis on job security is perhaps the highest in developing countries, where jobs are scarce and there is no system of social security to take care of employees who cannot find employment in other jobs. In such countries, layoffs and retrenchments are difficult to implement, because both union and government pressures tend to be strongly against them. Moreover, industry practices in developing countries do not permit layoffs, especially of the type witnessed in the United States, where companies routinely lay off thousands of employees either to improve profitability, restructure the organization, or because demand for the products has fallen off. In fact, to prevent worker hardship, many governments have in the past nationalized operations of MNCs who have decided to lay off large numbers of workers. In developed countries, job security is important, although not quite to the same extent as developing countries. Among the industrialized countries, Japan and Germany place a particularly strong emphasis on job security. Japanese industry has been long noted for its tradition of lifetime employment. Although this is no longer true of a large number of companies in Japan, substantial benefits are available to Japanese workers who lose their jobs, especially because of corporate policies. These benefits include salary payments, retraining, assistance in finding alternative employment, and relocation assistance. Similarly, in Germany assistance is provided to workers who lose their jobs because of corporate decisions. In many instances companies must seek approval from the government and come to an understanding with unions before affecting any significant layoffs of employees.

Labor productivity

Labor productivity is a critical issue for MNCs. It determines, to a significant degree, the level of competitiveness an enterprise can hope to achieve in the local and international markets. Labor productivity varies greatly in different countries, but this variance is not only because of differences in labor quality. In fact, seven factors can be identified, that are crucial to improvement of labor productivity:

1 *Worker quality and skills*. The labor force must be constantly upgraded through training in the latest methods and technologies.

130 *International staffing and labor issues*

2 *Research and development.* A high level of R&D is needed to remain abreast of and preferably ahead of the competition. New products and information must continue in a steady stream.

3 *Business savings and investment* are a major source of capital, R&D, and training.

4 *Personal savings and investment* provide a pool of funds to be used for investments by commercial banks, which in turn stimulate the economy's growth.

5 *Natural resource development and substitution.* Obviously, there is a limit on the amount of natural resources that can be utilized. Thus, new sources must be developed to provide for the needs of business.

6 *Production techniques and systems must be constantly upgraded and changed* because of the high rate of obsolescence. The personal computer industry is a good example.

7 *Management techniques and philosophy.* Management must take a long-term view of the future. Short-term goals have proved to be ineffective and costly, and productivity can only be increased over the long term.

Exhibit 6.2 provides indices of manufacturing productivity and other measures for some of the industrialized countries.

Technology

Of the many issues that affect labor productivity, technology is one of the most important and presents major problems to MNCs seeking overseas locations for their plants. Many less-developed countries (LDCs) have major unemployment problems and are eager to develop industries that are labor intensive and provide maximum job opportunities. Modern technology is often capital intensive, however, and relies on reducing the role of human effort in accomplishing production goals with minimum costs and maximum efficiency. As a result, in many instances MNCs have to use technology that is relatively less advanced to meet host country requirements of providing greater job opportunities. Thus, a certain amount of productivity and efficiency have to be sacrificed to gain entry into a new market.

Labor unions

The concept of collective bargaining is central to the functioning of labor unions. After a union is certified by workers and recognized by management, it is the sole representative of those workers. It represents all the workers collectively when negotiating with management for compensation and working conditions and signs agreements into legally binding labor contracts. The contracts cover such issues as wages, fringe benefits, holidays, vacations, promotion policies, layoff policies, job security provisions, stipulations regarding working conditions and safety, administration of the contract, and grievance and dispute settlement.

International staffing and labor issues   131

(average annual rates of change)

	Productivity				Labor Compensation (U.S. dollar basis)			
	1973–1987	1982–1987	1993–2003	2000–2014	1973–1987	1982–1987	1993–2003	2000–2014
United States	2.5	4.5	5.0	1.3	7.4	3.5	4.3	2.6
Canada	2.1	4.3	2.6	1.1	7.2	3.3	1.3	2.9
Japan	5.3	4.8	3.5	0.9	12.9	15.2	3.3	−0.1
France	3.9	3	4.3	0.7	10.5	9.2	2.7	2.5
Germany	3.3	3.3	2.7	0.8	10.2	11.4	3.2	2.0
United Kingdom	3.2	5.5	2.7	0.3	10.8	6	3.8	2.3

	Unit Labor Costs (U.S. dollar basis)				Unemployment Rate (in % annually)			
	1973–1987	1982–1987	1993–2003	2000–2014	1983	1993	2003	2000–2014
United States	4.8	−1.0	−0.7	1.6	9.6	6.9	6.0	7.1
Canada	5	−1.0	1.3	2.2	11.5	10.8	6.9	7.0
Japan	7.3	10.0	0.3	−0.9	2.7	2.5	5.3	4.3
France	6.4	6.0	−1.4	1.8	8.6	11.3	9.3	8.6
Germany	6.7	7.8	0.5	1.2	6.9	8.0	9.3	7.4
United Kingdom	7.4	0.5	1.1	1.9	11.8	10.4	5.0	6.6

Exhibit 6.2 Annual rate of change for manufacturing productivity, compensation, unit labor costs, and unemployment rates

United States

Labor-management relations in the United States are relatively nonpolitical, in that the government is not a part of the collective-bargaining process, but legislation does establish and enforce rules regarding the framework of collective bargaining (for example, both parties must bargain in good faith). The labor contract is enforceable through the courts, and either side can be sued for any breach of the contract. For the most part, collective bargaining takes place at the company or plant level, that is, on a company-by-company basis. Some exceptions include the trucking and construction industries, which have regional contracts, and the steel industry, which has a national contract.

The contract agreed upon is usually very extensive and covers almost every contingency. Its terms apply to all workers in the bargaining units, and individual workers cannot negotiate individually with management to obtain better terms. During the life of the contract, strikes and lockouts are usually banned, but if an old contract expires and a new one is still being negotiated, strikes and lockouts are allowed. Strikes occur when the workers walk out and refuse to work. **Lockouts** occur when the employer closes or locks the plant, and bars workers from entering. Fans of professional hockey may recall the

132 *International staffing and labor issues*

lockout during the 2004-2005 season, when the owners and the players could not agree on an appropriate salary cap. The owners initially wanted a payroll cap of $31 million, while the players wanted the teams to set their own payroll levels. The entire season was eventually cancelled when the two sides could not agree on the maximum salary cap. Strikes are generally more frequent than lockouts. A **wildcat strike** occurs when the workers strike during the life of an existing contract and give little or no notice. There are relatively few strikes in the United States, but they tend to last a long time. The emphasis in labor relations in the United States is on keeping the firm going and profitable.

Great Britain

Labor-management relations in Great Britain are much more political and contentious than in the United States. Unions see the negotiation process as more of a class struggle and going on strike as an exercisable right. The unions are guided by the principle of voluntarism, which states that workers alone will define and pursue their self-interest, which makes them militant and abrasive with authority, and they have very little regard for the welfare of the enterprise. They have historically been seen as a powerful political force, as the Labour party has traditionally espoused this class-struggle mentality. Today, Great Britain's unions have been subject to new legal constraints and have lost much of their erstwhile unity, while membership has dwindled.

Germany

In Germany union membership is purely voluntary. There is typically only one union for all workers in a single industry. Labor agreements cover only major issues such as wages. All the other issues, such as vacations and shifts, are negotiated at the plant level. Legally established work councils are able to codetermine issues involving safety and plant practices with management. Members of the work council are elected by the firm's workers. Strikes and lockouts during the life of an existing contract are illegal, regardless of the contract's provisions. They are legal when the existing contract has expired or is being renegotiated. A unique feature of German labor relations is that an individual worker can negotiate individually with management to try to obtain better terms.

Japan

Japanese unions are usually company unions, organized by enterprise. A union is made up of employees within a single company or single operational unit, regardless of occupations or positions. There is legislation in Japan that determines minimum wages, hours per week, overtime, vacation, sick leave, sanitary conditions, and layoff policies and procedures, which leaves little for collective bargaining. Thus, negotiations are limited mostly to wages, but wages, positions, and promotions are usually determined through seniority. Every spring all the unions from every company embark upon **shunto**, or the **spring wage offensive**, when the few negotiations take place. Unions want companies to remain profitable for the good of the groups, so they will never ask for too much. This attitude is diametrically opposed to the attitude of the unions in Great Britain. *Shunto* is an effort by the unions to raise wages across the country, so that no single firm will become less competitive than another. There are very few strikes in Japan, and what strikes there are usually take place during *shunto*. The strikes are for very short periods of time, sometimes only half a day, and merely demonstrate worker support for the unions. Japanese workers in the unions also promote a company's well-being and profitability because its success benefits the whole group.

Given the recession, deflation, and fall in union membership in Japan in recent years, the *shunto* has not been as successful in achieving wage increases on an annual basis. In fact, the recent focus has been on maintaining the existing structure and level of wages, rather than pushing for annual increases as has been done in the past.

MNC tactics

Over the past several years, the AFL-CIO has maintained that MNCs have several detrimental effects on U.S. industry. First, MNCs use capital resources for foreign investment that are needed for domestic investment and expansion. Second, MNCs export U.S. technology to other countries in order to take advantage of low-cost foreign labor, which denies American workers from gaining the rewards of using the technology. Third, MNCs replace U.S. exports with foreign-produced goods, which worsens the trade balance and decreases domestic employment. Fourth, MNCs use imports from their subsidiaries in low-wage countries instead of using domestically produced goods. Finally, many MNCs have outsourced jobs to areas of the world with much lower wage rates such as India and China.

Unions feel threatened by the rising power of MNCs and the advantages they have because of multiple production locales. When a firm decides to locate operations abroad, it is no longer dependent on only domestic plants, and the domestic union will have no control over what happens half a world away. Most of the concerns of unions are in part because of the huge amount of resources at the command of MNCs. More important, an MNC's power and decision-making capabilities are outside every country in which they operate except headquarters. Some of the specific concerns unions have regarding MNCs include:

- The ability of MNCs to relocate facilities if a contract is not agreeable to them.
- Restricted access to data by unions, especially financial data, to combat MNCs. For example, if an MNC says it is losing money on overseas

134   *International staffing and labor issues*

operations and thus needs to cut labor costs, the union cannot confirm or deny this statement.

- The ability of an MNC to pick and choose where to locate and thus take advantage of differences in the amount and level of benefits they are required to provide by law.
- The ability of an MNC to withstand strikes by threatening to close the facility and relocate, and because that factory is only one part of the corporation, the MNC will be able to obtain cash and production from other plants.

Counter-tactics by labor

The only hope for unions to compete with MNCs lies in international rules and regulations and international cooperation. There are three main international labor organizations that make efforts in this direction.

The International Labor Organization

The ILO was established in 1919 under the Treaty of Versailles. It is now affiliated with the United Nations and is composed of government, industry, and union representatives. Its premise is that the failure of any country to promote humane working conditions is an obstacle to nations that want to improve the conditions in their own countries. The ILO tries to define and promote international standards regarding safety, health, and other working conditions.

Organization for Economic Cooperation and Development

The OECD also consists of government, industry, and union representatives. It has developed a set of voluntary guidelines for MNCs and for host countries regarding labor conditions and fair practices. The organization is based in Paris, but does not have any enforcement mechanisms in international jurisdictions.

The European Union

The EU also attempts to coordinate the evolution of industrial relations standards within the member countries by issuing directives on issues of common concern. These directives are approved by the council of ministers before they become effective. Existing directives cover such issues as employee participation on company boards and the safeguarding of employee interests and the right of employee representatives to information and consultation in the event of a change of ownership of a business. Some of the EU directives, once accepted by the council of ministers, are incorporated into the national laws of member states. The impact of EU directives on national labor laws of member states has increased over time.

International staffing and labor issues 135

International unions

The prospect of international unions may offer solutions for improvement. International unions may increase or decrease in influence subject to an emerging new paradigm in industrial relations systems in both highly industrialized economies and emerging economies. International unions could employ transnational bargaining, which would mean a centralized and coordinated collective-bargaining strategy between an employer and a union or group of unions for employees in facilities located in two or more nations. In other words, one union could negotiate for all the plants that a single firm has around the world, thus guaranteeing equal treatment for all workers and restoring the power of the unions. In the real world, this is much easier said than done. The few international unions that exist are in similar countries, such as the United States and Canada. In order for international unions to affect global wage increases or improved worker conditions, all countries would need to comply.

Codetermination

One final possibility of increasing the impact of workers on firms is the concept of codetermination. Codetermination means employee participation in management. An early example of codetermination was in the German coal and steel industries in 1951. By law, codetermination gave the representatives of workers and shareholders 50% each of the directorships, with one neutral director to break any ties. Codetermination has gained importance in many other countries as the emphasis of collective-bargaining shifts, little by little, to agreements and counterbalancing of labor-management interests.

Perspective 6.1 The Managerial Grid

Now that we have finished our discussion on international staffing and labor issues, we would like to point you in the direction of a free online quiz that you can complete to assess what type of manager you are. A classic example of managerial classification is the **Managerial Grid** by Blake and Mouton. Exhibit 6.3 highlights the general characteristics of this model. Readers interested in completing their own assessments are instructed to search the internet for free sites catering to this assessment.

The Managerial Grid questionnaire consists of questions where respondents have to classify themselves on a zero to five scale (zero is "never" and five is "always," based on various circumstances. Things like "nothing is more important than completing the goal or task" and "I enjoy coaching people on new tasks or procedures" are answered in order to tally results for each respondent. The responses are then classified as "people oriented" and "task oriented" such that data points can be calculated to assess where on the grid the respondent falls.

Please see this chapter's appendix for websites offering a free questionnaire.

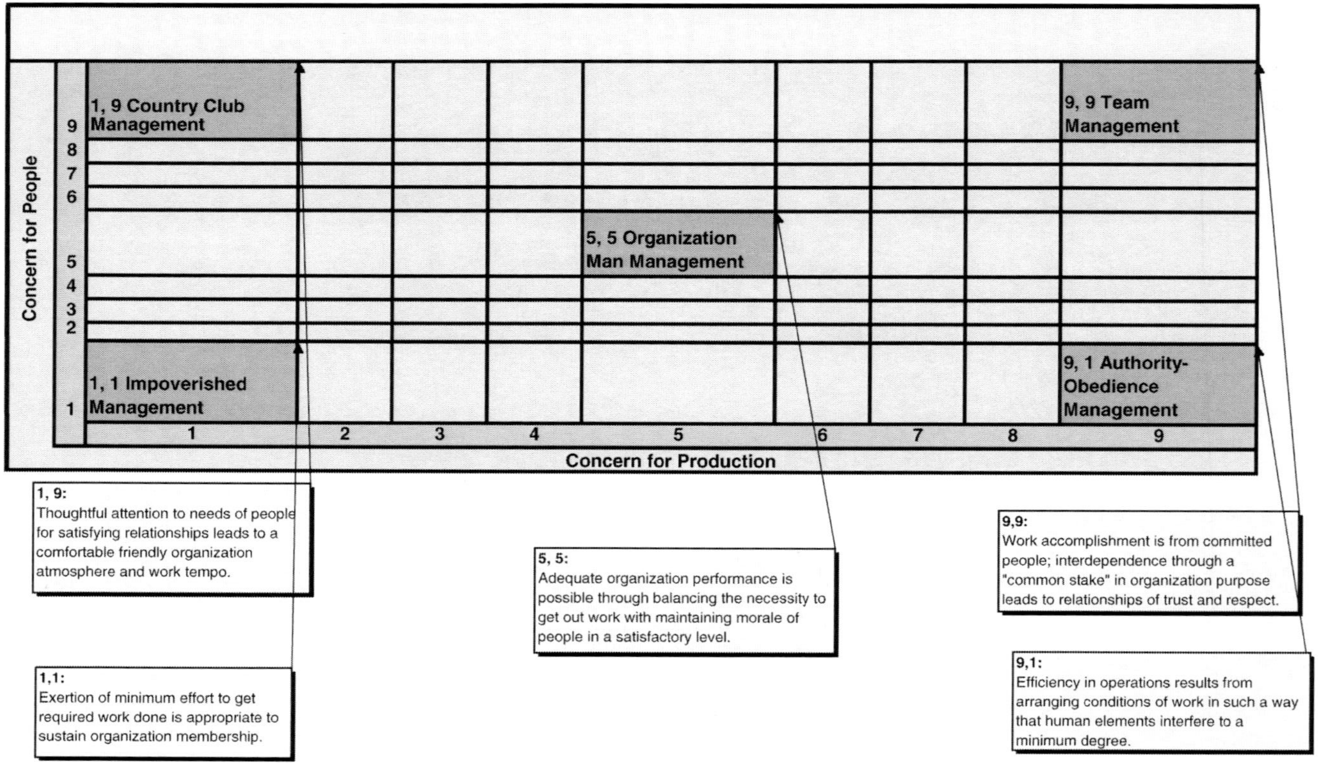

Exhibit 6.3 The Managerial Grid (Blake & Mouton, 1964)

Concern for People

9
8
7
6
5
4
3
2
1

1, 9 Country Club Management

1, 1 Impoverished Management

5, 5 Organization Man Management

9, 9 Team Management

9, 1 Authority-Obedience Management

1   2   3   4   5   6   7   8   9

Concern for Production

1, 9:
Thoughtful attention to needs of people for satisfying relationships leads to a comfortable friendly organization atmosphere and work tempo.

1.1:
Exertion of minimum effort to get required work done is appropriate to sustain organization membership.

5, 5:
Adequate organization performance is possible through balancing the necessity to get out work with maintaining morale of people in a satisfactory level.

9.9:
Work accomplishment is from committed people; interdependence through a "common stake" in organization purpose leads to relationships of trust and respect.

9.1:
Efficiency in operations results from arranging conditions of work in such a way that human elements interfere to a minimum degree.

Summary

The four most common structures used by MNCs to organize and manage operations are functional, regional, product line, and matrix structures. Staffing is crucial for MNCs because of technological advances, worldwide competition for skilled labor, and the constant need to increase productivity, the need to reduce costs, and the need to increase intra-company communication and information flows. International staffing involves recruitment, selection, training, and motivation and requires a bi-cultural sensitivity toward the host country environment. High failure rates among expatriate managers have caused MNCs to carefully select and train global managers.

International staffing may involve filling the management position with expatriates, host country nationals, or third-country nationals; each selection offers different advantages and disadvantages. Staff selection is affected by the availability of trained candidates in the host country location, corporate policies regarding local versus corporate control, a candidate's knowledge of the local environment, the local image the MNC wants to project, and employment incentives. Also, the candidate's technical skills, language abilities, and adaptability must be evaluated. Adaptability assessment through an early identification program test is important in order to minimize the effects of management, culture shock, and ineffectiveness on local operations. Cross-cultural training techniques are useful in reducing candidate failure rates and help ensure their success.

Specialized compensation arrangements for international managers make these positions very attractive. Income taxes and repatriation, however, are additional problems for an international manager. Gender biases in many countries may slow foreign assignments for female managers. The dumping of inefficient personnel in international positions may occur, but can harm the long-term interests of an MNC.

International managers are faced with a diversity of nationalities, languages, cultures, and work ethics, which can complicate motivation and management of the local labor force. To develop management–labor relations essential for efficient operations, local managers must have sufficient authority and flexibility. Centralized corporate control, through industrial relations policy, however, is required to achieve MNC-wide cohesion. Host country laws and practices also may limit local management flexibility.

Wage and fringe benefit systems should reflect local costs of living and the extent of existing social welfare benefits. Further, MNCs must be careful not to exploit less-developed countries in terms of wages and benefits to prevent criticism from host governments, local media, and trade unions. Policies and procedures for employee layoffs, suspensions, and terminations must also reflect the traditions and practices of the host country.

Labor productivity can vary in different countries. Improvements in productivity are a function of government support, worker quality and skill, research and development, innovation, business savings and investment, personal savings and investment, natural resources, production systems, and

138 *International staffing and labor issues*

management techniques and philosophies. Because modern technology is capital intensive and may be unavailable, MNCs can sacrifice productivity and efficiency for low labor costs when expanding production into new markets. Labor relations and the role of unions also differ between nations (with some having a strong union presence, and others not as strong). International unions are seeking greater cooperation across national boundaries, but nationalistic attitudes, different goals, and physical distance has impeded their growth. Codetermination is a recent development that attempts to increase worker influence and responsibilities in MNC operations.

Discussion questions

1 When staffing an MNC for positions outside the home country, what are some advantages and disadvantages of hiring host country nationals? Expatriates?
2 Who is a global manager?
3 Why do expatriate managers frequently receive additional compensation over their colleagues at equivalent positions in the corporate office? Why are these packages more complicated than packages provided to domestic employees?
4 What problems do expatriates face at the completion of their foreign assignments?
5 What obstacles do women executives encounter when seeking international staff positions?
6 Before investing in a production plant in a foreign country, what are some of the questions concerning labor management that should be addressed?
7 What is collective bargaining? How does collective bargaining differ in the United States, Great Britain, Germany, and Japan?
8 How is productivity affected by a shortage of skilled labor?

Bibliography

Adler, Nancy. 1984. Expecting International Success: Female Managers Overseas. *Columbia Journal of World Business* 19(3), 79–85.

Blake, Robert R., and Mouton, Jane S. 1964. *The Managerial Grid: The Key to Leadership Excellence*. Houston: Gulf Publishing Co.

Campbell, Duncan C. 1989. Multinational Labor Relations in the European Community. *ILR Report* (Fall): 7–14.

Charnovitz, Steve. 1987. The Influence of International Labor Standards on the World Trading Regime. *International Labor Review* (September/October): 9–17.

Clarke, Christopher J., and Kieron Breenan. 1990. Building Synergy in the Diversified Business. *Long Range Planning* (April): 9–16.

Daniels, John D. 1986. Approaches to European Regional Management by Large U.S. Multinational Firms. *Management International Review* (Second Quarter): 27–42.

Dolins, Ilene L. 1998. 1998 Global Relocation Survey: Current Trends Regarding Expatriate Activity. *Employee Relations Today* 25(4): 1–111. DOI:10.1002/est.3910250402

Dowling, Peter J. 1987. Human Resource Issues in International Business. *Syracuse Journal of International Law & Commerce* (Winter): 255–271.

Dowling, Peter J. 1989. Hot Issues Overseas. *Personnel Administrator* (January): 66–72.

Duff, Mike. 1985. Hands Across the Water. *Supermarket Business* (February): 45, 47.

Economist, The. "Déjà vu?", June 5, 2003, http://www.economist.com/node/1826029, accessed July 17, 2017.

Expat.Com website, Expat US Relocation Survey 2014, www.expat.com/, accessed July 17, 2017.

Fanning, W. R., and A. F. Arvin. 1986. National or Global? Control versus Flexibility. *Long Range Planning* (October): 84–88.

Gellerman, Saul W. 1990. In Organizations, as in Architecture, Form Follows Function. *Organizational Dynamics* (Winter): 57–68.

GMAC Global Relocation Survey. 2006. Global Relocation Trends: 2005 Survey Report. Woodbridge, IL: GMAC Relocation Services.

Harris, Phillip R., and Robert T. Moran. 1987. *Managing Cultural Differences.* Houston: Gulf Publishing Company.

Hogan, Gary W., and Jane R. Goodson. 1990. The Key to Expatriate Success. *Training and Development* (January): 50–52.

Leontiades, James. 1986. Going Global – Global Strategies versus National Strategies. *Long Range Planning* (December): 96–104.

Levine, Marvin. 1987/1988. Labor Movements and the Multinational Corporation: A Future for Collective Bargaining? *Employee Relations Law Journal* (Winter): 47–57.

Morgenstern, Felice. 1985. The Importance, in Practice, of Conflicts of Labor Law. *International Labor Review* (March/April): 119–113.

Narasimhan, Ram, and Joseph R. Carter. 1990. Organization, Communication and Coordination of International Sourcing. *International Marketing Review* 7: 6–20.

OECD Statistics, https://data.oecd.org/, accessed July 17, 2017.

Ray, George F. 1990. International Labor Costs in Manufacturing, 1960-88. *National Institute Economic Review* (May): 67–70.

Savich, R. S., and W. Rodgers. 1988. Assignment Overseas: Easing the Transition Before and After. *Personnel* (August): 44–48.

Schultz, T. Paul. 1990. Women's Changing Participation in the Labor Force: A World Perspective. *Economic Development & Cultural Change* (April): 457–488.

Servais, J.-M. 1989. The Social Clause in Trade Agreements: Wishful Thinking or an Instrument of Social Progress? *International Labor Review* 128: 423–432.

Staiger, Robert W. 1988. Organized Labor and the Scope of International Specialization. *Journal of Political Economy* (October): 1022–1047.

Tung, Rosalie. 1984. Strategic Management of Human Resources in the Multinational Enterprise. *Human Resource Management* (Summer): 129–143.

U.S. Department of Labor, Bureau of Labor Statistics.

Weisz, Morris. 1988. A View of Labor Ministries in Other Nations. *Monthly Labor Review* (July): 19–23.

Appendix
Managerial grid – free questionnaire sites

As noted at the end of Chapter 6, below are some site links which offer free Managerial Grid questionnaires.

Free Internet Site Managerial Grid 1: https://www.bumc.bu.edu/ facdev-medicine/files/2010/10/Leadership-Matrix-Self-Assessment-Questionnaire.pdf

Free Internet Site Managerial Grid 2: http://www.stellarleadership.com/ docs/Leadership/assessment/Managerial%20Grid%20Questionnaire.pdf

Free Internet Site Managerial Grid 3: http://www.nwlink.com/ ~donclark/leader/matrix.html

Free Internet Site Managerial Grid 4: http://www.thevisioncouncil.org/ sites/default/files/members/Leadership%20Matrix%20Employee%20 Questionnaire.pdf

Free Internet Site Managerial Grid 5: http://my.ilstu.edu/~llipper/com329/ activity_bm.pdf

All were accessible as of 08/10/2017.

7 Managing operations and technology

> Delight is a very fleeting factor which vanishes like yesterday when that day is gone.
>
> (Soren Kierkegaard)

Chapter objectives

This chapter will:

- Present the interrelated nature of the operations process and technology.
- Identify efficiencies achieved through standardization of the international production process.
- Describe key inputs for designing and developing the local operations system.
- Discuss the question of centralized or decentralized control in the context of the multinational corporation.
- Briefly discuss the evolving Asia-Pacific managerial production systems.
- Examine the role and importance of management information systems within MNCs.
- Examine the role technology holds in maintaining a competitive advantage.
- Discuss the methods multinationals use to acquire, transfer, and protect technology.
- Present a definition of global strategy and its importance to the long-term success of an MNC.

Operations, technology, and international competition

With increasing worldwide competition, the strategic implications of decisions concerning the choices of an MNC for operations and technology become even more important. These two elements influence where and how a company will operate. Decisions as to what and where it will produce to maintain a competitive edge are closely related to its technological and operational resources. Although some international business experts have chosen to treat

142   *Managing operations and technology*

technology and production in the international arena as separate factors, the two are interrelated issues because of the impact that technology has on international production decisions.

International production and operations

International management of operations and production may be very similar to the operations and production in a home country. Common to both are considerations regarding the efficient use of all the factors of production, productivity improvements, research and development, and the extent of horizontal and/or vertical integration. The international environment, however, includes other considerations. Before making production decisions, an MNC must consider such additional factors as different wage rates, industrial relations, sources of financing, foreign exchange risk, international tax laws, control, the appropriate mix of capital and labor, access to suppliers, and the production experience curve in each country. While many MNCs attempt to standardize their production systems on a worldwide basis by transferring production processes and procedures unchanged from the parent, these environmental influences often make such standardization unsuccessful or at best difficult.

Worldwide standardization

On one hand, there is strong justification for worldwide standardization. First, the capacity of management to develop a successful organization is improved, primarily by making it easier to carry out the home office management functions. Organization and staffing are simpler when overseas production facilities are replications of existing facilities because future plants are reduced or enlarged versions of existing plants, and there are fewer labor hours and fewer costs involved with plant design. In addition, because technical assistance workers are familiar with the standard plant design, the overseas technical staff can be smaller, and home-based technical workers can assist the foreign operation on an as-needed basis. Furthermore, production specifications are more easily maintained and updated. If changes are necessary in production specifications, there is no need for a plant-by-plant evaluation to determine which operations are affected, which also implies cost savings in specifications maintenance for unified production processes.

Supply

The second area that experiences direct benefits from standardization is supply. Increased profits are realized when all production facilities can be organized into one logistics system for supplies. This single system would detail the activities between suppliers, facilities, consumers, and the corresponding requirements for raw materials and inventory (parts and finished products). In

Managing operations and technology 143

addition, with production processes standardized, machinery and parts necessary for the process would also be standardized, allowing for some interchangeable parts and machinery.

The option of using a production rationalization strategy is available if a company chooses to standardize product offerings, even if only regionally. Under **rationalization**, a subsidiary changes its purpose for production from manufacturing for its own market to manufacturing a limited number of component parts for use by several or all subsidiaries. This strategy has the advantage of production and engineering economies of scale and allows for higher-volume production with lower production costs than if the subsidiary manufactured for only end-product sales in its local market.

Control

Control is also affected by worldwide standardization. When all manufacturing facilities are expected to adhere to the same standards, quality control is easier to monitor, with quicker response to variances in quality control reports. Similarly, while human and physical factors will affect production and maintenance standards, machinery will be expected to produce at the same rate of output and with the same frequency of maintenance service. It will be possible to schedule maintenance of equipment based upon historical records of similar equipment to avoid costly unexpected breakdowns.

Planning and design of production facilities under standardization strategies are also simpler and quicker to complete. Donald A. Ball and Wendell H. McCulloch, Jr. list five steps in the process for planning a new plant based on a standardized system:

1 Design engineers need only copy the drawings and lists of materials that they have in their files.
2 Vendors will be requested to furnish equipment that they have supplied previously.
3 The technical department can send the current manufacturing specifications without alteration.
4 Labor trainers experienced in the operation of machinery can be sent to the new location without undergoing specialized training on new equipment.
5 Reasonably accurate forecasts of plant erection time and output can be made based on the experience with existing facilities.

With all of the advantages, it would appear that MNCs would strive for standardization, but environmental forces affect host nation operations, resulting in a variety of sizes, equipment, and procedures for plant operations of the same company. In addition to the environmental forces, the plant designer must consider economic, cultural, and political forces that may limit or at least affect direct alternatives.

144   *Managing operations and technology*

Controlling strategically

Areas to control

The control process involves continuous monitoring of the strategic plan to measure its effectiveness and to make corrections where necessary, in either the plan itself or in compliance.

Three major areas of importance to an MNC with regard to controlling international operations include controlling foreign exchange risk, adjustments needed in routine control systems because of differences in various branch operating environments, and control of risks arising out of foreign operations, including relations with host governments.

Establishing systems of internal control in an MNC is far more difficult than in a domestic enterprise. The communication of goals and objectives and corrections may be impeded by the distance between the parent company and its branch or subsidiary, as well as by differences in languages and operating procedures. The form of an operation may be such that a firm may have only partial ownership and not have full authority to impose control measures. Similarly, the operating environment may have such external characteristics that the control measures may be unachievable. For example, an attempt to bring sales profitability levels up to corporate objectives by raising prices might be stymied in a foreign environment because of controls on price levels set by governments.

Locating decision authority

The key factor in the control process for an MNC is the location of the decision-making authority between headquarters and subsidiaries. This problem is often referred to as centralization versus decentralization of control. Centralized decision-making vests all-important decisions with the headquarters of the firm, while decentralized decision-making means that decisions are made entirely under the authority of subsidiary heads. These situations represent extreme ends of a continuum, but there is middle ground, where some decisions come from headquarters and others remain within the subsidiary.

The structuring of the locus of authority for decision-making includes a tradeoff between the realization of different objectives. While centralized decision-making provides for the overall integration of objectives and potential efficiencies for a firm in worldwide operations, it also distances subsidiary management from making valuable inputs to the process and adding their own expertise to provide for local operating efficiencies. Total decentralization of decision-making may provide for local efficiencies, but it could also result in a loss of control by headquarters and in overall systems-wide sub-optimal operations.

The types of decisions involved include resource allocation, acquisition of capital equipment, employment of personnel, and use of liquid or capital assets.

Managing operations and technology 145

Other decisions involve the use of profits, determination of prices, reinvestment or repatriation of earnings, and determining the sources and prices to be paid for raw materials or inventory goods. Decision authority regarding marketing and production, such as adaptations to products and product lines, markets served and methods of serving those markets, types of promotion and distribution, and channels to be utilized must be allocated between the parent and the subsidiary or affiliate.

The degree of autonomy accorded to subsidiaries by MNCs depends on a number of factors, one of which is the mode of international operations. International activities, such as licensing and export functions, are usually carried out from corporate headquarters, but affiliates or subsidiaries based abroad require some degree of localized decision-making to keep operations efficient.

Another factor is the nature of the industry and its technology. If a company's advantage is based in product development and the marketing of these products using the same technology worldwide, the firm is likely to have centralized decision-making.

The size and maturity of an MNC also help place decision-making authority. An older, larger MNC might concentrate experienced personnel at headquarters and coordinate activities and decision-making from that centralized location, while a younger, smaller operation might be operating in an ad hoc manner and would continue to locate decision-making authority in the subsidiary because the company lacks experienced personnel to run those functions from the central location.

The competence of subsidiary managerial staff plays a large part in the determination of whether decision-making authority should be placed there or not. If local personnel are of high quality with good experience and business judgment, they will be given more authority.

Similarly, centralization of decision-making is affected by the local political environment and the sensitivity of an industry. An industry such as telecommunications is more sensitive to local political pressure because it is deemed essential to the welfare of the host country. Thus, local powers would impose pressure for more decentralized than centralized authority in the subsidiary.

In some countries the vesting of authority in local personnel may be an issue of political sensitivity with regard to the welfare of home country nationals. In many situations, the host government feels that centralized authority and decision-making by an MNC disenfranchises host country nationals from authority, retarding their educational and career growth and, in turn, the development process overall.

If a decision needs to be made quickly, it is more likely to be made locally. Similarly, the importance or magnitude of a decision also influences its reference to headquarters or not. Generally, headquarters gets into the act of making decisions about large amounts of assets or strategic activities, such as the expansion of production capacity, the acquisition of capital assets, and the introduction or development of new products.

146　*Managing operations and technology*

Branch goals versus headquarters goals

In addition to the factors that are characteristic of an industry, a subsidiary, and the decisions themselves, the locus of decision-making is also affected by two potentially opposing forces: the objectives of the parent firm and the subsidiary. Subsidiary managers may, for example, be directed to set prices at certain levels or to allocate the results of production to other subsidiaries and not to high-profit markets. These decisions may benefit an MNC in the aggregate but reduce the performance of a subsidiary. Thus, any benefits to the overall firm through the centralization of decision-making may be negated by increasing frustration at the subsidiary level, which may lead to a lack of motivation or performance problems on the part of the subsidiary staff. The result of opposing pressure is a balancing act between the efficiencies to be achieved through centralization; the allocation of resources, assets, and profits among subsidiaries; the allocation of resources, assets, and profits between branches of a firm; and the operating integrity of the subsidiary. If an MNC truly operates from a global perspective, the overall coordination of the operations must be integrated in a worldwide system.

Other control concerns

Other control concerns arise in situations where firms lack full ownership of a subsidiary and operate instead in a cooperative agreement or a joint venture. In these instances, an MNC may find its hands tied in efforts to centralize operations control of the affiliate.

An MNC must decide at the outset its minimum required level of control, but it must be realistic about limitations on its ability to control, and accept that it may not be able to make unfettered decisions regarding the allocation of production from the subsidiary or the repatriation or reinvestment of its resources.

Another control concern deals with the selection of managerial staff for a subsidiary. While an MNC can gain additional control from the use of expatriate corporate staff, it could lose access to the home-country operating environment. Thus, some firms make it a practice to use host country nationals in subsidiaries, but also provide training and exposure to operations in corporate headquarters in order to familiarize them with the corporate culture, objectives, policies, and procedures. The goal is to provide subsidiary executives a common basis with headquarters staff.

Evaluation of branch managers is a final important aspect of international control. The optimal situation is one that balances the objectives of an enterprise and its subsidiary in determining performance criteria. Thus, a subsidiary manager's performance should not be judged according to profits from sales if the MNC objective (as determined centrally) is to gain market share through lowered prices in the market served by the subsidiary, or if the central authorities determine that production should be allocated to other arms of the company.

Instead, the manager's performance should be evaluated according to relevant criteria, which are both quantifiable and qualitative. In this way, performance appraisal is divorced from operational profitability and is linked instead to criteria more relevant and appropriate to the situation.

Designing the local operations system

The local operational system will be somewhat reflective of the parent organization. For example, a foreign subsidiary is usually a smaller version of the parent company and will have a similar organizational structure. If a parent company is structured according to functional divisions, for example, the foreign subsidiary will also be organized by functional departments. Furthermore, because the local operational system is most likely to be smaller than the parent company, it will not be integrated vertically or horizontally. **Vertical integration** combines the stages of production typically done by different companies, while **horizontal integration** combines firms which are at the same stage of the production cycle. Because of the increased investment necessary for vertical integration, it is often only conducted to the extent necessary to obtain scarce raw materials. Also, countries such as Mexico require foreign manufacturers to purchase inputs from local suppliers and legally restrict vertical integration. As for horizontal integration, the subsidiary is unlikely to expand in such a way because it often becomes a conglomerate in its own right.

There are four elements in the design of a production system: plant location, plant layout, materials handling, and staffing. These elements, while directly applicable to the production of tangible goods, can also be applied to the design of a system for the production of services.

Plant location

Factors affecting plant location include government incentives, land and labor costs, location of competition, employee preference, location of suppliers and infrastructure (such as ports), and conditions imposed by local authorities. Which particular factors will be most important will depend to a great extent on the type of investment, such as market-seeking, labor-efficiency, or extraction mining. Because production and distribution costs are often in conflict, a plant designer often must choose between locating away from a major city because of government incentives and lower land and labor costs or locating near an urban center because of the availability of skilled labor, access to consumer markets, and a better infrastructure to support transportation.

Plant layout

Plant layout should be determined before the construction of buildings. The plant will not only need to accommodate current production needs for maximum utilization and return on investment, but also must include

148　*Managing operations and technology*

possibilities for future expansion. Accurate forecasts become crucial in terms of estimating future plant requirements, but plant layout may also be dictated occasionally by acquisition of an existing building.

Materials handling

Management may be able to achieve considerable production cost savings by careful planning for materials handling. Materials handling includes obtaining necessary inputs and maintaining appropriate inventories. If materials handling is inefficient, management may find surplus parts inventories at some sites, while other sites are shut down because of a lack of parts. The logistics of the production system, or coordination of the movements and storage of inputs and outputs, are an intricate part of the materials handling function. The objectives of the logistics system of MNCs are to minimize costs, secure supplies, and satisfy demand. For the **ethnocentric** MNC, logistics are confined to exporting with the least cost and in the least amount of time. **Polycentric** MNCs, on the other hand, have a tendency to de-emphasize logistics. The foreign subsidiary of such an MNC may not have rapid response to the introduction of new products by competitors or to excess demand or production shortfalls. The geocentric MNC will most likely maintain a separate logistics department that coordinates the activities between the markets, production location, and suppliers of its many subsidiaries.

Staffing

The labor element is often overlooked in the design of a production system. The human factor, however, can be the key to the success of a production plant. Because temperature, lighting, noise level, and aesthetics in a plant can affect the productivity of workers, an evaluation is needed for these aspects of the work environment and their respective impact on workers. Decisions made in this regard are typically a function of host country norms.

Production and operations management

There are two categories of activities inherent to production, productive activities and supportive activities. In terms of productive activities, given a period of introduction and orientation, managers of the productive activities expect the system to operate at a sufficient and prescribed level of output in order to meet demand. If the system fails to produce at such levels, managers, including the line organization, must determine where or what the impediment is and how to correct it. Potential obstacles with which management must work are low output, inferior product quality, and excessive manufacturing costs.

Managing operations and technology 149

Productive activities

First, management must verify supplies of raw materials. In addition to poor quality, the failure of vendors to meet delivery dates or to supply materials according to specifications may cause disruptions in the production process. Although this is a problem in both developing and industrialized countries, it is often more common in the developing countries, where the raw materials supply is a seller's market. When such a problem is identified, it is the responsibility of the purchasing department to educate suppliers, notifying them of exact standards and delivery date requirements and providing technical assistance when needed. It is necessary often to pay a higher price to obtain better service.

In addition to problems with outputs to the production system, management may find scheduling problems within the system itself. In a system of sequential steps, for example, poor scheduling will result in bottlenecks and excessive inventories in some areas and work stoppages because of a lack of work in others. If back orders are a problem, a company may be running many small batches to fill these orders, thereby perpetuating the problem. This situation has been found to be an even greater problem in many cultures where long-term planning is frowned upon culturally or socially. To rectify the situation, management may incorporate additional training for the scheduling staff, which includes stressing the importance of their work, providing additional supervision, or encouraging more cooperation between the marketing and production departments to avoid a back-order problem.

High absenteeism also may contribute to a low-output problem. In many developing countries, production workers are often called away from work to assist in seasonal family business, such as helping with the harvest. Furthermore, where transportation systems are inadequate, it may be very difficult for workers to commute; management may need to organize its own transportation for workers. In addition, where absenteeism is caused by sickness, management may choose to provide in-house lunch programs to provide better nutrition, which, besides reducing the instances of absenteeism because of illness, also reduces the risk of work injuries. In a situation where absenteeism is a result of low morale, management must again evaluate cultural factors. While some international production managers accept high absenteeism and low productivity as problems inherent in the foreign environment, others have found solutions to these problems by utilizing the same techniques found at home with modifications for their local environment.

Another obstacle to maintaining production standards designed for the foreign production system is that of inferior product quality. Because perceived quality is relative to the standards of a particular environment, it may be impossible to meet standards set up by home office managers. The marketing staff should evaluate the quality standards demanded by the market and then set the price–quality combination that reflects this demand, which would also include quality standards for inputs of raw materials. When a home office is

150 *Managing operations and technology*

concerned about global reputation for its name brand quality standards, it may be possible for the foreign subsidiary to produce under a different name. The other alternative is for the home office to require the same level of quality as produced abroad as is required in the home market.

Excessive manufacturing costs will affect the ability of production management to meet the prescribed standards for the system. Anything that is of significant variance from the projected budget is of concern. Again, low output may be the culprit, perhaps the budget assumptions were completely out of line with the market, or poor inventory control of inputs and finished products may exist (imported supplies may be necessary because of the uncertainty or quality of supplies in the local market).

Supportive activities

Supportive activities include quality control, inventory control, purchasing, maintenance, and technical functions.

Production depends on the purchasing department obtaining raw materials, component parts, supplies, and machinery to produce a finished product. If a firm is unable to obtain these things, the production facility may experience costly shutdowns and lost sales. If such inputs are obtained at a higher cost than that paid by a competitor, a company must either charge more for its finished products or price competitively and realize a smaller profit. Purchasing agents must search for suppliers that will provide quality inputs and reliable service at the lowest possible price. If the quality of raw materials is low, the quality of the finished product will also be low. As the saying goes, garbage in, garbage out.

Purchasers must be able to locate vendors and, if necessary, be familiar with the process and players associated with importing. A company that is establishing a production facility in another country must decide between hiring purchasing staff from the home country or within the host country. While natives have knowledge and acquaintance advantages, they may be susceptible to cultural influences, such as favoring family or extended family members for sourcing supplies.

In order to prevent unexpected work stoppages caused by equipment failures, maintenance must be conducted on buildings and equipment. While preventive maintenance will help to avoid unexpected breakdowns, many less-developed countries are subject to the cultural influences that often cause the attitude, "Why fix it if it isn't broken?" In addition, the maintenance team is under pressure from marketing and production to keep the machinery running constantly, which perpetuates a short-term view of the maintenance role.

The local environment may necessitate more frequent maintenance than that mandated by headquarters. Temperature and climate and the handling of equipment by locals may cause unforeseen wear and tear not experienced in the home production plant.

The last element of the supportive function is technical assistance. The technical assistance staff is responsible for providing production with manufacturing specifications and for checking the quality of the inputs and the finished products. Often, the technical staff must find substitutes for hard to find raw materials or may be required to visit suppliers to educate or train them so that they can meet requirements and delivery dates.

Just–in–time system

During the late 1980s to the mid 1990s, some experts felt that the Japanese advantage existed due to culture (societal and corporate), quality circles, lifetime employment, or other socio-cultural factors; today, more and more experts are identifying the abilities of Japanese companies to manage effectively as the key to their success. Some have stated that the Japanese advantage in production costs and product quality stems from the superior organization and administration of their production.

One such element of superior organization and administration that has been implemented for the last decade in many American and European companies' production systems is the **kanban** or just-in-time (JIT) inventory system. JIT requires that externally sourced inputs never arrive at the production plant before they are needed. Parts arrive exactly when they are needed, suppliers know the production schedule, and parts arrive from suppliers several times a day. Although JIT schedules are frozen for a certain period, the system is still fairly flexible. There are many benefits to such a system when it is carefully implemented, primarily because many costs are reduced as the work-in-process inventory and warehousing space requirements are greatly reduced. JIT works toward zero inventories, reducing warehousing, handling, and financing costs and time for tracking stocks and movements. Companies using JIT perceive buffer stocks as a hidden inefficiency that only adds costs to production. Being successful in this type of system requires having a strong relationship with the company's suppliers.

While the Japanese example illustrates the importance of efficiency in operations systems, other methodologies have been implemented elsewhere. In China, for example, a cost-based manufacturing system has been implemented with great success in world export markets. India has utilized its abundant labor surplus to succeed in service operations structures, while Mexican maquiladoras highlight the importance of proximity to a larger developed country market (i.e. United States). Regardless of the operating system chosen, companies must assess the capabilities of the countries where they operate and how those capabilities lead to competitive advantages in today's marketplace.

152 *Managing operations and technology*

Perspective 7.1 International piracy

An issue of increasing importance for all internationally active companies is the prevalence of maritime piracy worldwide. The International Maritime Organization provides statistics concerning acts of piracy and armed robbery against ships located in port, in territorial waters, or in international waters. Exhibit 7.1 provides a historical perspective for areas of concern across the globe.

Regional Acts of Piracy & Armed Robbery Against Ships														
	2009	%	2010	%	2011	%	2012	%	2013	%	2014	%	2015	%
Arabian Sea	2	0%	16	3%	28	5%	38	11%	6	2%	12	4%	15	5%
East Africa	222	55%	172	35%	223	41%	61	18%	20	7%	3	1%	4	1%
Indian Ocean	27	7%	77	16%	63	12%	33	10%	31	10%	44	15%	18	6%
Malacca Strait	0	0%	0	0%	22	4%	24	7%	17	6%	81	28%	134	44%
North Atlantic	0	0%	0	0%	2	0%	1	0%	1	0%	1	0%	2	1%
Persian Gulf	0	0%	2	0%	0	0%	1	0%	2	1%	3	1%	1	0%
South America (A)	15	4%	20	4%	12	2%	2	1%	1	0%	2	1%	0	0%
South America (C)	6	1%	5	1%	4	1%	8	2%	6	2%	6	2%	4	1%
South America (P)	15	4%	15	3%	13	2%	11	3%	10	3%	1	0%	1	0%
South China Sea	71	17%	134	27%	113	21%	90	26%	142	48%	93	32%	81	27%
West Africa	46	11%	47	10%	61	11%	64	19%	54	18%	45	15%	35	12%
Mediterranean Sea	0	0%	1	0%	2	0%	6	2%	8	3%	0	0%	2	1%
North Pacific	1	0%	0	0%	0	0%	0	0%	0	0%	0	0%	2	1%
Caspian Sea	1	0%	0	0%	0	0%	0	0%	0	0%	0	0%	0	0%
China Sea	0	0%	0	0%	1	0%	0	0%	0	0%	0	0%	0	0%
Far East	0	0%	0	0%	0	0%	2	1%	0	0%	0	0%	0	0%
Yellow Sea	0	0%	0	0%	0	0%	0	0%	0	0%	0	0%	4	1%
Total Incidents	**406**	100%	**489**	100%	**544**	100%	**341**	100%	**298**	100%	**291**	100%	**303**	100%
Source: International Maritime Organization Annual Piracy Reports 2009-2015														

Mostly in Intl Waters	
Mostly in Terr Waters	
Mostly in Port	
Tie Intl/Terr Waters	
Tie Port/Terr Waters	

2014	2015	Location
82	36	Int'l Waters
119	141	Terr Waters
90	126	In Port
291	303	Totals

Exhibit 7.1 Maritime piracy statistics

While losses from pirated shipments can eventually be recouped via maritime insurance, companies that maintain lean inventory levels could experience customer impact if piracy were to affect expected delivery times. While the overall incidence of maritime piracy has declined over the last few years, the primary activity appears to be centered in the Indian Ocean, Singapore and the Straits of Malacca, the South China Sea, and West Africa. Given MNC operational decisions to locate manufacturing facilities in these regions, one detriment to these location decisions has been the continued problem of maritime piracy. The stakes could not be higher, especially in light of China's "Maritime Silk Road" which includes investment of $ 4 trillion in an effort to connect China with Europe via China's One Belt, One Road program.

International technology

An integral part of any production system is the technology used in the manufacturing process. Technology also may be separate from the production system itself in the form of the end product or finished good. After World War II, government officials and experts believed that increasing capital inputs was the key to rapid economic growth, but the basis for this belief weakened as capital became more accessible and developments were not always successful. The importance of technology for stimulating expansion then became more important, and technology transfer became an issue in world economies. As a result, developing, exploiting, and maintaining technological advantages became crucial issues for MNCs.

The question for an MNC and for a government official is "How will we obtain the desired technology?" Often the choice for a firm is either through its own research and development efforts or by acquisition from another firm. For the government of a developing country, on the other hand, the choice is more limited. The technology usually must be transferred from sources other than those within the country. Within industrialized countries, the main focus is the protection of technology and the creation of new technologies. Lesser-Developed Countries (LDCs), however, must be concerned with the opposite: restrictions on transfers, royalty limitations, lack of patent protection, and other legal constraints. For LDCs, international firms are responsible for a large share of technology transfers, but there are also noncommercial organizations that provide international transfers, such as development programs funded by other industrialized nations.

Definition of technology

Technology has been defined as a perishable source comprising knowledge, skills, and means for using and controlling factors of production for the purpose of producing, delivering to users, and maintaining goods and services for which there is no economic and/or social demand.

There are several elements of technology that can be used for classification purposes. First, there are three types of technology: product technology, which is knowledge used to make a product; process technology, which is knowledge used in the process of making a product, including the organizing of the inputs of machinery and equipment necessary for the production process; and management technology, which is knowledge used in running the business, including managerial skills that make the firm competitive.

A second level of classification within technology concerns the particular characteristics of the technology. These include hard/soft technology, proprietary/nonproprietary technology, front-end/obsolete technology and bundled/unbundled technology. Hard technology includes the physical hardware, capital goods, blueprints and specifications, and knowledge necessary to use the hardware, while soft technology encompasses the management,

154 *Managing operations and technology*

marketing, financial organization, and administrative techniques that can be combined with the hard technology to serve the needs of the user. Technology that is owned or controlled by an individual or organization is proprietary and may be either controlled as a trade secret or patented. An example of proprietary technology that is controlled as a trade secret is the formula developed by the Coca-Cola Company for the production of its soft drink of the same name. Nonproprietary technology is knowledge found in technical literature, hardware, and services that may be copied without infringing on proprietary rights. This reproduction often is achievable through reverse engineering, where the technology is broken down to learn how it was created. State-of-the-art technology is considered front-end, while old technology is termed obsolete. Bundled technology is another aspect of controlled technology, where the owner is only willing to transfer it as part of a package or system. Unbundled technology is available separate from the total system of technology of the supplier.

Technology development

There are three stages of *technology development*. *Invention* is the first stage. At this level, new knowledge is created that may be applied to business or industry. The next step is *innovation*, where the new knowledge is introduced into the marketplace. It is not uncommon for a technology to complete the first stage and not reach the second or third stages. In fact, most inventions never reach the innovation stage. If they do, the next step is *diffusion*, or the spread of the new knowledge throughout the marketplace. For example, telecommunications is well into the diffusion phase, but with developments in wireless technology, this industry is experiencing new invention and innovation stages, and diffusion is well underway in some other high-tech industries.

A technology advantage is one held by a firm whose employees possess a superior business knowledge (product, process, or management) that is not held by other firms. In the interest of maintaining this advantage, a firm may seek to protect their proprietary possession of the technology, usually through patents. It is necessary for firms to continually develop new technology to perpetuate their advantages, because most patents are of limited duration.

Research and development is the prime source of a company's technology advantage. An MNC will find pressure from a host country to combine research and development facilities with production facilities. One motivation for establishing research and development in a foreign country is that such facilities can aid in the transfer of technology by making easier product and process modifications for local markets and by strengthening the competitive stance of a subsidiary by offering local technical assistance to purchasers. Foreign research and development sites also allow subsidiaries to develop products in accordance with local market needs and to identify those needs that differ from the perception of the home country. Local knowledge and

Managing operations and technology 155

skills can also be a benefit that is derived from locating the research and development abroad. Before a company can complete its decision to locate a research and development function in a host country, an evaluation must be made of host government controls and incentives. The ultimate question is whether or not such controls or incentives justify the economics of a research unit, in light of the availability of adequate universities, infrastructure, and local supply of technical skills.

Technology transfer

Technology transfer is the process by which knowledge is diffused through learning from its place of origin and introduction to other world markets. Depending on the characteristics of the technology to be transferred, the time and expense involved will vary, and the choice of transfer method must incorporate such factors as the nature of the technology, the capabilities and objectives of the parties involved, and the elements of the socio-cultural environment that enable the recipient country to assimilate and synthesize the technology. The transfer process also has distinct phases, from planning, product, and facility design to personnel training, engineering for quality control, and technical support for local suppliers.

The transfer of technology may take place through market transactions, which creates issues for both governments and for international managers. Host governments are concerned with obtaining up-to-date technology at low cost from MNCs, while companies are interested in protecting and realizing benefits from their technology.

Noncommercial ways of transferring technology usually involve foreign study in university programs, which enable foreign nationals to acquire knowledge and then bring the knowledge back to their own country. There are also government-to-government agreements for technology transfers. Some examples are development aid programs for infrastructure, nuclear energy programs, and space research programs. Commercial methods for transferring technology are more varied, including foreign direct investment, turnkey projects, trade in goods and services, contracts and agreements, research and development programs located in foreign countries or through joint research efforts, migration of trained personnel or employment of local nationals by foreign firms, international tender offers, and industrial espionage.

In general, strategies for conducting technology transfers and exploiting technology advantages fall within two broad categories. Which strategy the firm chooses is determined by the type of business and the type of technology. The first type of strategy involves extending the firm's own operation, which is known as internalizing. Internalizing requires a company to utilize foreign subsidiaries and affiliates in different markets to sell its products or services in local markets. In smaller markets, a company trying to internalize will attempt to meet demand through exports. This approach is best when:

156   *Managing operations and technology*

- The firm makes new products that are not easily copied by others.
- Outside firms also use the technology and serve part of the market, because economies of scale the firm achieves on products would be lost.
- The firm depends greatly on the sale of the product or service that uses the technology.
- The firm is so small that it does not have the personnel to both use the technology internally and sell it to outsiders, or the firm is so large that it can easily exploit the technology through its own affiliates.
- The technology is more important to the firm than to potential buyers of the technology.
- The technology is costly to transfer from one firm to another.

This strategy is the same approach as for finding and exploiting other sources of competitive advantages, but another approach the firm might choose is that of externalizing. Using external markets has become increasingly important in light of the wave of **outsourcing** to developing countries, which occurred over the last decade, to capture significantly lower wage rates than are required in the developed world. Through this strategy, a company would contract with other firms to sell the technology itself, rather than sell the final product which results from such technology. Such contracts may be in the form of licensing agreements or management contracts.

There are two approaches, in particular, that have become more common external market strategies: turnkey projects and licensing. **Turnkey projects** are contracted projects that encompass all elements of the project, usually including training. When the project is completed, the contractor turns the entire system over to the purchaser. A popular strategy in such industries as chemicals, petrochemicals, and petroleum refining, this method often includes an equity position for the contractor, which enables the firm to reap the benefits of their technology over a longer period of time.

The other external market strategy that has increased in practice is licensing. Exhibit 7.2 explains the appropriate situations in which licensing would be considered the best strategy. For small companies that have inadequate capital or management expertise for international expansion via foreign direct investment, licensing is an advantageous option. There are, however, several arguments against using licensing. The strongest argument is that a licensor may lose its competitive advantage to a licensee over time and, in the process, be prohibited from future direct investment in the market served by the licensee. On the other hand, if the licensor is a participant in the foreign venture, there is an infusion of protection against such an event. Furthermore, trademarks can be utilized as part of the licensing agreement, because trademarks remain the property of the licensor in perpetuity despite the fact that the license is for a limited time only.

Strategic concept	Conditions
1. Product cycle standardization	Obsolescing products considered for licensing Imminent technology or model change Increasing competition in product market
2. Environmental constraints on FDI or FDI income	Government regulations restricting FDI to specific sectors only High political risk in nation Market uncertain or volatile, licensor lacking in requisite marketing abilities, or market too small for FDI.
3. Constraints on imports into license nation	A high ratio for transport cost to value for item Tariff or non-tariff barriers
4. Licensor firm size	Licensor firm too small to have financial, managerial, or marketing expertise for overseas investment. Licensor firm too big (see 12 below)
5. Research intensity	Licensor firm will remain technologically superior, so as to discount licensee competition in other markets.
6. High rate of technological turnover	Change so rapid, and technologies so perishable that even with equally proficient licensees, a design or a patent may be transferred with little fear of significant competition.
7. Perpetuation of licensee	Even without or beyond the licensing agreement, dependency effective licensee dependency maintained by trademarks, required components or licensee hunger for technical improvements.
8. Product vs. Process Technologies	Licensing opportunities are auxiliary processes (e.g. galvanizing in the steel industry, or anodizing aluminum) even if the basic product technologies are not licensed.
9. Reciprocal exchanges of technology	Licensing as a valuable tool for obtaining technology of market rights in industries characterized by high R&D and market development costs and product diversity.
10. "Choosing" competition	With a patent about to expire, licensing gives a head start to a licensee firm favored by the present patent holder (may be illegal in some countries).
11. Creation of auxiliary business	Even if direct royalty income is inadequate, margins on components to or from licensee can be handsome (in the extreme case, licensing is tantamount to disguised imports). Other auxiliary business can be turnkey plants, joint bidding with licensee, etc.
12. Diversification and product-line organization in licensor firm	Especially in large diversified firms, with dimensional attention focused on the "product imperative", a centralized examination of the product/country matrix reveals neglected market penetration possibilities via licensing, (especially where considerable diversification puts a constraint on the financial and managerial resources available for equity ventures overseas).

Exhibit 7.2 Licensing as a preferred strategy

Source: F. Contractor, "The Role of Licensing", *Columbia Journal of World Business*, Winter 1981, page 76.

158 *Managing operations and technology*

In general, externalizing is best when:

- The firm's products are not central to the ability to survive in competition.
- The firm's greater skill is in creating the technology than in producing and marketing the final products.
- The firm's financial and personnel capabilities make it desirable to let another firm use the technology.
- The firm cannot protect its technology with a patent, and it could lose the benefits of that technology unless it is compensated for the technology's use by rival firms.
- The firm's technology is not costly to transfer between firms.

Choice of production technology

Once a company has decided to internalize, it often obtains its competitive advantage through overseas production facilities, and a company must determine the choice of technology to implement in such plants. This issue becomes particularly controversial in developing countries, where many government officials are concerned that technology transferred by foreign firms for local production be appropriate to the resources of the country and not necessarily the same technology that is used in capital-rich countries with large markets or the home country of the foreign firm. In most instances, this results in pressure from host governments to establish smaller, more labor-intensive facilities. In other situations, however, host country policies may invite capital-intensive production technologies in order to obtain state-of-the-art systems.

Before the choice is made, a firm must consider the availability of production technology alternatives that are, in reality, commercially feasible for operation. In some industries, this may mean many more options than for others, depending on the nature of the product. Cost and availability of information concerning specific technologies also will impact the decision. It is much easier to obtain information regarding capital-intensive equipment because information and technology flows are more likely to be from industrialized countries to developing countries than between developing countries.

Market sizes, which vary from one country to the next, also influence the plant design choice. Capital-intensive technology incorporates automated, high-output machinery, but it is often severely limited in flexibility regarding the production and size range of products. A capital-intensive system can produce in a few days what may be a year's supply in some markets. For these smaller markets, the design choice may be to install only one machine. Unfortunately, in some cases, the capacity of one such machine would still greatly overproduce for the demand in a particular market. Labor-intensive technology, on the other hand, employs more people and incorporates semi-automated general-purpose equipment with lower productive capacity.

Labor and capital intensity are not the only contributing factors to the technology decision. The decision must include quality control maintenance,

Managing operations and technology 159

waste minimization, response-time to market demand fluctuations, training costs, labor relations, and the image or prestige factor of front-end equipment.

Until recently it was thought that a choice between labor and capital intensity was the only available option. There is a third alternative which, despite its high costs and high technological content, is utilized by industrialized nations. Such technology would create a mix of labor and capital and is known as hybrid plant design. In addition, when faced with the need for a production design that incorporates both labor and capital requirements, there are the options of intermediate technology and appropriate technology. Hybrid designs also offer solutions to the problem of choosing between labor and capital-intensive production technologies. These designs are geared toward obtaining a certain product quality, while ensuring a labor-intensive production method. In such a design, the production process includes both types of technology in distinct phases. Intermediate technology uses a combination throughout the process. It is not a question of using capital intensity in some steps of production and labor intensity in others, but it is the utilization of a less than fully automated process. In recent years, many LDCs have looked to intermediate technology as a means to create more jobs, use less capital, and still be able to produce the desired product quality. Although many governments are urging investors to implement intermediate technology, it is not easily accessed from industrial nations. There is often miscommunication between developed countries and the developing world regarding technological transfer. Industrialized nations often are looking for a place to sell their older technology, while developing nations are looking for the most up-to-date technology, which can allow for a more rapid industrialization. Moreover, there may be higher start-up costs associated with intermediate technology implementation than can be justified by the savings in reduced capital costs.

Appropriate technology considers the optimum technological mix by matching a country's markets with its resources and ability to produce certain components. Unlike an approach that would use intermediate technology, the emphasis is on applying the technology that is most appropriate to the immediate economic, socio-cultural, and political variables. This approach may range from the most primitive of production processes to high-tech systems, and takes into consideration that with some products the superiority in productivity and quality of a modern process is so significant as to make labor-intensive methods completely inappropriate. It is often the government that must choose between the use of less capital-intensive technologies to save scarce capital resources and create new jobs and more capital-intensive methods that will provide less expensive products for its citizens.

Pricing technology transfers

Unlike most free-market transactions where market demand and supply determine price, there is relatively little information available regarding pricing of technology transfers. In most instances, negotiating parties do not have

160 *Managing operations and technology*

access to data regarding previous sales or transfers of technology for similar products or between similar parties. Furthermore, because technology transfers may include many different types of services and, therefore, payments, even if price information were available, it would be difficult to discern what products, services, and prices would be comparable to the technology transfer negotiations currently underway.

Pricing of technology in recent years has become a controversial issue, especially for developing countries. Host government intervention is common because it is commonly assumed that such transfers are overpriced to developing nations. Transfer pricing is also suspected when payments are made to parent companies by foreign affiliates.

Developing countries often see themselves in a vulnerable and weak negotiating position and assume that higher prices are set than for similar technology transfers between industrial countries. In addition, there is a common belief that technology is protected by a patent monopoly that enables a seller to set excessive monopoly prices. It is the opinion of the governments of these developing countries that the sunk costs of developing the technology have already been amortized over the home market sales, and international transfers do not need to compensate for much more than the incremental costs of the transfer.

To combat these fears of host governments, there has been an increasing exchange of information among national agencies that are trying to better prepare a host country for negotiations. In defense against the patent monopoly claim, it is argued that this point confuses the concept of a patent as a monopoly with monopoly power in the marketplace. Despite the fact that the technology is patented, it still faces competition in the market from substitute technology. Furthermore, the claim that development costs have already been amortized does not consider the fact that several industrialized countries, including the United States, have tax agencies that instruct that such costs should be shared by all users of a technology in order to avoid the loss of income tax revenues that would result if companies expended all sunk costs within the home country. Companies involved in research and development plan that the pricing of currently available technology will cover sunk costs plus future research and development.

Protecting technology

There are different issues imbedded in the problem of protecting technology. Primarily, there is the question of how an MNC can implement control measures for proprietary technology. Obtaining patents is one way to protect one's technology. In most countries, if the knowledge possessed by a firm is a manufacturing process and it produces a new product, that process and the product can be protected with a patent. Patents are usually held for limited periods of time (up to twenty years in the developed world). There are recent attempts by beneficiaries of this earlier system as well as others who are arguing

Managing operations and technology   161

that the number of years should be altered. **Copyrights** are another tool available for protecting proprietary technology which covers knowledge which is embodied in text. Similarly, **trademarks** will protect knowledge that is embodied in a product that can be sold. Trademarks usually imply a high standard of quality or expertise in services. There are other methods available such as hiding the technology, e.g., Coke's secret "formula," requiring key technical or research and development employees to sign agreements whereby they are prohibited from using new technology which they acquired outside the firm, or rapid exploitation of the technology which would establish a large market share and discourage competitors from entering the market.

Despite these mechanisms for establishing and maintaining control, it is not uncommon for a firm to lose control. For example, companies in countries such as China have reputations for manufacturing branded copies of products that have been patented, copyrighted, or otherwise protected. Similarly, industrial espionage is almost considered merely a modern inconvenience, often depicted in television and screen productions as normal corporate behavior. Also, the mobility of employees makes it almost impossible to control 100% of a company's proprietary technology. Even in the absence of malice, an employee may unwittingly incorporate some of the learned technology in future projects with other companies.

Protecting technology is not only an issue for an MNC, but also for national governments. The private interests of the parties involved in buying and selling technology may not be compatible with the national interests of a government. The home country or seller's country is concerned with the control of technology for national security reasons, while the host country becomes more active in monitoring international transfers as a guideline for future negotiations.

In reality, because of these issues, an international manager must constantly be aware that negotiations regarding technology transfer are between four players: the buyer, the seller, the home country, and the host country – without losing sight of the fact that this is not necessarily a win–lose situation. There may in fact be an arrangement that is mutually beneficial to all parties.

Management information systems

MIS in an MNC

The appropriate transfer and analysis of information regarding markets, operations, customers, and enterprise activities can be a crucial factor in the success or failure of a firm and its international activities. In the best of circumstances, the use of relevant information can provide a multinational concern with competitive advantages over its competitors by allowing it to develop a strategic position of strength.

On a more routine level, an MNC must manage its information flows from subsidiaries about operations, markets, and potential just to maintain its existing operating strengths in current markets across the globe. This is a major challenge

162   *Managing operations and technology*

for an MNC, considering the distance involved, both physical and cultural, and the need to transfer data and information from a variety of environments. Moreover, information must be comparable and standardized, if it is to be aggregated for analysis by an MNC.

Corporate reports

One method of control used by MNCs is the establishment of reporting requirements and procedures for staff and departments within the organization. These reports constitute a steady stream of information that flows to headquarters and is analyzed to provide input in strategic decision-making about overall corporate resource allocation by senior management. Because written reports often represent the only formal presentation of information from the subsidiaries or operating branches regarding their activities, and because these reports often provide the basis for performance evaluation, it is crucial that subsidiary managers understand the reporting requirements, format, and purposes.

In order to be effective tools of control and decision-making, it is imperative that reports from branches and arms of the firm be timely, so that an MNC is able to respond with adjustments and corrections. Similarly, reports must contain complete information that is relevant to the needs of an MNC in its evaluation of the subsidiary's performance. Information must be presented in an understandable, comparable format and include data that is usable by top management and strategic planners. Accuracy of data is critical because some mistakes in reports from one region may upset calculations for the entire corporation.

Corporations require a variety of reports on activities in their worldwide operations, which fall into four categories: financial reports, operating reports, in-country reports, and market-based reports. Financial reports provide an MNC with information regarding the flow of funds within the subsidiary and between its suppliers and customers. They quantify the results of operations and provide information on the status of the onsite currency. These reports must be presented in an established form, use standardized currency conversions, and use the same conventions to permit comparison with the results of other corporate segments. This presentation of financial data may not be in the same format as that required by the host government regulatory standards. In many instances, therefore, it is necessary for a subsidiary to maintain separate sets of books for official reporting requirements in the host country.

Operations reports give management a view of the performance of subsidiaries and an indication of such information as production volumes, inventory levels, supply contracts negotiated, and expended raw materials and energy. These reports frequently also note staffing changes, technological developments regarding operating procedures and compliance with local laws, such as environmental or social welfare reporting requirements. The reports comprise the core of the information sent to headquarters, and they chronicle the day-to-day achievements, problems, and status of the operating arms of an

Managing operations and technology 163

MNC, and give it a basis of comparison from reporting period to reporting period. From formal operating reports and informal communications with branches, top management can keep its finger on the pulse of the enterprise and be aware of what resources are being utilized where, to what end, and how efficiently.

Subsidiaries also perform a valuable function by giving the managers at headquarters key information from the foreign operating environment. These in-country reports provide information on developments in the host country on economic, political, and social fronts. Such information provides a firm with timely data on which to base revisions of risk factors or to limit or increase operations in the host country. They can also provide the firm with an advantage in the event of potential crises, such as political or military upheavals, by providing top management with early warning signals, so that the loss of company assets and danger to company personnel can be minimized.

Subsidiaries also provide an MNC with information regarding activities in the market it serves. This information concerns the actions of a firm's competitors in existing market areas, consumer behavior, buying patterns, and demand and pricing structures. Onsite personnel often also provide information to a firm about potential market development through the examination of new markets or the development of new products to satisfy different needs of consumers in existing markets.

The information provided by these reports assists a firm in its efforts to develop and fine-tune its implementation of strategic and operating objectives. Consequently, to ensure that it is interpreted and used correctly, it is essential that the information provided in these reports be accurate, reliable, and consistent across all arms of a firm in terms of the use of the same standards of measurement, accounting principles, and definitions.

Formal written reports are also supplemented with informal reports made in face-to-face contacts with subsidiary managers and through frequent telephone conversations. These channels of informal reporting are also important because they provide a subsidiary manager with methods for reporting on smaller occurrences that might not warrant formal reporting, but which may be significant. They also keep communication lines open in the event that there is need for further information on more important issues. To encourage this interaction (and to provide nontraditional support for expatriate or subsidiary managers), some firms assign managers a corporate mentor, who is charged with staying in touch with the manager so that he is involved in the activities of the firm at headquarters.

Despite the care that is taken to ensure comparability and compatibility of reports from all arms of an MNC, problems nevertheless arise in the management of information systems across international borders. Some firms assume that they can use the same reporting systems abroad as they do at home. This is not always the case because of differences in the operating environments. For example, in some countries where computer skills are low, the use of computerized reports by overseas employees is not feasible. Similarly, if a system requires the use of computerized data collection or report transmittal, a myriad of compatibility problems arise.

International data processing: integration issues

There is a constant interchange of information between the parent office and subsidiaries in every MNC operation. Figure 7.3 illustrates the process of information interchange between a parent and a single subsidiary. The interchange pattern becomes vastly more complex when multiplied by a number of subsidiaries involved in the overall structure of an MNC.

The complexity of these networks and the involvement of the international component of information management raise several issues of concern to MNCs. These issues stem mostly from problems regarding compatibility of data processing systems, the establishment of controls on data compilation and its transfer across national borders by host governments, and the risks involved in using multinational computer networks.

An MNC often has problems in sharing information with its subsidiaries because of differences in data processing capabilities and sophistication of systems. While an MNC may have highly sophisticated fast computer systems, its subsidiaries may be equipped with much less sophisticated equipment, either because a subsidiary's information management needs are less extensive or because the capabilities of the personnel in a subsidiary do not allow for the efficient use of such equipment. Alternatively, a subsidiary may have different software and hardware.

Another problem in integrating information systems of a parent and subsidiaries is the high costs of centralization of information systems. Moreover, an attempt by MNCs to impose tight controls upon their branches with respect

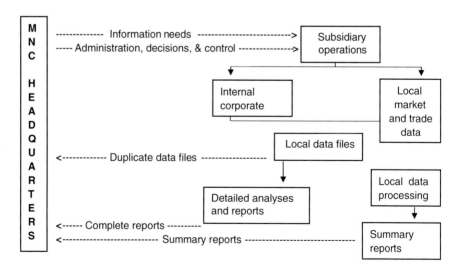

Exhibit 7.3 Typical information flow between an MNC and its subsidiaries

Managing operations and technology 165

to data processing and transmittal leads to additional administrative costs, delays in having information or data files transmitted, the need for extensive and expensive computer systems, and the need to protect against loss of data during transmittal by piracy.

Through the decentralization of information management, an MNC can avoid these higher costs and allow subsidiaries to make their own decisions regarding computer systems. The tradeoff, however, is a lack of parental control over the management of the system. As with all aspects of the centralization versus decentralization debate, an MNC must balance these opposing outcomes in an effort to reach an appropriate level of managerial control over the information system for efficiency's sake without sacrificing subsidiary autonomy.

Another enormous problem for MNCs in the management of data and information is a result of forces in the external environment on the use of information systems. These are primarily the forces that emanate from political or governmental entities in host countries, which have concerns about national security in their country, protection of economic forces, and, to some degree, about cultural independence. In recent years, cyber-security has become a large concern for all businesses, so the complexities of a global presence only increase the need for safeguards of information from unwanted intrusion.

These concerns may lead to host country union requirements regarding the employment of local data processors, and laws regarding privacy and the carrying of data across national borders. For example, some countries do not allow data to be transmitted for processing elsewhere across their borders. These restrictions are intended to retain employment in the country and to force firms to use local labor to satisfy the labor requirements of their data processing.

In some firms or businesses, this function can be a very large component of overall business activity. International banks are a prime example of a business that is based on the fast, reliable, and accurate use of computer systems to chronicle individual banking transactions. International banks frequently spend millions of dollars to establish data processing systems and computer networks to facilitate the flow of information and data processing from branches around the world. In these instances, the speed of processing has a very real economic effect on business because the slow transfer of invested funds means losses in interest earned.

International firms can also be affected by government controls imposed to deal with the treatment of the issue of privacy of personal information. Such treatment usually includes limits on the uses of computer systems by firms in order that individuals have control over the content of personal information, can correct it when necessary, and must give consent for it to be used by other parties. Such information could include personal data regarding sex, religion, race, or political orientation, but could also include personal academic, criminal, and financial information.

Limits on the transmittal of such information affect an MNC in the area of transmitting personnel records to headquarters, and may result in additional

166 *Managing operations and technology*

resources to insure compliance with local laws or act as barriers to having complete records at centralized locations. In Norway, for example, a centralized data inspectorate must be given notice each time that personal information is sent abroad.

Governments use other methods to control transnational data flows. Some countries have attempted to limit the flows by considering the imposition of a tax on information leaving the country. Such taxation is difficult to implement because it is virtually impossible to determine objectively the value of economic information except on a case-by-case method. Other countries merely make it expensive to move data out of the country. In Japan, for example, Control Data Corporation was forced to pay for its own private telephone line between that country and the United States (at a cost of $33,000 per month) and, because of restrictions, could only use that line at 1% of its capacity.

Besides these additional costs and procedural problems involved in operating information systems in an international setting, MNCs also face a high level of risk in managing transnational information networks. The biggest problems a firm faces are maintaining the integrity of data through a control process that oversees data inputs to the system, and the management of the information at the local level to correspond to data needs at the corporate level. Other risks involved are the loss of data in transmittal because of unreliable channels or through the piracy (or theft) of the data. Developing protection against such risks is very expensive for a firm and involves such measures as the establishment of a company's own computer network, or the purchase of private communication lines.

The goal of an MNC is to take advantage of its operation as an integrated system, of which the management of information is a major part. The aim of the firm is to minimize duplication of efforts and facilities and to maximize operating efficiencies by coordinating information concerning operations and business opportunities around the world. Issues raised in the control of transnational data flows have the potential of adversely affecting the ability of MNCs to pursue these objectives by placing limits on their ability to exchange and analyze this crucial information or by imposing additional operating costs through restrictions on the processing, location, and transmittal of data. These controls are a significant issue for the modern MNC that attempts to develop an information management system that strikes a balance between costs and benefits, and has the capability of synthesizing data from worldwide operations while maintaining the appropriate technology at the subsidiary level.

Should international firms go global?

The process of controlling international operations is a formidable challenge for a firm attempting to make the best of its corporate strengths while simultaneously remaining aware of its limitations. Some analysts believe, however, that the progressive firm should not content itself with an international focus, but should adopt a global orientation toward operations and planning.

Managing operations and technology 167

Some companies are merely international; they operate a variety of subsidiaries in a number of countries. In such a portfolio approach, individual operating arms or companies in a conglomerate are ranked according to criteria, such as their individual market strength and market growth, not as part of the global system, such as those within the Boston Consulting Group matrix of business units, which are categorized as "cash cows", "stars", "dogs", and "question marks". This focus and orientation is limited and leads to sub-optimization of operations and resources, and to the company's missing opportunities to be exploited by integrating all operations worldwide. Rather than comparing individual units against each other in terms of a firm's entire portfolio of business activities, a firm would be better off if it looked at international factors from a global perspective to identify possibilities for operating synergies.

Similarly, a firm must consider worldwide competition in designing its strategy; the forces of global competition that may lead a firm toward the establishment of less profitable business units as a defensive posture, rather than an offensive move toward profitability. Such a defensive action could be costly in the short-term, but pays dividends from a long-term, global perspective.

By accurately assessing the forces of global competition and a firm's relative advantages and strengths, an enterprise can devise a global strategy to become effective in world markets. Such a strategy may hinge on competing in all product lines, or in a product area that is protected from competition, or on a global strategy area focusing on a specific market (global niche), or on a particular national or regional area market. Although the process of planning and subsequent implementation and control is highly complex because of the assimilation and analysis of information about a variety of operating and supply environments, it can provide incomparable strategic advantages for a corporation willing to take on such a global challenge.

Summary

In the international business arena, production and technology can influence how and where a company will operate. International production management for an MNC may in fact be very similar to production in the home country. The international environment, however, includes other considerations. Before making production decisions, an MNC must consider such additional factors as different wage rates, industrial relations, financing sources, foreign exchange risk, international tax laws, control, and the production experience curve in each country. While many MNCs attempt to standardize their production systems on a worldwide basis, local environmental influences often make such standardization unsuccessful or at best difficult. The benefits of standardization are ease and simplification, which result in cost savings in organization and staffing, supply systems, options for rationalization, control, and planning. There are four elements in designing a local production facility-plant location, plant layout, materials handling, and the human factor. MNCs

168   *Managing operations and technology*

must determine whether to centralize or decentralize decision-making authority, which is influenced by the mode of international operations, the nature of industry and technology, the size and maturity of the MNC, the competence of the branch managerial staff, the local political environment, and the required speed of decision-making and the magnitude of the decision.

Operations management encompasses two categories of activities: productive activities and supportive activities. Productive activities require that deviations from expected output are investigated and corrected. Low output, possibly caused by inadequate raw materials or poor scheduling, inferior product quality, or excessive manufacturing costs, is an indication that corrective actions are necessary in order to achieve planned output objectives. Supportive activities include quality control, inventory control, purchasing, maintenance, and technical functions.

Technology is knowledge that can be applied in a business environment. It is an integral part of any production system, although it may be separate from the production system itself in the form of the end product or finished good. Technology can be created through research and development or acquired with experience in business operations and transactions. In addition, technology may be purchased from the individuals or firms that have developed the technology, and it is often transferred between parties and across national boundaries for a cost. In terms of production technology, the choice of technology that is implemented in a foreign country depends on the cost-benefit evaluation of capital-intensive versus labor-intensive methods. Such evaluation must also consider the environmental (economic, political, and cultural) influences that affect technology. Information and data flows can be slowed by the incompatibility of hardware and software systems used in the corporate and branch offices as well as by political or governmental regulations.

The competitive advantage of any MNC is considerably dependent on technology advantages, whether they are a process, a product, or a management technology. An MNC must constantly be concerned with maintaining and improving this advantage. The perishability of technology requires that an MNC continue to make gains in technology improvements. For an MNC, technological advances can be transferred between affiliates and subsidiaries in different countries.

Pricing of international technology transfers has become a major issue between the governments of developing countries and owners of technology in industrialized countries. In the future, it is expected that such governments will share information regarding technology transfers and pricing among themselves in order to become better equipped to negotiate for such transfers.

For an MNC, control over proprietary technology is a difficult management task. Although there are protection measures and tools available to assist in control, there are also many instances where protection has been inadequate and a firm has lost its proprietary advantage. Because technology is closely associated with national security, governmental controls also affect an MNC and its ability to transfer technology.

Discussion questions

1 Why are production and technology so important to maintaining a multinational corporation's competitive edge?
2 Discuss the three key production issues as they relate to following types of firms:
   - Manufacturer of trucks
   - Manufacturer of welding equipment
   - Consumer electronics manufacturer (PCs, mobile devices)
   - Textiles manufacturers
3 You are the CEO of a U.S. automobile manufacturer who is interested in building a new production plant in Eastern Europe. What are the factors that you should review in order to make your decision?
4 What advantages do manufacturers have when implementing emerging production systems out of the Asia-Pacific economy? How do you think suppliers respond to changes from their standard distribution approaches?
5 How can MIS make or break a multinational corporation?
6 What data problems might occur between the parent office and its subsidiaries?

Bibliography

Baden-Fuller, Charles, and John M. Stopford. 1988. Why Global Manufacturing? *Multinational Business* (Spring): 15–25.

Ball, Donald A., and Wendell H. McCulloch Jr. 1988. *International Business*. Plano, TX: Business Publications.

Carnoy, Martin. 1985. High Technology and International Labor Markets. *International Labour Review* (November/December): 643–659.

Contractor, Farok. 1981. The Role of Licensing. *Columbia Journal of World Business* (Winter): 73–83.

Davidson, W. H., and D. G. McFetridge. 1985. Key Characteristics in the Choice of International Technology Transfer Mode. *Journal of International Business Studies* (Summer): 5–21.

Dunning, John H. 1981. *International Production and the Multinational Enterprise*. London: Allen & Unwin.

Goshal, S., and C. A. Bartlett. 1987. Innovation Processes in Multinational Corporations: Proceedings of the Symposium on Managing Innovation in Large Complex Firms. *INSEAD* (September).

Goshal, S., and C. A. Bartlett. 1988. Creation, Adoption, and Diffusion of Innovations by Subsidiaries of Multinational Corporations. *Journal of International Business Studies* (Fall): 365–388.

Grosse, Robert, and Duane Kujawa. 1988. *International Business*. Homewood, IL: Richard D. Irwin.

Håkanson, Lars, and Udo Zander. 1986. *Managing International Research and Development*. Stockholm: Mekanforbund.

Hall, Robert. 1983. *Zero Inventories*. Homewood, IL: Dow Jones-Irwin.

170 *Managing operations and technology*

International Maritime Organization. 2016. "2014 Annual Piracy Report", http://www. imo.org/en/OurWork/Security/PiracyArmedRobbery/Reports/Documents/219_ Annual_2014.pdf, accessed March 17, 2016.

International Maritime Organization. 2017. "2015 Annual Piracy Report", http://www. imo.org/en/OurWork/Security/PiracyArmedRobbery/Reports/Pages/Default.aspx, accessed March 29, 2017.

Johanson, Jan, and Lars-Gunnar. Mattison. 1987. Internationalization in Industrial Systems: A Network Approach. In V. Hood and J. E. Vahne, eds., *Strategies in Global Competition*. London: Croom Helm.

Keller, Robert T., and Ravi R. Chinta. 1990. International Transfer: Strategies for Success. *Academy of Management Executives* (May): 33–43.

Munkirs, John R. 1988. Technological Change: Disaggregation and Overseas Production. *Journal of Economic Issues* (June): 469–475.

Paris, Costas. 2017. China Takes Ahold of Trade Route. *Wall Street Journal*, April 8: B2, print edition.

Porter, Michael, ed. 1986. *Competition in Global Industries*. Boston: Harvard Business School Press.

Rastogi, P. N. 1988. *Productivity, Innovation, Management, and Development: A Study in the Productivity Culture of Nations and System Renewal*. New Delhi: Sage Publications.

Robock, Stefan H., and Kenneth Simmonds. 1983. *International Business and Multinational Enterprises*. Homewood, IL: Richard D. Irwin.

Rugman, Alan H., Donald J. Lecraw, and Laurence D. Booth. 1985. *International Business*. New York: McGraw-Hill.

Smith, Charles. 1990. Two's Company: Mitsubishi and Benz Plan Wide Links. *Far Eastern Economic Review* (May 24): 67–78.

Stobaugh, Robert B., and Louis T. Wells Jr., eds. 1984. *Technology Crossing Borders: The Choice, Transfer, and Management of International Technology Flows*. Boston: Harvard Business School Press.

Wells, Louis T. Jr. 1974. Don't Over-automate Your Foreign Plant. *Harvard Business Review* (January/February): 84–97.

8 Global case studies

One always fishes best in troubled waters.

(Soren Kierkegaard)

Chapter cases

Competitiveness cases

- Myanmar: The last global frontier
- Attractiveness of global markets
- Increasing market share at Acme Industries
- Hedging with foreign exchange

Sustainability cases

- Lilly Pharmaceuticals: triple bottom line and values-based leadership
- International real estate investor
- Cooperative workforce development: public–private sustainable linkages
- Privilege Capital

This final chapter provides international business case studies focusing on international competitiveness and sustainability issues. From a competitiveness standpoint, the first set of case studies represents perspectives from both the developed and developing world. These real-world cases have in common issues which arise when businesses expand internationally. The second set of cases presents issues of sustainability that businesses fail to address at their peril. Things such as ethical leadership, understanding the limitations of social responsibility, value perception differences, and efforts to utilize public and private linkages for a sustainable future are all addressed.

172 *Global case studies*

Myanmar: the last global frontier

G. Jason Goddard

The annual performance review meeting at the headquarters of International Credit Bank had not gone very well for Gregory Fuller, regional vice president for Asia. He had expected trouble at the meeting, but he had not expected the kind of intensely negative feedback he received from Timothy Martin Jr., the bank's president and chief executive officer. Fuller's area of responsibility included the bank's overall operation in Southeast Asia, and the bank had not done very well in the region during the past two years. Martin was extremely upset about this, because the entry of International Credit Bank into this region was his idea, and he had visualized spectacular growth for the bank in this region, which he felt was going to be the main growth area for the next two decades. In fact, Martin had felt that the only real chance for the bank to grow internationally was in this area and other options were practically nonexistent. Africa had been doing so badly that even such international lending agencies as the World Bank seemed to be losing heart. Latin America had also been plagued by economic troubles over the years. He, for one, was not going to commit the bank to these parts of the world, at least for now, which meant that for the foreseeable future Latin America and Africa were forbidden territories for any international expansion plans for International Credit Bank. This left Asia and the growth juggernaut of Southeast Asia as the likely candidate for expansion.

International Credit Bank was a major commercial bank based in the United States. Founded in 1920, it had survived the Depression years and had become an important player in the international banking markets by the 1960s. The bank's international approach, exemplified by its strong presence in Europe and Australia, had enabled it to grow rapidly in the 1970s and the 1980s. Commercial banks in general, however, were hit by the growing securitization of international financial markets, and International Credit Bank was no exception. Growth during the 1990s and 2000s was slow, with some level of market share erosion occurring in Western Europe which predicated Martin's desire for market entry in Southeast Asia. Although it was a large bank, it was quite conservative in its approach and had historically not wished to set up overseas investment banking subsidiaries to take advantage of new opportunities that were becoming available in the financial markets. As a matter of policy, the bank had decided to expand its commercial banking operations into other countries, both to keep growing and to offset the decline in its European commercial banking business.

The bank, and especially Martin, had great expectations from its move into Southeast Asia. The growth prospects were good, the infrastructure was in decent shape, and the Asian economies had, for the most part, recovered from their financial crisis of the late 1990s. Most countries had proven to be good hosts for foreign direct investment and had done very well on the international

Global case studies **173**

front, especially in exports. The region had seen improvement in its banking sector, primarily as a result of the Asian financial crisis. Both the increasing domestic prosperity, led by industrialization, and rapid international trade growth signaled important opportunities for a commercial bank such as International Credit Bank, which had excellent facilities for financing both domestic and cross-border transactions.

The bank faced few problems in establishing a presence in most of these countries. Corresponding banking relationships were already there, and the bank's Southeast Asia representatives had maintained excellent contacts with the senior government officials in these countries. Approvals for establishment of branches were therefore fairly easy to come by, and within two years the bank had a network of seven branches in four countries of the region. Early business development was greatly facilitated by the presence in all four countries of a number of international companies that were the bank's clients in Europe and North America. After the initial progress, however, the bank's business did not increase as rapidly as Martin had anticipated. His frustration grew as after three years of relatively rapid expansion the bank witnessed only very slow growth for two years. Based on the annual review discussion, there was a difference of opinion as to the probable cause of the slowdown in growth. Fuller felt that cutthroat competition was the culprit, while Martin felt the lack of bold action was a more likely reason.

Martin shared with Fuller during the meeting that he had recently read articles in the *Economist* and *Financial Times* touting Myanmar as the "last frontier of globalization" as the economy opened up after more than fifty years of political and economic isolation. Martin shared that a recent article in the *Journal of Asia-Pacific Business* had reviewed the strengths and weaknesses of the Myanmar economy, and had identified commercial banking as an area of much needed growth. Fuller said he had not considered Myanmar as a viable option for business expansion in the past owing to their autocratic regime. Martin wondered why Fuller was not more excited about pursuing the first mover advantage that foreign entry into Myanmar would provide. At the end of the meeting, Martin directed Fuller to read the *Journal of Asia-Pacific Business* article as a starting point for the new growth strategy focused on Myanmar. Given the anemic growth experienced by the bank over the last few years, Martin asked that Fuller consider whether it was time to open a foreign bank branch or a representative office in Myanmar, rather than pursuing their familiar route of pursuing a correspondent banking relationship in the country. Martin then provided Fuller with a copy of the article along with other recent economic surveys of Myanmar for his consideration.

Exhibit 8.1 summarizes some of the notes that Fuller jotted down in his pad when reading the various reports on Myanmar.

As Fuller read the articles, one doubt after another rose in his mind and he began to feel uneasy about the whole proposition. Just then, the phone rang. It was Julia Peterson, Martin's executive assistant. It appeared that Martin wanted Fuller to stop by and discuss it right away. Oh no, thought Fuller, as he collected

174 *Global case studies*

Government Progress	Business Pros
History of human rights abuse	Last Frontier of Globalization!
Former "pariah state"	Strategic location (between India and
Tight import controls	China)
Limited investment in 50 years	Linkage of East Asia to Western world?
Severe shortage of office/hotel space	Deep sea ports, abundant natural resources
2012 Foreign Investment Law to open	Large, youthful, low-cost, English-speaking
things up	workforce
Government control of most agricultural	Very few commercial banks
production	Record FDI of $8 billion in 2014-2015
Much red tape to start a business as foreign	80% of population does not have a bank
entity	account
Many new regulations and restricted	
investment sectors	

	Business Cons
Local worker hiring requirements (non-	
skilled positions)	Overall poor infrastructure
Corporations must train locals to upgrade	Poorly developed telecommunications/
skills	transportation structure
Limited private property rights/protection	Frequent power outages
Foreigners can only lease land, not own it	Lack of international bank cards with few
Government controlled entity only for	ATMs
insurance	Only one in ten people have a phone
Yangon Stock market opened in December	Limited electronic payment systems, hard
2015	cash preferred
	Joint Venture primary option for foreign
	firm
	Return to authoritarian rule could lead to
	asset confiscation

Exhibit 8.1 Gregory Fuller's notes on Myanmar

his ideas en route to Martin's plush office. This is going to be quite a difficult endeavor if Martin has made up his mind on this. In any case, I have no choice but to say my bit, since there is no way I am going to take the blame for this whole thing if it goes awry.

Martin welcomed Fuller quite warmly, apparently very pleased with the prospect of market entry into Myanmar. "This is going to really get us a jump start on the competition," he told Fuller. "It seems that none of the foreign banks in that part of the world are on the ground in Myanmar. So with one stroke not only will we increase our business, but we'll also get ahead of the competition. And I am sure the local governments are going to love this, since we will be bringing in modern technology in order to improve their computer systems and ATM service. The costs do appear quite high, but then that is to be expected. You can't really get the returns unless you make the investment and I believe this is one investment that is really worth making. I am sure you agree, don't you, Gregory?"

Fuller spoke with some difficulty. It was obvious that there was a crisis in his mind. Here was the boss, upset with him over the performance of the bank

Global case studies   175

region, now wanting to boost it through a means that Fuller saw as highly risky. Nevertheless, he must be honest with himself and Martin and speak his mind. "Well, sir," he began, "market entry into Myanmar is technically sound as it is conceived, but there are a number of problems on the ground as referenced in the materials that you provided. The authors of the articles are academically sound, but they really do not have an appreciation of the realities as they exist in the field. I know you are concerned about performance there and are of the view that the answer lies in rapid market entry. Nevertheless, I feel very strongly that we should not ignore the problems that may arise whereby we create a presence that may cause more harm than good."

"Well," said Martin, sounding a bit dubious, "it's really your area. Why don't you specify the problems you feel are going to arise and let me have a small executive brief on this by Tuesday morning."

Questions for discussion

1   Review the items in the references to this case along with other internet sources. Is now the time to enter Myanmar?
2   Prepare a brief outlining the benefits and weaknesses of market entry into Myanmar as well as whether those risks could be averted by the type of market entry employed (i.e. correspondent bank, foreign bank branch, representative office, brownfield vs. greenfield strategies, etc.).
3   If your decision is to delay market entry, what developments must transpire before market entry into Myanmar's banking sector is a reasonable risk? If your decision is to proceed into Myanmar, how is risk best avoided in this situation?

References

Economist, The, "Special report Myanmar: A Burmese spring", survey, pp. 1–12, May 25, 2013, print edition.

Goddard, G. Jason. 2013. Doing Business in the New Myanmar. *Journal of Asia-Pacific Business* 14(4): 361–368.

Hook, Leslie. 2013. Natural gas starts to flow between China and Myanmar. *Financial Times,* p. 2, July 30, print edition.

Peel, Michael. 2016. FT Big Read Myanmar. *Financial Times,* p. 7, February 2, print edition.

Robinson, Duncan. 2013. BAT lines up $50m factory on its return to Myanmar. *Financial Times,* p. 14, July 9, print edition.

Thomas, Daniel. 2013. Myanmar in first mobile deals. *Financial Times,* p. 13, June 28, print edition.

176 *Global case studies*

Attractiveness of global markets: a case study on how businesses analyze and select international markets as export targets

Van R. Wood (Ph.D.) – Virginia Commonwealth University (VCU)

Whitney Harrison (M.S. – VCU School of Business Graduate Program)

Jesse Myrick (M.B.A. – VCU School of Business Graduate Program)

Introduction

This case study overviews and demonstrates a three-step approach by which worldwide countries/markets can be analyzed and compared for their relative attractiveness in terms of export targets. The case focuses upon Photos Photiades Breweries (PPB), the market leader in Cyprus for its flagship product, Carlsberg beer, as well as its bottled water brand, Agros. This analysis indicates that China, France and the United Arab Emirates are the most promising targets for PPB's exporting efforts. Readers are asked to consider how these results might have changed given different interpretations of the significance of each country's legal, political, economic, infrastructure, sociocultural and market potential dimensions.

Photos Photiades Breweries (PPB) is the market leader in Cyprus for its flagship product, Carlsberg beer, as well as its bottled water brand, Agros. It has reached such success by focusing on its core capabilities, which include producing products of exceptional quality, establishing itself as a leader in technical know-how and expertise and investing in new technology and machinery to increase capacity.

However, the company is battling with external factors to maintain its top position. Specifically, in order to combat fierce competition, a saturated market in Cyprus, and to utilize the company's new investments in machinery, PPB charged a consulting team with identifying viable export markets within five regions of interest, namely Asia, Middle East/North Africa, Sub-Saharan Africa, Mediterranean, and Latin America/Caribbean. Due to the highly seasonal nature of the Cypriot market, the brewery functions at only 40% of capacity during the slow winter months. Thus, it is expected that exporting its private label beverages, Leon and Krauzer Bräu beers, ENA juice and Agros water, will help solve the problem of the under-utilization of production capability. The company does not expect to reach market leader status internationally but envisions its export opportunities to serve as a supplemental form of revenue and a way to maximize production, especially during the winter months.

To aid PPB in its export decision making, the consulting team utilized three stages of analysis (i.e., Stage 1: Market Size Analysis, Stage 2: PEST Analysis, and Stage 3: the "Method" Analysis) to filter 45 countries to the three most attractive export markets in which the company can successfully

Global case studies 177

compete. This report provides the company with the tools and a framework by which it can continue its discovery and evaluation of export markets, as it strives to utilize its investments in new technology and machinery and to operate at full capacity.

Ultimately, the analysis undertaken indicates that China, France and the United Arab Emirates are the most viable markets for PPB. More specifically, it is recommended that PPB export beer, juice and water to France and China, and export water and juice to the United Arab Emirates (UAE). Nonetheless, while the brewery uses market share of Carlsberg beer (over 53%) as a success factor, the primary factor at stake in this case is production capacity. The brewery produces 65% of the island's local beer production and has a total capacity of 30 million liters of beer per year. However, due to competition and insufficient demand in Cyprus, the brewery is unable to reach its total annual capacity of 30 million liters of beer. The brewery operates near or at 100% capacity during the summer months as beer consumption is seasonal, and only at 40% capacity during the winter months. The purpose of this case is to identify export opportunities for the brewery's private label beer, water and juice that would drive production capacity to 100% year-round, even in the winter months, in order to reach a capacity of 30 million liters. Therefore, success is also measured by the brewery's ability to reach 100% production capacity (30 million liters) supported by robust demand in export markets.

Overview

Founded in 1942, Photos Photiades Group has become one of the largest, fastest growing, and leading private companies in Cyprus. Its current portfolio includes investments in beverage production, beverages and goods distribution, real estate projects, and financial services domestically. With such a dynamic portfolio of products, brands, and services, the Photo Photiades Group's presence currently extends outside of Cyprus to countries such as Greece, Romania, Croatia, and Slovenia.

In 1968, the Photos Photiades Group entered into the beverage production industry by obtaining the first ever license to produce Carlsberg beer outside of Denmark. This pioneering partnership established Photos Photiades Breweries Ltd. (the parent company of the Cyprus Carlsberg Brewery) and eventually kick-started the production of PPB's private label beers, Leon and Krauzer Bräu, in Cyprus. In 2001, the brewery invested heavily in new technologies inside its Brewhouse, which successfully resulted in improved production performance. Currently, the brewery is the largest in Cyprus, boasting approximately 65% of the island's local beer production and a capacity of 30 million liters of beer per year. In addition, it remains one of the most successful Carlsberg breweries in the world.

The Photos Photiades Group added the ENA juice brand to its list of beverages in 1996. The brand features a 100% natural juice line (ENA Orange

178   *Global case studies*

and ENA Apple), a nectar juice line (ENA United Fruits) which includes a mixed blend of flavors, and ENA fruit drinks for kids. In 1998, the Photos Photiades Group launched Agros water to the Cypriot market under Blue Sky Mountain Springs Ltd. This natural mineral water comes from the perennial springs along the Troodos mountain range in the Cypriot village of Agros. Currently, Agros water is the market leader in Cyprus.

Later that year, the Photos Photiades Group opened Kyperounda Winery, which produces roughly 300,000 bottles per year and is the most awarded vineyard in Cyprus. In 2012, the Photos Photiades Group further diversified its beverage portfolio to include the private label spirit, Tazovksy Premium Vodka, introducing it first to the Romanian market. Based on an age-old Russian recipe, the "spirited" beverage is more refined in its distillation which differentiates it from its competition.

Problem statement

Although Photos Photiades Breweries (PPB) has made significant investments in new technology and machinery, which has improved process efficiencies and increased brewery capacity, these investments are currently underutilized, especially during the winter months. PPB management is very interested in finding markets that would allow the brewery to operate at a constant rate throughout the entire year. Typically during the summer months, the company runs two shifts to maintain production; however, during the winter months, the facility operates at only 40% capacity.

PPB has also experienced a growing number of external factors that have influenced its decision to pursue external markets. In addition to local brands, imported brands and EU Carlsberg wholesalers taking advantage of the EU Open Borders policy have created significant competition for PPB, and it now finds itself in a fierce battle to remain the market leader in the Cypriot beer and bottled water markets.

Lastly, having saturated the highly seasonal Cypriot market, PPB is looking to utilize the brewery's excess capacity by exporting both of its privately branded Leon and Krauzer Bräu beers into attractive new markets (PPB is not authorized to export its flagship product, Carlsberg beer, which is the leading beer in Cyprus with over 53% market share, to external markets due to its licensing agreement with the Carlsberg Group). In addition, the company is looking to export both its Agros natural mineral water along with its ENA juice brand.

Regions of Interest: In order to utilize its newly invested technology/ machinery and to operate at full capacity, PPB's management expressed interest in evaluating export opportunities in the following five regions: Asia, Middle East/North Africa, Sub-Saharan Africa, Mediterranean and Latin America/ Caribbean – and requested that the three most promising markets/countries within these regions be uncovered. All countries within these broad regional areas of interest were initially evaluated on whether or not meaningful and reliable data exists. Since sparse or questionable data can severely limit the veracity of market analysis results, any countries with insufficient data were eliminated from the subsequent analyses. Only those countries wherein robust data exists were further analyzed.

Two assumptions also guided the research, including (1) since beer, in and of itself, can be barred from a country (for religious and/or regulatory reasons), it was assumed that if PPB was indeed allowed to sell its beer to given export markets, it would also be allowed to sell water and juice to such markets, and (2) since the countries in the Middle East/North Africa have populations comprised of over 75% Muslims, the market for beer in such countries would not be viable for PPB. Only bottled water and juice would be feasible in such markets.

Based on the data requirements and the two aforementioned assumptions, an evoked set of 45 countries within the five regions of interest were further examined.

Market Analysis: Three subsequent stages of analysis were undertaken in order to ultimately filter the initial 45 countries to the three most appealing export markets for PPB. Extensive use of data from the *Euromonitor International Database* (and other sources) guided each stage of this investigation.

Stage 1 – Market Size Analysis

Each of the 45 countries (as shown in Exhibit 8.2) was evaluated based on their respective market size in terms of total volume of beer and/or bottled water consumed in liters per year. The logic underlying this analysis was that the largest markets (volume-wise) would have the highest demand and would allow for more beer and bottled water brand diversification, thus presenting the most opportunity for PPB's exports. This analysis produced the top three countries with the largest market size within each of the five regions. In this way, the 45 initial countries were narrowed down to 15 possible markets (see Exhibit 8.3 and Appendix 8A).

Stage 2 – PESTL "PEST" Analysis

Next, a PEST analysis (see Exhibit 8.4) was undertaken to evaluate each of the 15 countries' external environments as they relate to political, economic, sociocultural, technological and legal indicators. A PEST analysis is a useful tool for market research that takes into account various macro-environmental factors in potential markets and assesses whether said markets would present viable business opportunities.

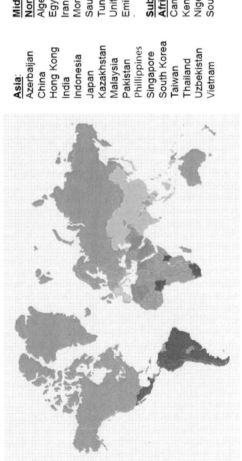

Asia:
Azerbaijan
China
Hong Kong
India
Indonesia
Japan
Kazakhstan
Malaysia
Pakistan
Phillippines
Singapore
South Korea
Taiwan
Thailand
Uzbekistan
Vietnam

Middle East & North Africa:
Algeria
Egypt
Iran
Morocco
Saudi Arabia
Tunisia
United Arab Emirates

Sub-Saharan Africa:
Cameroon
Kenya
Nigeria
South Africa

Latin America & Caribbean:
Dominican Republic
Argentina
Bolivia
Brazil
Chile
Colombia
Costa Rica
Ecuador
Guatemala
Mexico
Peru
Uruguay
Venezuela

Mediterranean:
Spain
Italy
Greece
France
Israel

Exhibit 8.2 Regions/countries examined for export potential

The following 15 countries proceeded to Stage 2 – PEST Analysis:

Middle East & North Africa:
Saudi Arabia
Tunisia
United Arab Emirates

Sub-Saharan Africa:
Cameroon
Nigeria
South Africa

Mediterranean:
Spain
Italy
France

Latin America & Caribbean:
Brazil
Colombia
Mexico

Asia:
China
Japan
Vietnam

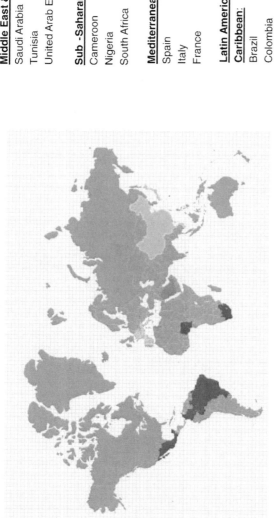

Exhibit 8.3 Stage 1: Market size analysis results

The following 5 countries proceeded to Stage 3 – Country Attractiveness / Competitive Strength Analysis.

Asia:
China

Middle East/North Africa:
United Arab Emirates

Sub-Saharan Africa:
South Africa

Mediterranean:
France

Latin America/Caribbean:
Mexico

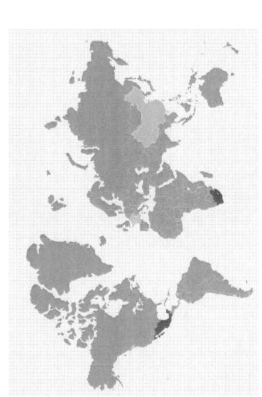
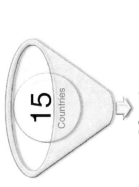

Exhibit 8.4 Stage 2: PEST Analysis Results

Global case studies 183

Based on the nature of PPB's business and its desire to export abroad, the PEST indicators used in this analysis were as follows:

Political Environment:
- Corruption Perceptions Index score (0 = highly corrupt; 100 = very clean)

Economic Environment:
- Cost to import (EUR per 20ft. container)
- GDP (in bn EUR)
- Imports of goods and services (%) of GDP

Sociocultural Environment:
- Total sales volume of beer/water in mn of liters

Technological Environment:
- Logistics performance (overall) (1 = low; 5 = high)

Legal Environment:
- Strength of legal rights (0 = weak; 12 = strong)

As shown in Appendix 8B, the PEST indicators for the countries in each region were ranked from 1 to 3 (1 being worst; 3 being best). The results of the PEST analysis provided the highest scoring country in each region as follows: Asia – China; Middle East/North Africa – United Arab Emirates; Sub-Saharan Africa – South Africa; Mediterranean – France; Latin America/Caribbean – Mexico. These five countries proceeded to Stage 3 of the analysis.

Stage 3 – Country Attractiveness/Competitive Strength Analysis

The final stage of the analysis requires the selection and examination of specific "drivers" of success as they relate to exporting to the five selected markets (again, China, United Arab Emirates, South Africa, France and Mexico). This analysis is based on the works of Harrell and Kiefer (1981) and Wood and Robertson (1999), wherein two primary dimensions of analysis, Country Attractiveness (of each of the five selected markets) and Competitive Strength (of PPB in each of the five markets), were evaluated and compared, and an ultimate decision was made as to which specific countries offer the most promise for PPB's exports. This analysis consists of a five step process, as follows:

Step 1: Select Country Attractiveness and Competitive Strength Variables: The Country Attractiveness "drivers" for export success include: (1) Market Potential (as measured by market size and market growth); (2) Political Stability (as measured by each country's Corruption Perceptions Index score as well as the strength of its legal rights); (3) Economic Strength (as measured by the cost to import, GDP and the imports of goods and services as a percentage of GDP); and (4) Infrastructure (as measured by each country's overall logistics performance). In a similar manner, the Competitive Strength "drivers" for PPB include: (1) Competitive Landscape (as measured by the number of existing breweries/bottled water manufacturers in each market); (2) Product

184 *Global case studies*

Fit (as measured by the total volume sales of mid-priced lager/bottled water (mn liters) and the price of these products); (3) Contribution Margin (as measured by the shipping cost from Limassol port in Cyprus to the main commercial port in each country as well as the transit time for each route); and (4) Market Representation (as measured by the total import volume of beer/ bottled water (mn liters)).

Step 2: Rank Country Attractiveness and Competitive Strength Variables: The next step in this method of analysis required the ranking of all the comparative data for each market's country attractiveness and competitive strength variables from best to worst. The country with the best score received a 10, second place scored an 8, third place scored a 6, fourth place scored a 4, and the country with the worst score received a 2. If there was a tie, the two scores were averaged, and the countries received the same score. For example, if there were two first place countries, the countries each received a score of 9 (10, for first, + 8, for second, divided by 2). A detailed analysis of the variable rankings is found in Appendices C and D.

Step 3: Develop Linear Equations for Country Attractiveness and Competitive Strength: After ranking each of these variables, linear equations for country attractiveness and competitive strength were developed. Each variable was weighted based on the subjective estimates of the relative importance of each factor in analyzing a country's attractiveness and PPB's competitive strength within that country as it relates to export opportunities. The equations and respective variable weights are as follows:

Linear Scale for Country Attractiveness:

> Country Attractiveness = (.40 × Market Potential) + (.05 × Political Stability) + (.45 × Economic Strength) + (.10 × Infrastructure)
> Market Potential = (.50 × Market Size) + (.50 × Market Growth)
> Political Stability = (.50 × Corruption Perceptions Index Score) + (.50 × Strength of Legal Rights)
> Economic Strength = (Cost to Import + GDP + Imports of Goods & Services as a % of GDP)/3
> Infrastructure = 1.00 × Logistics Performance Overall

Linear Scale for Competitive Strength:

> Competitive Strength = (.10 × Competitive Landscape) + (.40 × Product Fit) + (.40 × Contribution Margin) + (.10 × Market Representation)
> Competitive Landscape = 1.00 × Number of existing breweries
> Product Fit = (.50 × Sales of Mid-Priced Lager) + (.50 × Price of Mid-Priced Lager)
> Contribution Margin = (.50 × Shipping Cost from Limassol Port) + (.50 × Shipping Transit Time)
> Market Representation = 1.00 × Total Import Volume (mn liters)

Global case studies   185

Countries	Competitive strength	Country attractiveness
China	6	7.375
UAE	5.2	7.1
South Africa	5.8	4.5
France	7.2	5.2
Mexico	5.8	5.825

Exhibit 8.5 Stage 3: Country attractiveness/competitive strength analysis results

Step 4: Compute Total Country Attractiveness & Competitive Strength Scores: The rank (2, 4, 6, 8, or 10) of each variable is then entered into the equations in order to generate total country attractiveness and competitive strength scores for each of the five markets. The results of this calculation are displayed in Exhibit 8.5.

Step 5: Plot Key Countries on a Two-Dimensional Matrix: The final step of the analysis requires the plotting of the five key countries on a two-dimensional market matrix with country attractiveness on the y-axis and competitive strength on the x-axis. The matrix shown in Exhibit 8.6 is an example taken from the work of Harrell and Kiefer (1981). This parsimonious model presents the combination of each country's attractiveness and competitive strength and provides a visualization as to which countries are ripe for investment and growth (i.e., ranking high in both country attractiveness and competitive strength (green)) and those countries for which companies should forgo direct foreign investment (i.e., ranking low in both country attractiveness and competitive strength (red)).

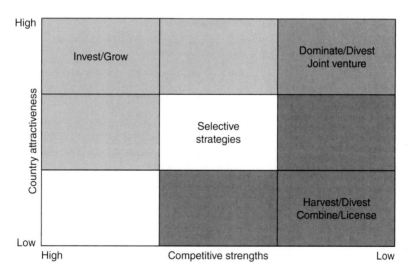

Exhibit 8.6 Harrell & Kiefer country plotting matrix

186   *Global case studies*

The results

As can be seen in Exhibit 8.7, the countries scoring high in both country attractiveness and competitive strength fall in the green shaded portion of the matrix and are markets for which PPB should proceed to export. A country falling in the yellow portion of the graph should only proceed to export with caution. For these countries, the market is particularly attractive; however, the chances of the company being competitive in that market are low. Lastly, it is not recommended that PPB export to any countries falling within the red portion of the matrix, as these countries would score low in both country attractiveness and competitive strength and, thus, would not present viable export opportunities. As evidenced by Exhibit 8.7, China, France and the United Arab Emirates have "gone green" and would be viable markets for export. No countries fell into the yellow (proceed with caution) and red zones (do not export). Those countries falling in the middle of the graph, South Africa and Mexico, presented only mediocre opportunities for export and should not be PPB's first focus when exporting.

Recommendations: Photos Photiades Breweries is currently looking to export its locally branded beers (Leon and Krauzer Bräu), ENA juice, and Agros bottled water to attractive markets outside of Cyprus. Exporting will assist the brewery in maintaining a more consistent production schedule, especially during the winter months when utilization is only 40% of capacity. The underutilization of its facility, compounded by fierce competition and a saturated Cypriot market, urged the company to undertake an analysis of export markets in its five areas of interest. A three-stage analysis filtered 45 prospective countries down to 3 countries (China/France/UAE), which present viable exporting opportunities for PPB. The market analysis shows China as the strongest market for beer consumption, France as a viable market to export all three products, and the UAE as another attractive market to export its water and/or juice brands.

Although the "method" presented herein provides a mathematical approach by which to systematically and objectively analyze international export markets, such analysis should also be coupled with an evaluation of the consumer trends in each country, as consumer behavior is dynamic and always changing. Though advancements in communications technology and transportation have made geographical barriers virtually disappear, the notion of exporting globally still remains an overwhelming and daunting task for most businesses. Thus, it is imperative for companies to take such a systematic approach when screening and evaluating international markets.

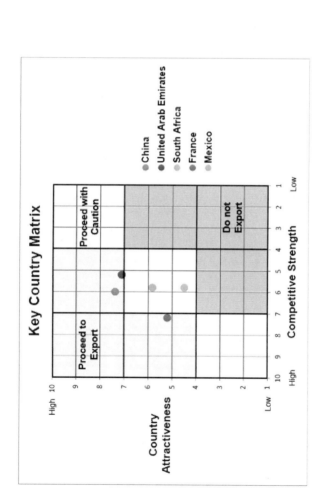

Exhibit 8.7 Stage 3: Country attractiveness/competitive strength analysis

188 *Global case studies*

Questions for discussion

1 Does the analysis in this case seem rigorous and complete?
2 What other tools might be used to improve this analysis?
3 If we changed the ranking of dimensions in the analysis, how might the ultimate results be influenced?
4 Outline the "next steps" for PPB's market penetration into the markets recommended for PPB in this analysis (e.g., what agent or strategic alliance relationships might be best for PPB to realized international success and explain why this is so?).

References

1 Euromonitor International Database. *Statistics & Analysis*. Information retrieved June 2015. http://www.euromonitor.com/
2 Harrell, Gilbert D. and Richard O. Kiefer. 1981. *Multinational Strategic Market Portfolios*.
3 MSC Routefinder. Information retrieved June 2015. https://www.msc.com/cyp/help-centre/tools/routefinder
4 Oanda Currency Converter. Information retrieved June 2015. http://www.oanda.com/currency/converter/
5 Photos Photiades Group. Information retrieved June 2015. http://photiadesgroup.com/
6 The World Bank. *Indicators*. Information retrieved June 2015. http://data.worldbank.org/indicator
7 Transparency International. *Corruption Perceptions Index 2014: Results*. Information retrieved June 2015. https://www.transparency.org/cpi2014/results
8 Wikipedia. *Islam by Country*. Information retrieved June 2015. https://en.wikipedia.org/wiki/Islam_by_country
9 Wood, Van R., and Kim R. Robertson. 2000. Evaluating International Markets. *International Marketing Review* 17(1): 34-55.
10 World Freight Rates. *Freight calculator*. Information retrieved June 2015. http://worldfreightrates.com/freight

Global case studies 189

Market		Market share	
		Market size – Beer (mn litres)	Market size – Water (mn litres)
Mediterranean:	Spain	3,377.1	
	Italy	1,546.5	
	France	1,936.3	
North Africa/Middle East:	UAE		1,112.1
	Saudi Arabia		2,724.5
	Tunisia		1,288.5
Southern Africa:	Cameroon	719.2	
	Nigeria	2,179.4	
	South Africa	3,401.0	
Asia:	China	52,213.2	
	Japan	6,049.1	
	Vietnam	3,625.6	
Lating America & Carribbean:	Brazil	13,997.7	
	Colombia	2,236.8	
	Mexico	7,203.5	

Appendix 8A Stage 1: Market size analysis

Region	Countries	Political		Economic						Social				Technological		Legal		TOTAL
		Corruption index score	Rank	Cost to Import (EUR)	Rank	GDP (in billions EUR)	Rank	Imports of goods and services (%) GDP	Rank	Total Beer Sales (mm litres)	Rank	Total Bottled Water Sales	Rank	Logistics Performance Overall	Rank	Strength of Legal Rights	Rank	
Mediterranean																		
	Spain	60	2	1,243	2	1,236.48	1	28.1	2	3,356.70	3			3.72	2	5	3	1.875
	Italy	43	1	1,016	3	1,907.90	2	26.3	1	1,617.20	1			3.69	1	2	1	1.25
	France	69	3	1,283	1	2,491.02	3	29.8	3	1,878.70	2			3.85	3	4	2	2.125
Middle East/ North Africa																		
	Saudi Arabia	49	2	1,162	2	664.33	2	30.6	1			2,609.80	3	3.15	2	5	3	1.75
	Tunisia	40	1	808	1	1,236.48	3	56.2	2			1,167.50	2	2.55	1	2	1.5	1.5625
	UAE	70	3	555	3	357.12	1	77.7	3			1,048.40	1	3.54	3	2	1.5	1.9375
Asia																		
	China	36	2	710	2	8,201.76	3	23.8	2	50,850.30	3			3.53	2	4	1.5	1.9375
	Japan	76	3	906	1	4,366.66	1	19	1	6,148.50	2			3.91	3	4	1.5	1.6875
	Vietnam	31	1	533	3	152.13	3	79.8	3	3,214.00	1			3.15	1	7	3	1.625
Sub-Saharan Africa																		
	Cameroon	27	1.5	2,012	1	26.25	1	28.9	2	653.1	1			2.3	1	6	2.5	1.25
	Nigeria	27	1.5	1,740	3	463.16	3	13	1	2,048.10	2			2.81	2	6	2.5	1.875
	South Africa	44	3	1,846	2	324.92	2	33.2	3	3,445.30	3			3.43	3	5	1	2.125
Latin America/Caribbean																		
	Brazil	43	3	2,046	2	1,978.17	3	15	1	13,368.50	3			2.94	2	2	1	1.875
	Mexico	69	1	1,663	3	1,110.71	2	32.4	3	6,876.30	2			3.13	3	8	2	2
	Colombia	37	2	2,176	1	333.34	1	20.2	2	2,194.70	1			2.64	1	12	3	1.375

Glossary of Indicators:

- Corruption Index Score: 0 = highly corrupt; 100 = very clean

- Logistics Performance Overall: 1 = low; 5 = high

- Strength of Legal Rights: 0 = weak; 12 = strong

Appendix 8B Stage 2: PEST analysis

Country Attractiveness = (.40 x Market Potential) + (.05 x Political Stability) + (.45 x Economic Strength) + (.10 x Infrastructure)

Market Potential = (.50 x Market Size) + (.50 x Market Growth)
Political Stability = (.50 x Corruption Index Score) + (.50 x Strength of Legal Rights)
Economic Strength = (Cost to import + GDP + Imports of goods & services as a % of GDP)/3
Infrastructure = 1.00 x Logistics Performance Overall

Country Attractiveness

Regions:	Countries:	Market Potential				Political Stability				Economic Strength							Infrastructure	
		Market Size (beer/water)	Rank	Market Growth (beer/water)	Rank	Corruption Index Score	Rank	Strength of Legal Rights	Rank	Cost to import	Rank	GDP	Rank	Imports of goods & services (% of GDP)	Rank	Logistics Performance	Rank
Asia	China	52,213.20	10	2.5	8	36	2	4	5	710	8	8,201.76	10	23.8	2	3.53	6
Middle East/North Africa	UAE	1,112.10	2	6.5	10	70	10	2	2	555	10	357.12	4	77.7	10	3.54	8
Sub-Saharan Africa	South Africa	3,401.00	6	0.8	4	44	4	5	8	1,846	2	324.92	2	33.2	8	3.43	4
Mediterrean	France	1,936.30	4	0.6	2	69	7	4	5	1,283	6	2,491.02	8	29.8	4	3.85	10
Latin America/Caribbean	Mexico	7,203.50	8	1.9	6	69	7	8	10	1,663	4	1,110.71	6	32.4	6	3.13	2

	Market Potential	Political Stability	Economic Strength	Infrastructure	Country Attractiveness Final Score
China	9.00	3.50	6.67	6.00	7.38
UAE	6.00	6.00	8.00	8.00	7.10
South Africa	5.00	6.00	4.00	4.00	4.50
France	3.00	6.00	6.00	10.00	5.20
Mexico	7.00	8.50	5.33	2.00	5.83

Glossary of Indicators:

- Market Size of beer/bottled water (UAE) (mn litres)
- Market Growth of beer/bottled water (UAE) (%)
- Corruption Index Score: 0 = highly corrupt; 100 = very clean

- Strength of Legal Rights: 0 = weak; 12 = strong
- Cost to import (EUR)
- GDP (EUR)
- Logistics Performance Overall: 1 = low; 5 = high

Appendix 8C Stage 3: Country attractiveness variable rankings

Competitive Strength = (.10 x Competitive Landscape) + (.40 x Product Fit) + (.40 x Contribution Margin) + (.10 x Market Representation)

Competitive Landscape = 1.00 x Number of existing breweries
Product Fit = (.50 x Sales of mid-priced lager) + (.50 x Price of mid-priced lager)
Contribution Margin = (.50 x Shipping cost from Limassol Port to Main Port) + (.50 x Shipping Transit Time)
Market Representation = 1.00 x Total Import Volume (mn litres)

Competitive Strength:

Regions:	Countries:	Competitive Landscape		Product Fit				Contribution Margin				Market Representation	
		Number of existing breweries/ bottled water lager/bottled water manufacturers	Rank	Sales of mid-priced lager/bottled water (mn litres)	Rank	Price of mid-priced lager/ bottled water per litre (EUR)	Rank	Shipping cost from Limassol Port to Main Port (20ft container) EUR	Rank	Shipping Transit time (days)	Rank	Import Volume (mn litres)	Rank
Asia	China	530	4	7,169.20	10	1.51	4	817	8	51	2	182.3	8
Middle East/North Africa	UAE	100	6	1,048.40	4	0.28	2	1,588	6	33	10	N/A	2
Sub-Saharan Africa	South Africa	8	10	2,276.30	6	1.60	6	2,751	4	40	6	31.6	4
Mediterrean	France	544	2	694.1	2	3.18	10	508	10	38	8	749.3	10
Latin America/Caribbean	Mexico	46	8	6,616.60	8	1.96	8	2,866	2	46	4	140.5	6

	Competitive Landscape	Product Fit	Contribution Margin	Market Representation	Competitive Strength Final Score
China	4	7	5	8	6
UAE	6	3	8	2	5.2
South Africa	10	6	5	4	5.8
France	2	6	9	10	7.2
Mexico	8	8	3	6	5.8

Ports: China – Tianjin; United Arab Emirate – Jebel Ali; South Africa – Cape Town; France – Fos-Sur-Mer; Mexico – Veracruz

Appendix 8D Stage 4: Competitive strength variable rankings

Global case studies 193

Increasing market share at Acme Industries

Gregory M. Kellar, Wright State University

Acme Industries manufactures a single, differentiated consumer product in Taiwan. It began operations in 1999 and expanded its operations to sell its products in India in addition to Taiwan in 2001. Its manufacturing operations are located in Northern Taiwan. The company now has four sales areas, Northern Taiwan, Central Taiwan, Southern Taiwan, and India. Although sales have been growing steadily over the past two years, competitive pressures are increasing. Five direct competitors exist with four competitors having entered the marketplace within the past two years. Only three companies (including Acme) compete in all four markets. The remaining companies are smaller and only operate in some of the markets and only sell locally. Globally, no other markets are served with competitive offerings. Competitive analyses show that excess capacity exists in the industry. Competition exerts pressures on product price, product quality, product feature set, product availability, and customer service. Because of the competitive landscape, the perception is that the probability of new entrants entering the market is low.

India has enjoyed a fairly stable economy over the past several years. However, signs of excessive inflation have surfaced in the recent past. Several competitors have frozen prices with the apparent fear of loss of market share preventing them from increasing prices to offset decreasing currency value.

Nian Sur, President of Acme Industries, wants to balance the pursuit of increased market share with the maintenance of profitability and stock prices. While Acme finds sales increasing across all markets, its profitability and stocks prices have been eroding for the past five quarters. Also, its market share is decreasing. Mr. Sur believes that increased price pressures and decreasing market share are explained by increasing competitive forces. Additionally, he suspects that much of the profitability concerns can be explained by the inflationary forces found in India.

Mr. Sur has charged Hyun Li, Marketing VP and Jungbo Yang, Production VP with investigating solutions to the company's recent profitability and stock price difficulties.

After several weeks of considerable efforts, Hyun and Jungbo report in an executive meeting that, in some markets, competitive pressures prevent the company from pricing their product above total costs. However, their prices can be maintained above variable costs in all markets. India applies the greatest pricing difficulties. If Acme chooses to exit the Indian market because of these competitive pricing pressures, reentry costs, competitive pressures, and the legal and regulatory environment might prevent Acme from reentering the Indian market in the foreseeable future.

At the same meeting, Hyun and Jungbo report that production could be moved from Taiwan to India. Capital costs associated with this move would be about $10 million. Variable costs would be reduced from $6 to $5 per unit.

194　*Global case studies*

Fixed costs per unit would not be influenced by the move. Assuming that current sales of about 1.5 million units per quarter continue to grow at existing rates, the breakeven time period for this move will be less than seven quarters (independent of transportation or holding costs). Transportation costs will be about 10 cents per unit to Taiwan and they will be eliminated in the Indian market as the finished goods warehouse will be adjacent to the production plant. Holding costs will be about 7 cents per unit per quarter. The political climate, education level, and skills of the Indian workforce increase concerns for stability and efficiencies of the manufacturing process but quantifying these concerns has proven elusive.

Several executives express concerns about abandoning the Indian market. This gives rise to an informal brainstorming session in which several ask if the Indian market should be subsidized by the Taiwanese market. Others ask if moving production to India, with its improved production efficiencies resulting in reduced variable costs, would offset any required subsidies to the Indian market. After a lengthy discussion, Mr. Sur asks if perhaps the company should subsidize the Indian market while also transferring production to India. He asks for timeframes and cash flow statements to support recommendations. The meeting is adjourned with a follow-up meeting scheduled two weeks later in which specific plans will be discussed.

During this two-week study period, new economic forecasts are released that predict inflation in India will increase over the next six quarters with an average of 2.65% per quarter. This represents an unexpectedly large increase as inflation has exceeded 6% annually only once over the past nine years.

Mr. Sur postpones the next meeting by two weeks so that recommendations can adequately consider the impact of the new inflation forecasts. He also asks everyone to be prepared to discuss the merits of further differentiating their product offering by increasing its relative quality and feature set so that they can potentially increase their prices in India at a rate that keeps up with inflation. R&D is charged with working with marketing to design these improvements and Hyun is asked to coordinate her efforts with R&D to present competitive pricing suggestions to accompany R&D's product improvement suggestions.

The next two weeks reveal that the finance department has been allocating fixed costs equally across all units being produced. The cost plus pricing mechanism that Acme has been using in all markets has never used any subsidy in any market. Fixed costs have been allocated equally on a per unit basis. Hyun observes that this allocation method might not be consistent with the recommended changes being pursued. In particular, Hyun suggests that allocating all fixed costs across the three Taiwanese markets will provide the required subsidies to the Indian markets to accomplish all objectives currently being pursued. Also, she points out that these fixed costs should be allocated on a per transaction basis. This will have the effect of securing their largest domestic accounts. While smaller accounts will be price penalized, product differentiation should allow for the price discrimination.

Global case studies   195

At the next meeting, a strong majority of executives and directors agree that Acme should relocate manufacturing to India, change fixed cost allocation schemes, subsidize products sold in India with no fixed costs being allocated to units sold in India, differentiate their product to support price increases, and increase prices in all areas to keep up with inflation.

One year later, all modifications have been implemented. The new production facility has been operating for a quarter. Product design improvements have been available to customers for two quarters. Prices have reflected management's subsidy and cost allocation decisions for over two quarters.

Several of Acme's main accounts have eroded. High level conversations with customers to understand the defections have revealed that the new product designs are not consistent with customer wants or needs. Previous customers were looking for a budget item for a budget price. The movement towards a premium product has forced the company to find a new set of customers. This unexpected exchange of target markets has proven painful and the short-term loss of sales has harmed short-term profits and stock prices. Also, the price increases in Taiwan because of the subsidy schemes appears to have contributed to reduced domestic sales. While long-term forecasts are promising, Mr. Sur wonders if the company should consider two expansion efforts to offset the impact of previous corporate decisions. The first effort would be to start producing two products, a budget product and a premium product. The premium model would maintain newly found customers and the budget model would recover customers that had defected. The second effort would be to expand sales to Indonesia where little competition exists. Sales would command premium pricing that would be high enough to provide much of the subsidy that India's economy currently requires. This would allow domestic sales to be restored to their previous lower price due to the reduced subsidy for Indian sales. The hope and belief is that these two efforts would improve sales, market share and profitability in all areas.

Memos are distributed to the executive team to consider these ideas and to be prepared to discuss the pros and cons at a follow-up meeting in two weeks.

At the follow-up meeting, Jungbo explains that moving to a two-product company will require significant changes to production operations such as facility expansion and scheduling. The required efforts will require about two quarters and $1 million in capital costs. R&D explains that it will take about one quarter to design a budget product because the one that was last offered is no longer competitive. Also, future R&D budgets will have to increase to maintain product development on two models instead of just one as in the past. Marketing explains the offering of two products will confuse some customers resulting in a loss of sales. This will have to be offset with an increased marketing budget. Also, Hyun notes that while the idea of global expansion makes sense, Indonesia might not be the best location to increase sales. Current conditions and long-term forecasts suggest that expansion into the United States would deliver better results. Also, Hyun asks for the team to consider increasing

196 *Global case studies*

expansion plans to include the US and Brazil within the near future due to economic opportunities and straightforward implementation paths. She brought five-year forecasts showing projections of improved corporate-wide sales and profits after the suggested expansions.

An ad-hoc team of three executives is created and charged with the creation of an expansion plan that considers pricing strategies, fixed cost allocation schemes, local economic conditions, competitive issues and roll out sequencing and timing. The team includes marketing VP Hyun Li, global economist Shen Wi and supply chain VP Jang Zhang.

The following data are compiled and found to be influential by the expansion plan team (see Tables 8.1 to 8.3).

Notice that while inflation in India has remained around 10% for six years, it is projected to decrease to levels that hover between 5.0% and 5.5% per year over the next five years. Further, competitive projections show that many companies will be offering budget products below Acme's full cost in India when fixed costs are allocated on a per unit basis across all markets. Also, if Acme expands to all markets identified and discussed, profits will increase over current levels. However, the Indian market shows a loss on all projections. Should the team suggest ceasing all Indian activities? Jang Zhang suggests that perhaps Acme should exit the Indian market until profitability can be secured. Shen Wi notes that since current Indian regulations lack transparency with

Table 8.1 Inflation rates in India

Year (20xx)	05	06	07	08	09	10	11	12	13	14	15
Inflation rate (%)	4.4	6.9	5.9	9.2	10.6	9.5	9.4	10.2	10.0	6.7	4.9

Table 8.2 Competitive offerings – end of 2014

Company	Acme	DEW Group	Emca	PBC Ltd.	Faliba	Crescent
Quality of offering	Medium	Medium	Low	High	Low	High
Features of offering	High	Medium	Medium	Medium	Low	Low
Global market share (%)	35	20	15	15	10	5
Markets served	Taiwan* India	Taiwan* India	Taiwan* India	Taiwan** India	Taiwan*	India

* serves all of Taiwan
** serves only central Taiwan

Table 8.3 Expansion projections

	AS IS	Brazil	Indonesia	USA
Global revenues ($ US)	75 M	90 M	85 M	100 M
Global profits ($ US)	15 M	18 M	17 M	20 M
Local revenues ($ US)	N/A	15 M	10 M	25 M
Local profits ($ US)	N/A	3 M	2 M	5 M

consequent limits to foreign entry into their markets, such an exit might be a one-way trip. Hyun Li suggests that the team should calculate overall corporate profitability including and excluding business in the Indian markets. Interestingly, when this is done, these calculations show that continuing operations in India is associated with increased profitability. The team finds this surprising since their calculations also show that with all subsidies removed, every unit sold in India loses money. This loss increases as more units are sold in India. The team wonders if they made mistakes in their calculations.

Further adding to their insecurities, the thoughts about expanding their product line cause concerns about confusing customers and harming Acme's brand. Would the two models cannibalize each other? Should Acme introduce a premium brand to accompany the introduction of a premium product? If so, what tactics should accompany the introduction of a premium product?

While the expansion to additional markets carries significant opportunities, several financial and operational questions need answers prior to implementation. For example, what are the capital requirements associated with market entry? How will management of the new markets be organized? What are the financial projections associated with the new market entries? What are the breakeven projections; how long will it take before Acme breaks even – how long will it take before Acme's profits offset its capital investments to enter the new markets?

As the team ponders and discusses answers to such questions, Shen Wi suggests that an optimized supply chain could allow Acme to minimize the time required to reach their breakeven points and secure corporate profitability. For example, packaging, kitting, and shipping schedules could be optimized to minimize total landed costs; maintaining system flexibility and reaction times would provide Acme with a competitive advantage that would translate into increased corporate profitability. He notes that the importance of these practices increases with the complexity of the system.

Shen Wi notes that full supply chain optimization will require the implementation of more sophisticated IT systems than the company currently has implemented. Enhanced systems would allow Acme to improve forecasting and virtually consolidate its inventory as appropriate. Costs and required time frames for IT system implementations are included in Table 8.4.

The team begins to get excited about the competitive opportunities of combining the multiple changes and improvements simultaneously, with IT improvements phasing in (as shown in Table 8.4). The virtual consolidation would reduce safety stock levels and simultaneously increase inventory velocity

Table 8.4 IT implementation plans

	Improved forecasting	Inventory virtual consolidation	Online sales
Implementation cost ($ US)	2 M	1 M	1 M
Time to implement	6 months	9 months	3 months

198 *Global case studies*

on rotating stock. The strategic subsidies will need to adapt to changes in competitive and economic conditions which should help preserve improved global profitability and a standardized corporate-wide IT system should improve aggregated forecasting which should improve production lot sizing and reduce production costs. The increasing number of markets should stabilize the economic swings experienced in individual markets by offsetting them with countercyclical swings in other markets also being served. The combination of these advantages feels significant to the team. The team needs to translate these feelings into specific recommendations and projections.

The team begins by compiling anticipated capital costs with their related schedules. These are listed in Table 8.5.

Breakeven analyses are presented in Table 8.6.

The team anticipates Acme executives being concerned with the sustainability of the competitive advantages gained through the proposed changes. In particular, how will Acme preserve any competitive advantages that these improvements bring? The concern is that while the improvements being proposed represent business practices and systems that are significantly better than the competition, are these advantages sustainable? What will prevent their competitors from duplicating Acme's new systems and reducing customers' purchase decisions to decisions based on price alone? How can Acme continue to differentiate itself? How can it make sure that the financial projections will be correct in a competitive environment in which the competition will adapt and copy any improvements that Acme brings to the marketplace? How long will it take before the competition copies or leapfrogs these improvements, and will this time frame be sufficient to recoup capital costs?

Jang Zhang illustrates the anticipated concerns by noting that recently their competitor, Emca, invested $10 million to implement a small-scale IT improvement with two-year breakeven projections. However, competitive

Table 8.5 Capital cost plans

	Improved forecasting	Inventory virtual consolidation	Online sales	New factory	Add new factory line
Capital cost ($ US)	2 M	1 M	1 M	10 M	1 M
Expected schedule for implementation to become available	6 months	15 months	18 months	12 months	15 months

Table 8.6 Breakeven analyses

	Improved forecasting	Inventory virtual consolidation	Online sales	New factory	Add new factory line
Capital cost ($ US)	2 M	1 M	1 M	10 M	1 M
Breakeven number of units	20 M		2 M	10 M	0.5 M
Projected time frame	32 months	11 months	4 months	20 months	3 months

Global case studies   199

responses to Emca's IT improvements were so quick that breakeven projections were necessarily and unexpectedly extended to five years. Further, what was originally a competitive advantage quickly turned into a competitive disadvantage as the competition improved on Emca's improvements.

With these opportunities and concerns, how should Acme proceed? Should they pursue a first mover strategy which will require consistent and prolonged efforts? Should they investigate forming corporate alliances, mergers or acquisitions to limit competition? Would any of the markets Acme currently serves or might enter limit or prohibit such inter-corporate activity? The team feels excited about several of their proposals but feels the need to present answers to questions identified and alluded to above. Also, they want to explain the synergistic opportunities of the proposals being developed. The leader of the team, Hyun Li, is in a quandary as to how they should proceed and what they should recommend at their next meeting, which is only a few days away.

Questions for discussion

1   Does it make sense to subsidize one sales area at the expense of the other? Explain why or why not.
2   What are the risks associated with changing the product line from a budget offering to a premium offering? What are the difficulties and risks of offering both a budget and premium product?
3   How does the choice of a fixed cost allocation scheme influence competitiveness?
4   What are the pros and cons associated with moving production offshore?
5   How should Acme manage inflation plaguing India? Should it continue to operate in India? What effect does the inflation rate have on the repayment of borrowed money used for plant relocation and expansion?
6   How can Acme afford to finance the growth plans being recommended by marketing VP Hyun Li?
7   What role does competition have on profitability of Acme?
8   Will Acme's expansion to other areas simplify or complicate its pursuit of market share and/or profitability? Is it easier to stay competitive when focusing on only one area or is it easier when multiple sales areas are in play? Explain your answer(s).

Hedging with foreign exchange

Johannes De Silentio, Silicatec

Background

Silicatec is a multinational, publicly held company that owns several subsidiaries that design, manufacture, install and service capital equipment serving several global industries, including the solar industry, a fast-growing, cyclical industry.

Silicatec, the parent company, with its corporate headquarters in Chicago, Illinois, has two domestic subsidiaries along with two foreign-based subsidiaries in Germany and China as is shown in Exhibit 8.8.

Silicatec's domestic subsidiaries serve non-solar markets worldwide, but they generally have no foreign currency exposure. They invoice and collect from their customers in US dollars and they pay their major suppliers in US dollars as they are all located in the United States.

Silicatec's Chinese subsidiary typically has no significant foreign currency exposure because their customers and suppliers are locally operated and transact business in local currency. The Chinese operation is consistently cash-positive and is generally self-sustaining. Historically, it has generated cash adequate to settle its liabilities to the parent company for shared services (described below). Charges for shared services, which are denominated in US dollars, are settled quarterly.

Silicatec's European subsidiary, Sub C, exclusively supplies the solar industry, a rapidly growing industry characterized by periods of heavy capital investment followed by periods of slow capital spending caused by under-utilization of capacity. Sub C invoices and collects the majority of its revenues in euros. It does, however, serve several small US-based customers who prefer doing business in US dollars. Additionally, Sub C deals with certain strategic US-based suppliers who require doing business in US dollars.

Silicatec's corporate offices in the U.S. supply significant support to the subsidiaries and maintain the infrastructure required of publicly held companies, therefore, the parent company charges the cost of these shared services to the subsidiaries. Shared services are invoiced to all subsidiaries in US dollars.

Shared services costs include the cost of corporate executive officers, including salaries, benefits, incentive stock compensation and travel. Shared service costs also include the cost of a centralized corporate finance and administration staff and corporate IT staff. The costs for the centralized corporate shared services include office space, salaries, benefits and travel as well as stock compensation plan administration, centralized human resources management, legal expenses, accounting and auditing fees and other professional services. Over the last 10 years, the primary source of Silicatec's cash has been from secondary public offerings.

The company's Corporate Director of Finance monitors the company's consolidated foreign currency exposure through data gathered from the subsidiaries on a monthly basis.

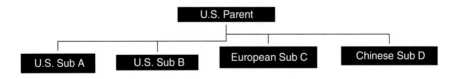

Exhibit 8.8 Parent-subsidiary relationships for Silicatec

Global case studies 201

Sub C's foreign currency exposure

Due to the extreme cyclical nature of the solar capital equipment industry, Sub C, Silicatec's European subsidiary, has realized significant profits in periods when customers are expanding capacity, however, they have realized significant losses for extended periods of time when Sub C's customers experienced significant under-utilization of their manufacturing capacity. The typical capital spending scenario of Sub C's customers has been one of overbuilding capacity, then filling that capacity over a period of several years.

During the 2013 through 2015 downturn in capital spending in the solar industry, Sub C has lost money and has depleted its cash reserves. Due to the extended downturn, they have also required periodic funding from Silicatec to remain liquid. They, therefore, have not been able to pay Silicatec for the shared services since 2014. Sub C's recent financial results have left them with very little external borrowing capacity.

Table 8.7 itemizes the recent history of Sub C's exposure to dollar-denominated assets and liabilities.

In reaction to the US dollar liability exposure in 2013 and 2014, Sub C converted available euro cash balances to US dollars, thus successfully hedging the exposure naturally. In 2015 and 2016, there were no euro cash balances available, therefore, Sub C is exposed to risk of foreign exchange gains and losses as the euro increases and decreases in value vs. the US dollar.

As noted above, given the prolonged downturn in demand for the equipment and services of Sub C, the following intercompany balances have accumulated on the balance sheet of Sub C. This intercompany balance is currently the main source of Sub C's exposure.

- Current liability (payable to the parent company) denominated in USD -$6.9 million

Sub C's annual charges for shared services are approximately $1.5 million. If the European subsidiary does not generate sufficient cash, then the current liability will grow by this amount each year. Due to the rapid growth in demand for solar energy, the upcycle of the solar industry is expected to be

Table 8.7 Sub C's foreign currency exposure (USD '000)

	12/31/2013	12/31/2014	12/31/2015	06/30/2016
Cash	$200	$100	$300	$100
Accounts Receivable	$200	$100	$100	$200
Accounts Payable	$(500)	$(500)	$(200)	$(400)
Intercompany Payable to Parent	$(1,000)	$(2,000)	$(5,900)	$(6,900)
Net Exposure USA Asset (Liab)	$(1,000)	$(2,300)	$(5,700)	$(7,000)

202 *Global case studies*

significant. Sub C expects to maintain and possibly increase its market share due to its recent successful development of equipment with leading edge technology.

Based on the current projections of Sub C, it is expected that they will generate adequate cash over the next 18 months to allow payment of $6 million of their liability to the parent company. These cash flow projections are based on the continuation of the current upcycle for at least 18 months. The capacity expansion of Sub C's customers is then expected to end, after which time the demand for Sub C's equipment will slow dramatically for a period of at least 12 months. Silicatec's cash management strategy is for the subsidiaries to maintain cash reserves locally in amounts that allow for expansion of the business as well as maintenance of reserves to locally fund the company's needs through the typical period of the solar industry's slowdown in capital spending.

As Sub C's sales volume grows, they need to finance the required increase in working capital (primarily inventory and accounts receivable). Given Sub C's business model, higher sales volumes do *not* generally require significant increases in capital spending, because a significant portion of production is outsourced.

It should be noted that Sub C's predictions of the timing, duration and magnitude of the up and down cycles of the solar industry have proven to be unreliable. Their foresight, as well as the foresight of expert trade publications serving the solar industry has not proven to be accurate. As a result, the forecast of generating significant cash over the next 18 months should be viewed with some skepticism.

As previously noted, Sub C does business worldwide, however, their selling prices are primarily negotiated in euros. The primary suppliers of Sub C are based in Europe, therefore purchase obligations are incurred primarily in euros.

- Since they generate and expend cash primarily in euros, Sub C's functional currency for accounting purposes is the euro.
- The functional currency of the Chicago-based parent company is the US dollar.
- Consolidated results of Silicatec are reported in US dollars.

Because Sub C has significant liabilities in a currency other than their functional currency, they are exposed to foreign currency gains and losses. As the exchange rate between the US dollar and the euro fluctuates, a gain or loss is recorded. As the euro declines in value versus the US dollar, the dollar-denominated liability grows. For example, if the exchange rate changes from $1.15 per euro to $1.00 per euro, the $6.9 million current liability grows from approximately €6.0 million to €6.9 million. This foreign currency loss of approximately €0.9 million or $1.0 million would result in an after-tax loss of approximately $0.85 million. Silicatec currently has approximately 13.0 million shares of common stock outstanding, therefore the foreign currency loss would reduce earnings per share of Silicatec by $0.065 per share.

Table 8.8 Historical price and earnings data

	2012	*2013*	*2014*	*2015*
Net Income (USD '000)	$9,500	$23,000	$5,000	$3,000
Shares Outstanding '000	12,700	12,800	12,900	13,000
Earnings per Share	$0.75	$1.80	$0.39	$0.23
Share Price	$11.00	$24.00	$5.00	$3.50
Price-Earnings Ratio	14.7	13.4	12.9	15.2

Table 8.9 Effect on share price of Euro decline

	2017 Sub C Projections		*Impact of*
	$1.15/€	*$1.00/€*	*Euro Decline*
Net Income (USD '000)	$10,005	$8,700	$(1,305)
Shares Outstanding '000	13,100	13,100	13,100
Earnings per Share–Sub C	$0.76	$0.66	$(0.10)
Share Price Impact			$1.50

Following is the recent history of Silicatec's earnings and share price. Based on the current expectations of potential growth, Silicatec's stock is commanding a multiple of approximately 15 times earnings (see Table 8.8). Therefore, a foreign exchange loss of $0.065 per share would have the effect of reducing Silicatec's share price by approximately $0.98 per share.

In addition to the foreign currency transaction exposure, Silicatec bears the risk that a decline in the value of the euro versus the US dollar would result in lower earnings. As the profits of Sub C are translated into US dollars for consolidated financial reporting purposes, the euro-based profits would translate to fewer US dollars, thus reducing Silicatec's earnings per share.

Based on current projections, Sub C is expected to earn approximately €8.7 million after tax in 2017. As illustrated below, the depreciation of the euro from $1.15 to $1.00 would result in a decline in earnings per share of $0.10. Assuming a price-earnings ratio of 15, the impact on the price of Silicatec's shares would be nearly $1.50 per share (see Table 8.9).

Silicatec's Corporate Director of Finance is evaluating alternatives for hedging Sub C's US dollar liability exposure. Following are some factors being considered:

- Is the exposure large enough to hedge?
- If so, what hedge instruments are appropriate?
- What contract period would be appropriate?
- Should the hedge be entered into by Silicatec or Sub C?
- Should the company retain the opportunity to profit from the increase in value of the euro vs. the US dollar?
- What are the risks of each hedge instrument?

204   *Global case studies*

- Under what circumstances could the company be required to come up with cash to settle the foreign exchange contract?
- If Sub C does not generate adequate cash to settle the contract, would Silicatec then be obligated to settle the contract.
- Does Silicatec want to assume this risk?

In deciding the most appropriate course of action, the Director of Finance is considering the following input from the board of directors and corporate management:

- As discussed, Sub C's forecast of generating significant cash over the next 18 months should be viewed with some skepticism. The decision must take into consideration the risk that Sub C may not have adequate cash to settle the contract.
- The level of risk that the board of directors will tolerate is a foreign exchange loss of approximately $0.03 per share.
- It would be preferable to retain the potential for some level of foreign exchange gains in the event the euro rallies vs. the dollar, provided that this does not have a significant cost.

One hedge instrument being considered is a simple forward contract which would allow Silicatec to lock in an exchange rate that approximates the current euro-to-dollar exchange rate. At the point in time that the contract is being considered, the cost of such a contract is nominal, because the premium on selling euros forward is insignificant. Locking in the current exchange rate precludes the company from participating in the benefits of a stronger euro should that happen.

Another hedge instrument being considered is a simple collar. The structure of the simple collar under consideration allows for a specified level of protection while retaining a similar potential for realizing some upside in the event of appreciation of the euro during the forward contract period. The structure of the simple collar is as follows:

- Buy a put option
  - The strike price will be set to limit the exposure to a tolerable level, protecting against the decline in value of the euro.
  - A premium will be paid for this protection.
- Sell a call option
  - The premium earned on the call option offsets the premium paid for the put option, making the collar a zero-cost alternative.
  - The strike price of the call option limits the upside potential in the event of a euro rally, however the company may participate in the benefits of a stronger euro, up to a defined exchange rate.

Global case studies 205

As a hypothetical example, when the spot exchange rate is $1.15 per euro, the strike price of the put option could be $1.12 while the strike price of the call option could be $1.18. In this case, Sub C remains exposed, but the exposure is limited. As a reminder, Sub C's exposure relates to US dollar-denominated liabilities, therefore, they will be converting euros to dollars.

- Foreign exchange losses on the current liability would be recognized when the euro declines in value. These losses are limited.
- Below $1.12, the put option protects Sub C from further losses.
- Foreign exchange gains would be recognized on the current liability when the euro increases in value up to $1.18.
- Above $1.18, the call option limits Sub C's potential for further foreign exchange gains.

Based upon the board of directors' preference to retain some upside potential, the Director of Finance is recommending hedging $7.0 million of Sub C's current liability exposure through a simple collar foreign exchange contract. The terms of the put and call include a range of $1.12 to $1.18 and a contract period of 18 months.

Additionally, the Director of Finance is recommending a similar simple collar instrument to protect the value of projected 2017 earnings. This hedge will limit erosion of earnings in the event the euro declines significantly, while it allows limited participation in the event the euro increases in value vs. the US dollar.

Questions for discussion

1 Should the company hedge its exposure to current intercompany dollar-denominated liabilities?
2 Should the company hedge its exposure to potential erosion of future profits generated by Sub C?
3 What hedging instruments would be advisable for each exposure?
   a   Current intercompany liability
   b   Future profits
4 What are the risks in entering into a zero-cost simple collar?
5 What are the advantages and disadvantages of each hedging instrument?
6 How should the company determine the appropriate range for a collar?

Lilly Pharmaceuticals: triple bottom line and values-based leadership

Joseph A. Petrick, Wright State University, USA

Lilly Pharmaceuticals is the tenth largest corporation by global pharmaceutical sales and was founded in May 1876 by Colonel Eli Lilly in Indianapolis, Indiana

206   *Global case studies*

in the United States. As a 38-year-old pharmaceutical chemist and a veteran of the U.S. Civil War, Colonel Lilly was frustrated by the poorly prepared, often ineffective medicines of his day. Consequently, he made the following three commitments to himself and to society: (1) he would found a company that manufactured pharmaceutical products of the highest possible quality; (2) his company would develop only medicines that would be dispensed at the suggestion of physicians rather than hucksters; and (3) his company would be based on the best science of the day.

Colonel Lilly and his pharmaceutical chemists laid the foundation for the Lilly tradition: a dedication that first concentrated on the quality of existing products and later expanded to include the discovery and development of new and better pharmaceuticals. Eventually, Colonel Lilly's son, Josiah K. Lilly Sr., and two grandsons, Eli Lilly and Josiah K. Lilly Jr., each served as president of the company, and each contributed a distinctive approach to responsible management of the firm. Even after the first non-family member became firm president in 1953 up to the present CEO, John C. Lechleiter, the Lilly tradition of responsibly implementing the company vision, mission and values has continued. The company vision is to make a significant contribution to humanity by improving global health in the future. The company mission is to make medicines that help people live longer, healthier, more active lives. The company values are integrity, excellence, and respect for people. In doing so, they upheld family honor and company values, while addressing the triple bottom line of respect for people, profits, and planet domestically and globally.

Triple bottom line: people

Lilly addresses the triple bottom line of respect for people by focusing on three stakeholder groups: customers, employees and communities. Lilly Pharmaceuticals currently conducts clinical research in more than 55 countries and has manufacturing plants in 13 countries. It has research and development facilities in six countries and products marketed in 120 countries. Lilly has four major product line divisions focused on human health needs: bio-medicines, diabetes, oncology, and emerging markets. First, Lilly Bio-Medicines represents the largest of Lilly's five business areas in terms of sales, and accounts for nearly half of Lilly's mid-to-late stage pipeline assets. This business unit is unique in that it focuses on multiple therapeutic areas. Unlike Lilly's other business areas, such as Lilly Diabetes or Lilly Oncology that focus exclusively on one therapeutic area, Lilly Bio-Medicines is diversified and includes the therapeutic areas of neuroscience, cardiovascular, urology, musculoskeletal and auto-immunity. Bio-Medicines is also home to Lilly's global marketing organization and Lilly's PRA (pricing, reimbursement, and access) function, which are leading development of capabilities, solutions and tools to ensure that all Lilly divisions deliver unparalleled customer experiences. Second, Lilly Diabetes remains committed to meeting the needs of people with diabetes from medicines to support programs, including investments in one of the world's

Global case studies 207

largest clinical diabetes pipelines. Third, Lilly Oncology is one of the top ten oncology companies in the world, focusing on speeding innovation and improving outcomes for individual patients, and boasts one of the largest clinical pipelines in the oncology industry. Fourth, Lilly Emerging Markets works to deliver innovative medicines that address unmet human health needs around the world. More than 6,000 employees in 30 Lilly affiliates work across the 70 countries that make up Lilly's Emerging Markets business. Lilly Pharmaceuticals has historically distinguished itself in the industry by having a high percentage of permanent research staff, inventing superior techniques for the mass production of medicinal drugs, and relentlessly focusing on quality at all stages.

These concerted efforts have resulted over the years in a remarkable number of milestones in medical research and profitable health care products. Lilly was one of the first companies to initiate a bona-fide pharmaceutical research program in the 1880s. In the 1920s Lilly collaboratively isolated and purified insulin for the treatment of diabetes, introducing Iletin, the world's first commercially available insulin product. Lilly also collaboratively introduced a new liver-extract product that served as a standard of therapy for anemia for decades, garnering its collaborators a shared Nobel Prize for the discovery of liver therapy against anemias. In the 1940s, Lilly was among the first companies to develop a method to mass-produce penicillin, the world's first antibiotic, marking the beginning of a sustained effort to fight infectious diseases. In the 1950s, the company introduced vancomycin, a powerful antibiotic that remains the last line of defense for patients suffering from serious hospital infections associated with certain types of resistant bacteria. Lilly also launched erythromycin, an antibiotic whose broad antimicrobial spectrum expands the alternatives for penicillin-allergic patients. In the 1960s, Lilly launched the first of a long line of oral and injectable antibiotics in a new class called cephalosporins. The company also introduced vincristine and vinblastine, anticancer drugs known as vinca alkaloids that are derived from the rosy periwinkle plant. In the 1970s, Ceclor®, a member of the cephalosporin family, was launched and eventually became the world's top-selling oral antibiotic. Lilly also introduced Dobutrex®, an innovative and lifesaving cardiovascular product. In the 1980s, the most significant breakthrough in diabetes care since the 1920s was marked by Lilly's 1982 introduction of Humulin® insulin identical to that produced by the human body. Humulin is the world's first human-health-care product created using recombinant DNA technology. Lilly later applied this technology to the introduction of Humatrope®, a new therapy for growth hormone deficiency in children. Lilly also launched Prozac®, the first major introduction in a new class of drugs for treatment of clinical depression. In the 1990s Lilly introduced a stream of innovative new products: Gemzar®, a drug for the treatment of pancreatic and non-small-cell lung cancer; ReoPro®, a cardiovascular drug that prevents blood clots following certain heart procedures, such as angioplasty; Zyprexa®, now the world's top-selling antipsychotic for the treatment of schizophrenia and Lilly's best-selling drug; Humalog®, a

208 *Global case studies*

fast-acting insulin product that offers greater dosing convenience to improve blood-sugar control; and Evista®, the first of a new class of drugs to be used for the prevention and treatment of postmenopausal osteoporosis. In 1999, Takeda Chemical Industries, Ltd. and Lilly successfully launched Actos®, an oral antidiabetes agent. In the 2000s Lilly launched another first-in-class product, Xigris®, for the treatment of severe sepsis in adult patients with a high risk of death. In 2002, Cialis®, a medication to treat male erectile dysfunction, was approved for marketing in the European Union; the U.S. launch followed in 2004. Forteo®, a first-in-class medicine for osteoporosis patients to stimulate new bone formation, also was approved. Strattera®, a non-stimulant, non-controlled medication to treat attention-deficit hyperactivity disorder received approval. In 2004, Cymbalta® was approved as a new treatment for major depressive disorder and diabetic peripheral neuropathic pain. In 2007, the FDA approved osteoporosis drug, Evista®, to reduce the risk of invasive breast cancer in two populations of postmenopausal women: women with osteoporosis and women at high risk for invasive breast cancer. In 2009, Effient® was approved by the FDA for the reduction of thrombotic cardiovascular events (including stent thrombosis) in patients with acute coronary syndromes.

These selected Lilly medicines and others have saved and/or improved millions of lives domestically and globally over the years.

In addition, Lilly addresses respect for employees by providing competitive compensation and maintaining an effective ethics and compliance system designed to meet external requirements and sustain an ethical work culture, guided by its three core values:

- *Integrity* – We conduct our business consistent with all applicable laws and are honest in our dealings with customers, employees, shareholders, partners, suppliers, competitors, and the community.
- *Excellence* – We pursue pharmaceutical innovation, provide high quality products, and strive to deliver superior business results. We continually search for new ways to improve everything we do.
- *Respect for People* – We maintain an environment built on mutual respect, openness, and individual integrity. Respect for people includes our concern for all people who touch or are touched by our company: customers, employees, shareholders, partners, suppliers and communities.

The institutionalization of an organizational ethics system at Lilly also includes the following components: (1) an appointed Chief Ethics and Compliance Officer (ECO) who has the ability to lead change within the organization and is responsible for developing, operating, and monitoring the compliance and ethics system. The Chief ECO reports directly to the Lilly Chief Executive Officer and to the Public Policy and Compliance Committee of the Board of Directors, with the advice of the Enterprise Risk Management Committee to assist in the implementation of the ethics and compliance system; (2) written standards contained in *The Red Book* which directs management and employees of the company globally to act in accordance with laws, other regulatory requirements, and applicable company policies. Lilly also provides for its employees more detailed policies, standards and procedures that establish expectations for ethical and compliant behavior. *The Red Book* includes references to company policies that apply globally, as well as examples to illustrate application of *The Red Book* principles; (3) ongoing training and education of employees on the application of the core Lilly values, and individual obligations under applicable legal requirements and company policies. Lilly trains all its employees on *The Red Book*, including its content and application to daily activities. Lilly also provides targeted training in key risk areas to those employees whose job functions are affected by those risk areas; (4) providing open lines of communication for reporting unethical actions available to employees 24 hours a day, 7 days a week, domestically and globally, while protecting individuals from retribution; (5) regular monitoring, assessment and response to unethical and non-compliant behavior with appropriate disciplinary actions; (6) annual auditing of system effectiveness with reports provided for continual improvement. In addition to imposing appropriate disciplinary action, the company also assesses whether a violation may be due in part to gaps in Lilly's policies, training, business practices, or other controls. If so, the company is committed to implementing corrective measures to enhance its controls to prevent further violations.

Lilly also addresses respect for communities through a wide variety of social responsibility initiatives including: (1) The Eli Lilly and Company Foundation which is a tax-exempt private charitable foundation established by the company in 1968. The Foundation awards cash grants for philanthropic initiatives aligned with the company's corporate responsibility priorities. Specifically, the Foundation is dedicated to improving the lives of people who lack the resources to obtain quality health care, with a primary focus on low and middle-income countries and strengthening public education in the United States, with an emphasis on science and math education; (2) significant partnership with United Way to leverage social assistance to local, regional and national communities; (3) Lilly matches employee donations to educational institutions, cultural organizations and select healthcare charities in the U.S., as well as various international non-profits through the partnership with Global Giving. In 2014, matching donations equaled \$6.2 million; (4) the Lilly NCD Partnership is the company's response to the rising burden of non-communicable diseases (NCDs) in economically developing countries. Through this partnership, Lilly is working to find new solutions to diabetes care for people living in impoverished communities; (5) the Lilly MDR-TB Partnership is focused on hard-to-treat tuberculosis, or multidrug-resistant tuberculosis (MDR-TB), which disproportionately afflicts people living in poverty; (6) Lilly offers a number of social programs that help patients and their families as they cope with disease, sickness and the healing process. This includes a broad number of programs, such as Lilly Cares, which helps people living in the U.S. who cannot afford or don't have access to Lilly medicines, and the

210   *Global case studies*

Lilly Oncology on Canvas program, which helps people who have been affected by cancer express their journeys through art; (7) Lilly provides many types of scholarships. For example, over the past 15 years, the Lilly Reintegration Scholarships, have assisted students living with mental illness by directing more than $4 million to cover their tuition, lab fees, and books at nearly 350 schools across the United States. The program specifically benefits individuals living with schizophrenia, schizoaffective disorder, bipolar disorder or major depressive disorder who wish to attain a certificate or degree from an accredited institution to help them secure employment and reintegrate into society; and (8) the Lilly Endowment, established in 1937, is a private charitable foundation supported by gifts of Lilly stock to advance the company mission. In 1998 it became the largest philanthropic endowment in the world in terms of assets and charitable giving and still remains in the top ten.

Triple bottom line: profits

Lilly addresses the triple bottom line of respect for profits by successfully being in the pharmaceutical business for around 140 years. Over that period of time it has faced numerous profit challenges and not only survived but thrived. From the latest annual report in 2015, the following public financial information was provided (in US dollars in millions, except per share data): (1) net sales – $19,958.7; (2) net income – $2,408.4; (3) earnings per share – $2.26; and (4) dividends paid per share – $2.00.

As of March 31, 2016, Lilly Pharmaceuticals employs 41,500 people at competitive salaries and benefits, 23,418 of which are outside the United States. Local and state wages are also generated by employing 10,975 in Indianapolis and an additional 1,231 in the state of Indiana (excluding Indianapolis).

The 2015 reported Lilly research and development (R&D) expenditures in U. S. dollars were $4,796 million/year. That amount was 24% of sales in the six countries that have Lilly R&D facilities. In accord with its values, 21% of its employees are directly involved in R&D activities, which amounted to over 8,800 activities domestically and globally in 2015.

Lilly Pharmaceuticals has also been vigorously engaged in anti-counterfeiting of medicinal drugs domestically and globally. Counterfeit drugs are produced and distributed by global criminal networks, and counterfeits have been reported in all major therapeutic areas, in all major geographies, and in more than 100 countries. Counterfeit drug sales generated an estimated $200 billion in illicit profits in one year alone. The internet is contributing to the problem, creating an anonymous, global marketplace for the counterfeit drug trade. Nearly 97% of online drug sellers are not legitimate. Furthermore, 62% of medicines purchased online are fake or substandard.

In addition to cooperating with domestic and global law enforcement and government regulatory agencies to stop counterfeiting, Lilly has also adopted its own quality, security, financial liability, and accountability measures including serialization of its products. Serialization is the term used to describe the unique identification of individual packs (cartons or bottles) of medications. As each batch of finished product is packaged, a globally unique code is assigned and physically marked on the packaging in the form of a two-dimensional code known as a datamatrix. At the conclusion of the packaging order, the serial numbers are electronically linked to the product's batch number in Lilly's global SAP environment. To track and trace the movement of individual packs, serial numbers can be recorded and electronically linked to outbound deliveries to customers. This is a regulatory requirement in some countries, where a documented chain of custody is further established by requiring wholesalers and pharmacies to record shipments and receipts of serialized products. Serialization not only helps secure the legitimate supply chain, but offers other potential benefits. These include automated checking of expiration dates, a way to record the batch number of specific medicines in a patient's electronic medical records, and other tools that offer value to patients and healthcare providers who serve them.

Triple bottom line: planet

Lilly is committed to continuously improving its policies and practices with respect to environmental responsibility. Lilly achieved its environmental management goals initially proposed in 2008 for best-in-class performance in the industry, using a base year of 2007. These goals included: improving energy efficiency and reducing associated greenhouse gases 15% by 2013; reducing waste-to-landfill 40% by 2013, with the ultimate goal of zero landfill; and reducing water intake 25% by 2013. Lilly has continued to focus on implementing cost-effective technologies and solutions to increase work efficiency and minimize environmental impacts with new 2020 goals including: improving energy efficiency by 20%; reducing greenhouse gas emissions by another 20% (i.e., reduce waste generation per unit of production) and measurably increasing recycling; and reducing phosphorus emissions to wastewater by 15%. Achieving the new environmental goals would also mean an estimated $175 million in savings.

Lilly uses a variety of leading edge environmental practices to achieve these goals, including: energy efficiency practices, design for process safety; product stewardship; green chemistry for source reduction; cross-functional use of lean six sigma; and sustainable packaging. First, since 2006, Lilly has invested nearly $18 million in 44 energy conservation projects that are delivering $10 million in annual savings. Successful energy efficiency projects include cogeneration, lighting management systems, and high-efficiency chiller systems. Second, Lilly designed and developed its Globally Integrated Process Safety Management System that goes beyond regulatory compliance by addressing hazardous processes from the design stage, during start-up, and throughout their operating life to ensure material containment. Third, Lilly developed a Product Stewardship Standard to prevent potential health, safety, and environmental

212   *Global case studies*

(HSE) disruptions along a product's value chain from initial discovery to disposal and assigning responsibility for managing HSE aspects across each value chain functional group. Fourth, by applying green chemistry techniques like using less hazardous alternative materials at the outset or employing new synthetic chemistry ingredients to reduce chemical process mass intensity (PMI), the ratio of material used per unit of active pharmaceutical ingredient produced is increased. A recent green chemistry process improvement for a product designed to treat anxiety and depression reduced hazardous waste material usage by more than 80%, saving more than three million kilograms of raw materials and six million liters of water per year at peak production. Fifth, by applying lean six sigma as a core cross-functional business tool to reduce statistical variation in processes, laboratory wastes have been minimized, emissions have been more exactly monitored and controlled, and a container recycling process established. Sixth, pharmaceutical packaging is critical to ecologically fulfilling many standards – providing information, resisting counterfeiting, meeting government regulations, and protecting against tampering or access by children. Lilly's innovative sustainable packaging approaches saved more than $14 million by reducing packaging mass and improving productivity.

Furthermore, a global division of Lilly, Elanco, demonstrates the company's deep commitment to another dimension of environmental responsibility – caring for animals. Elanco works to develop and market products that improve general animal health, protein production, and companion animal health and food safety in more than 75 countries across the globe.

Questions for discussion

1   Why has it been useful for Lilly Pharmaceuticals (or any corporation) to rely on its core values to address triple bottom line standards?
2   What are the costs and benefits of Lilly's ethics and compliance system to its internal and external stakeholders?
3   How has meeting Lilly's social and environmental responsibilities contributed to or detracted from meeting its economic responsibilities?
4   How would a new takeover CEO at Lilly Pharmaceuticals who wanted to eliminate corporate expenditures on social and environmental responsibilities and focus instead only on economic growth likely affect future corporate success?
5   Why would you or your family members want to work or not to work at Lilly Pharmaceuticals today?

References

Eli Lilly and Company Official Web Site (http://www.lilly.com/)
Madison, James H. (1989). *Eli Lilly: A Life, 1885–1977*. Indianapolis, IN: Indiana Historical Society

Loderhose, Gary (2001). *Legendary Hoosiers: Famous Folks from the State of Indiana*. Indianapolis, IN: Emmis Books.

Savitz, A. and Weber, K. (2006). *The Triple Bottom Line*. San Francisco: Jossey-Bass.

International real estate investor

G. Jason Goddard

On a hot and humid day in June after a long, boring presentation about internal performance metrics, an investment real estate lender's phone rings. "You have a group of investors who would like to discuss current loan terms with you," says the familiar voice on the line. "Please come down to the fifth floor and we can discuss. By the way, one investor is from Canada and the other is from Brazil." During the elevator ride downstairs, the lender thinks about how this conversation might go as he rarely deals with international real estate investors. "I wonder why they are interested in investing in the United States rather than in their home markets," he thinks to himself as the elevator doors open.

In the lobby stand three individuals. The first is a current customer from California who is brokering this transaction, while the second and third individuals are the foreign investors. Once in the conference room, the broker shares that he has been touring the local market with these new investors as they are interested in moving their money to the United States, and specifically to your home market, as the property values locally are much lower than what they have seen in their home markets. "As prices back home have increased, it is much more difficult to find a reasonably priced investment," the broker explains. The primary connection between these three individuals is cultural. The California broker is originally from Portugal, as are the Canadian and Brazilian investors.

"Twenty years ago, Jose came to me with money to invest from the sale of his dairy farm in Quebec," the broker continues. "Carlos has not invested with me before but his brother has." During the first few minutes of the meeting, the broker shares the various properties that he has shown the investors over the last few days. "We are interested in apartment properties as an investment, given the large increases in population in your state over the last ten years. When we compare the property values for apartments in this market with those back home, our money goes a lot further in your market than where we had traditionally invested. The property that we are interested in purchasing is an apartment where the loan is part of a mortgage-backed security, and there is a substantial pre-payment penalty should the seller wish to pay defeasance on the loan. The rate is fixed at 5.80%, but the pre-payment penalty burns off in one year," the broker continues.

"What have you done to compare prices between your home market and here locally?" asks the lender.

"The prices are so low here, we feel like we can spread our money over more investments than if we purchased properties at home," Carlos explains.

214 *Global case studies*

All goes well until the subject of loan pricing arises. "What would be the interest rate that you would charge me to finance this property should we close today with your bank?" the Canadian investor inquires.

"Right now we are looking at fixed rates around 4.50%," the lender responds.

"In Canada, I am only paying an interest rate of 3.25%, why are your rates so high?"

The lender responds by saying, "Interest rates have moved up by forty basis points over the last few weeks. Also it is hard to compare the interest rates from one country to another, as the rates are set domestically based on the expectations of inflation and also based on how well the economy is doing."

"In Canada, I can also get a better savings rate than what you offer," Jose exclaims.

"Well, we have recently come out of a large recession in the United States, and the Federal Reserve responded to that crisis by pumping large sums of new money into the economy. This led to lower interest rates over the last few years, but as quantitative easing has wound down, rates will tend to increase," says the lender.

"The rates are much higher in Brazil than what you have in the United States!" exclaims the Brazilian investor. "It makes sense to me that the difference in lending rates between the US and Brazil reflect the differences in inflation in both countries."

"What is the current inflation rate in Canada, Jose?" asks the broker.

"I am not sure, but I do not think it is very high," Jose responds.

"Given where the US exchange rate is, it does not make sense for the US to increase interest rates right now," the Canadian investor continues. "Why would the US increase their interest rates, as this will only slow down the economy?"

"Let's check the current inflation levels for the US, Canada and Brazil per the latest *Economist*," says the lender. "The current inflation rate is 0.40% in the US, 1.1% in Canada, and 7.9% in Brazil."

"What is the inflation rate in Portugal?" asks the broker.

"I don't see them listed on the page, but Spain is showing inflation of -0.4%, and believe it or not, Greece is showing an inflation rate of -0.9%" responds the lender.

"That is now but recently they were much higher," responds the Canadian investor. "Why would Portugal invest in Greece when they already had too much debt?" he asks.

"It would seem that investors in Portugal were attracted by the high returns in Greece, and knew that somehow Germany would make things right," exclaims the lender.

Exhibit 8.9 summarizes the data reviewed by the group in *The Economist*.

The discussion concluded with the lender mentioning the Fisher effect and the difference between real and nominal interest rates. "When you are looking at the rates on the screen, those are nominal rates, but if you adjust for expected

Global case studies   215

	GDP %	Prices %	Current Acc % of GDP	Govt Budget % of GDP	10 year Gov't Debt
United States	2.30%	0.40%	−2.40%	−2.50%	2.42%
Canada	1.80%	1.10%	−2.80%	−2.80%	1.91%
Brazil	−1.10%	7.90%	−4.10%	−5.50%	12.69%
Spain	2.70%	−0.40%	0.50%	0.50%	2.38%
Greece	1.40%	−0.90%	−0.90%	2.70%	11.64%
Germany	1.00%	0.50%	6.70%	0.70%	0.98%

Exhibit 8.9 Economic data from *The Economist* June 13, 2015 pg. 88

inflation, this is what leads to the real rate of interest. Depending on how strong a given country is economically, as shown indirectly in their exchange rate, this has an effect on the rate of interest offered in a given country," the lender explains.

"If I was to send you CDN $1 million today, how much would you give me?" asks the Canadian investor.

"It depends on what the exchange rate is today," responds the lender.

"Your bank in Canada will make the translation for you," says the broker. "That way when the funds arrive in the US bank they are already in US dollars."

"Your bank in Canada will charge you a fee, just like we would if the transaction was reversed," says the lender.

"My bank in Canada gives me an annual return on my deposits of 0.40%, but if I was to hold US dollars in the Canadian bank, they would only give me 0.25%," says the Canadian investor.

Everyone agrees that the depository rates in both locations are not very good and that they are also spurring investors to seek alternative forms of investment in the first place.

"I have CDN $900,000 spread over 4 banks in Quebec, but the returns that I am getting are not very good," says the Canadian investor. "I am seeking a nice apartment in a good location at a reasonable price, and the apartments that I am looking at are providing an annual return of from 6.00% to 8.00%."

The Brazilian investor smiles and then says, "If you are getting an 8.00% return but paying the lender 4.50%, you are doing pretty well."

"True," says the Canadian investor, "but I would be doing even better if the bank lending rate was 3.00%!"

"Everything is relative, Carlos," the lender exclaims. "If you assume the mortgage on the subject property for the next year, our current rate today will look pretty good relative to the 5.80% rate of interest that you will be paying for the next year! Of course, rates are expected to rise, so it may be unwise to wait a year to lock in your rate," the lender explains.

"I think we must assume the loan otherwise there is a $140,000 pre-payment penalty that must be paid. If the seller has to pay this defeasance fee, then the price of the property will increase," the broker responds.

216 *Global case studies*

Exhibit 8.10 shows a 30-year historical view of interest rates which was alluded to by the lender in the meeting. Based on this chart, rates look likely to increase over the near term.

The meeting closes with the lender requesting financial information on the investment being considered for purchase, along with the personal financial information for both investors. On the elevator ride back to his office, he wonders if he adequately explained why interest rates vary from country to country. Another thought that enters the lender's mind concerns the subjectivity of value. The international investors seem enamored with local market values, but lower prices don't always translate into a better deal. The lender remembers taking a course on Austrian economics in college, and when he returns to his office, he quickly reviews his notes from a speech that he attended at the local chamber of commerce on subjectivity in value. This is the perfect opportunity to use some of this information, the lender thinks. These investors aren't even questioning the property values and are moving straight to the interest rate question.

Below are samples of what the lender reviews from handouts from the presentation.

Menger contribution

The subjectivity in value owes its origin to Austrian economist Carl Menger, among others. Menger envisioned trade occurring when two parties exchange for items whereby they feel that the item obtained is of higher value to them than the item exchanged. Individuals may value a particular good for its use (i.e. an owner occupied property) or its exchange potential (i.e. a series of rental homes). If a good is valued higher for its use than for its exchange, the individual is more likely to retain that particular item. From a commercial real estate perspective, an investor may hold a property that others covet, but the current owner may have a desire to retain the asset owing to the cash flow being received from the property, or some other factor. This is not to say that a future price (or sales offer) might not change the individual's perception whereby the property is more readily sold than retained. This subjective ranking depends on the relative satisfaction that a given item provides to its owner. The following illustration was adapted from Menger to illustrate the individual satisfaction rankings whereby trade might occur:

As shown in Exhibit 8.11, the higher ranked a good is, the more satisfaction is provided to the owner. For our purposes, the salient points in this nascent theory of value subjectivity are that value is related to the person making the assessment, and that the value of a given object is not immutable and can change with circumstances and time. In our real estate example, a given property could be valued for its use until such time as this use is exceeded in value by another good, whereby exchange occurs.

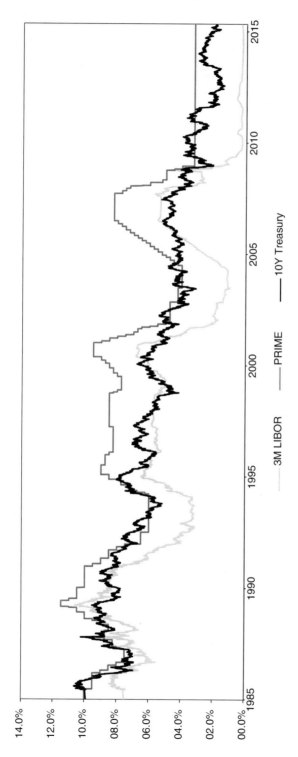

Exhibit 8.10 30-year views for 3-Month LIBOR, prime rate and 10-Year US Treasuries as of April 17, 2015 (data from Wells Fargo Securities via Bloomberg)

218 *Global case studies*

Good I	Good II	Good III	Good IV	Good V	Good VI	Good VII	Good VIII	Good IX	Good X
10	9	8	7	6	5	4	3	2	1
9	8	7	6	5	4	3	2	1	0
8	7	6	5	4	3	2	1	0	
7	6	5	4	3	2	1	0		
6	5	4	3	2	1	0			
5	4	3	2	1	0				
4	3	2	1	0					
3	2	1	0						
2	1	0							
1	0								
0									

Exhibit 8.11 Menger satisfaction scale (Menger, 1871 (Original German), English 1971)

Notes:
Goods ranked 10 are things on which life depends
Goods ranked 9-0 are less and less important
If Good I is food and Good V is tobacco, tobacco is desired once need for food is satisfied whereby future consumption would only register as a 6 on the importance scale.
Trade occurs when two parties exchange for items where they feel item obtained is higher than item exchanged

Radical subjectivism

The foundations of Menger were followed more recently by the radical subjectivist school of Austrian economic thought. Subjectivism is a research program of the social sciences which aims at elucidating social phenomena in terms of their inherent meaning to individual actors. In this context, even when different actors possess an identical knowledge about the same object, they will not necessarily make the same use of it since knowledge exists for each actor within a different frame of reference. Thus, the past differs for each actor whereby different weights are applied when making value judgments. Additionally, different actors will hold divergent expectations about the same future events. Ludwig Lachmann, a leading advocate of the radical subjectivist approach, stated that "in a world of unexpected change, investment is necessarily governed by expectation, not past results". The past is important as it provides us with points of comparison that make our present problems intelligible to us. Lachmann believed that we are living in a "kaleidic society interspersing its moments or intervals of order, assurance, and beauty with sudden disintegration" which will then "cascade into a new pattern".

Given these divergent patterns, "equilibrium analysis is hard to apply where the dependent variables of the system take a long time to respond to changes in data occurring frequently". One could venture to assume that this view lends credence to the idea that the value of a given object can vary depending on who is doing the valuing. In a recent study in the *Quarterly Journal of Austrian*

Economics, the subjectivity of value was discussed in light of appraisal theory utilizing the income approach. In that study, it was highlighted how the principle of subjectivity can affect the interest rate applied for discounting purposes, as well as the projected future benefits of a given investment option.

If subjectivity and objectivity is viewed as a spectrum, the radical subjectivists were very close to considering valuation an entirely subjective exercise. Other schools of valuation, such as the Physiocrats from 18th-century France, considered valuation to be almost entirely objective in that the cost of the goods equated to their value. For most market participants, valuation contains both objective and subjective elements, but the location on the spectrum will typically lie between these two outliers from history.

These thoughts lead us directly to the current situation: to illustrate how subtle value judgments can sway the final valuation whereby a range of possible values could represent a given property. What remains is the inclusion of a somewhat obscure Austrian economic model that helps illustrate a range in potential values.

Shackle possibility curve

The work of George Lennox Sharmin Shackle further contributed to our understanding of why human minds might differ on issues of valuation. Shackle, an English economist, spent considerable time in illustrating that the future is unknowable, given the actions of other market participants which may or may not resemble patterns of the past. Shackle conceived "time to come as the void needing to be filled by work of imagination using suggested elements but not bound as to their arrangement". In other words, as we have heard on countless investment marketing campaigns, past performance is not necessarily indicative of future results. Shackle believed that any choice involves valuation and that "we are prisoners of the present who must choose in the present on the basis of our present knowledge, judgments, and assessments". The past is helpful for interpreting present decisions, but often there exists a knowledge gap given the presence of other actors and variables which remain outside the control of the decision maker. Shackle called this knowledge gap "un-knowledge" that "liberates imagination which seizes and occupies the void of time to come". Enterprising individuals embrace "un-knowledge" whereby innovation is possible given a plurality of possible outcomes.

Therefore Shackle stated that the "process of valuation is beyond the reach of analysis by any apparatus which the formal theoretician as such disposes of". This reminds one of a quote from JK Galbraith, certainly not an Austrian economist: "the only function of financial forecasting is to make astrology look respectable". The Shackle possibility curve (our term) helps illustrate why this is the case.

The graph in Exhibit 8.12 depicts the situation facing anyone needing to make a choice for a given problem in the present. Let us assume for our purposes, that G_N on the graph above represents the initial neutral position for someone evaluating a commercial real estate property. The entirety of the graph represents all of the possible value choices that might exist for a given situation. The G axis represents "desired-ness" such that the individual's prior experience is perfectly suited in making the present decision. In Shackle terminology, no "un-knowledge" exists. Even in this perfect (unrealistic) situation, there can be present shocks that might cause the near term path which is entirely predictable by the recent past to veer off course. In the context of this case, un-knowledge is present as the investors are straying outside of their home markets when evaluating properties for purchase.

The Y axis represents disbelief, such that the further up the Y axis you venture, the larger the gap is between the chooser's existing knowledge and the theoretical leap needed to reach a particular choice. The wider this gap (or un-knowledge) is, the more there is for variability in choice. Y_0 represents perfect possibility in the judgment of the investor, or where the individual feels that they have all the necessary information to make a rational choice. represents perfect possibility, which sets the upper limit on the amount of un-knowledge that is seen as being too great for a pathway (or choice) to be selected. Thus the variability in response to a given choice is dependent upon the gap between the decision maker's knowledge and the knowledge required to make an informed choice. Temporary shocks, or "news from the field" in Shackle's terminology are positive (Y_G) or negative (Y_L) information which may sway the decision maker from the initial G_N position. For example, in the aftermath of the financial crisis, investors may have been much more risk averse when valuing investment properties than before the crisis as there was a lack of knowledge concerning which tenants could withstand the recession. A positive shock could be the willingness to accept more risk given the desire to obtain a good return for the investor in an otherwise lackluster yield environment.

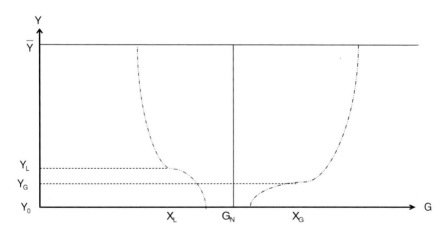

Exhibit 8.12 Shackle possibility curve (Shackle, 1966, 1969, 1970, & 1979)

Global case studies 221

These shocks, when combined with the decision maker's existing knowledge base and their risk tolerance, help set points X_L and X_G on the graph above. These points help determine the boundaries of acceptability for the investor. This boundary of acceptability reveals itself in the marketplace in the range of possible values for a given property.

The preceding discussion has illustrated that Austrian economic thought can teach us interesting things about valuation differences regardless of the overall economic circumstances. The lender realizes that this information, if conveyed appropriately, could aid the international real estate investors in their search for good deals in his local market.

Once his review of the Austrian economics material is complete, the lender decides to call his International Finance professor from college to see how close he came to doing justice to the academic theories of **interest rate parity**, the **Fisher effect**, and the **subjectivity of value**.

Questions for discussion

1   Research Interest Rate Parity and the International Fisher Effect. Explain in your own words what these theories have to say about the differences in interest rates in different countries.
2   What feedback do you think the Professor had for the Lender regarding his explanation to the international real estate investors?
3   How can the lender explain the subjectivity of value to the international real estate investors so that they can make more informed investment decisions?
4   What suggestions do you have for the lender in better explaining this situation?
5   What advice would you give the international real estate investors?

References

Economist, The. 2015. Economic Data from June 13, p. 88.

Fisher, I. 1928. *The Money Illusion*, Adelphi Company Publishers, New York.

Goddard, G. Jason. 2014. Kierkegaard and Valuation in a Business Context. *Business and Economics Journal* 5(2).

Hayek, F. A. 2014. *The Sensory Order*. Martino Publishing, Mansfield Centre.

Herbener, Jeffrey M., and David J. Rapp. 2016. Toward a Subjective Approach to Investment Appraisal in Light of Austrian Value Theory. *Quarterly Journal of Austrian Economics* 19(1), Spring: 3–28.

Lachmann, Ludwig M. 1986. *The Market as an Economic Process*. Basil Blackwell Ltd., Oxford & New York.

La Voie, Don, ed. 1994. *Expectations and the Meaning of Institutions: Essays in Economics by Ludwig Lachmann*. Routledge, London.

Mises, Ludwig von. 2006. *The Ultimate Foundation of Economic Science*. Liberty Fund, Inc., Indianapolis.

Mises, Ludwig von. 2007. *Bureaucracy*. Liberty Fund, Inc., Indianapolis.

222 *Global case studies*

Menger, Carl. 1971. *Principles of Economics, English Translation of original German Grundsatze der Volkswirthschaftslehre* (1871), New York University Press, New York and London.

Shackle, G. L. S. 1966. *The Nature of Economic Thought.* Cambridge University Press, London and New York: 162–186.

Shackle, G. L. S. 1969. *Decision, Order and Time in Human Affairs.* 2nd ed. Cambridge University Press, London and New York: 277–296.

Shackle, G. L. S. 1970. *Expectation, Enterprise, and Profit.* Aldine Publishing Co., Chicago: 122–169.

Shackle, G. L. S. 1979. *Imagination and the Nature of Choice.* Edinburgh University Press, Edinburgh.

Wells Fargo Securities. 2015. Derivative Desk 30 Year Views for 3-Month LIBOR, Prime Rate and 10 Year US Treasuries, as of April 17, 2015.

Cooperative workforce development: public–private sustainable linkages

Jennifer Winner, Air Force Research Laboratory

Dr. Riad A. Ajami, Wright State University

The need to educate the current and future workforce is shared by each organization. Although stakeholders may differ, organizations from different sectors have common goals and incentives related to workforce development. Primary among those are efficiency and effectiveness.

In the United States, organizations spent $164.2 billion training their employees in 2012, with the majority of those efforts being done internally for $100.2 billion. Across the 475 organizations surveyed, learning-focused per-employee spending averaged at $1,195 per employee. In 2014, spending per employee increased to an average of $1,229.

To maintain global competitiveness, multinational firms must find ways to develop and maintain their highly skilled workforce while minimizing costs. Accordingly, firms must look to capitalize on loosely coupled collaborations and leverage existing programs as a supplement to enhance human resource development.

Importance of a skilled workforce in a global economy

In 2015, the United Nations published a list of sustainable development goals, which included *inclusive and equitable education for all* and the *promotion of sustained, inclusive and sustainable economic growth*. The Organization for Economic Cooperation and Development (OECD) is focused on promoting policies to improve the economic and social fitness of people worldwide. OECD policy investigations cover topics ranging from statistical analyses to scorecards that depict trends and innovations in science, technology and industry.

Every three years, the OECD administers the Program for International Student Assessment (PISA), a formal look at the achievement of students from

Global case studies   223

across the globe with focuses on math, reading, and science. Similarly, the Survey of Adult Skills assesses the proficiency of adults on information-processing skill sets. The most recent results show that more favorable individual outcomes for workers (e.g., likelihood of employment, wages earned) are associated with higher proficiency in skills such as information-processing. The considerable efforts undertaken by the United Nations and the OECD highlight the widespread acceptance of the belief that workforce skills, including those related to science, technology, engineering, and mathematics (STEM) careers, are important for the global society and the economy.

The global economy has a significant impact on employment opportunities and the workforce within the United States. According to the International Trade Administration, exports supported 11.7 million U.S. jobs in 2014. Within the State of Ohio, 16,452 firms actively engaged in the export of goods and 242,900 workers were employed by foreign-controlled companies in 2013. In 2015, an estimated \$50.7 billion of merchandise was exported from Ohio to markets including Canada, Mexico, China, France, and the United Kingdom. In summary, these numbers highlight U.S. and, more specifically, Ohio's reliance on global markets. In today's economy, the local worker is impacted by local and global forces.

Think tanks such as the OECD have set their sights on globally competitive, sustainable economies, and they have highlighted the role of an adequately equipped workforce and technical skillsets in achieving these ends. How can organizations adequately address workforce development needs with limited resources? What linkages can be leveraged by multinational firms to build functional and sustained partnerships in support of a globally competitive workforce?

Using examples from the public sector, the present case study illustrates potential partnerships and how they may be leveraged to ensure a skilled workforce. This case study also includes an example of how the Balanced Scorecard (BSC) approach can be leveraged to strategically align and communicate about loosely coupled collaborations for workforce development.

Investment in the future public sector workforce

The U.S. Department of Defense (DoD) is among the leaders in workforce development spending. In recent years the DoD has engaged in strategic human capital management efforts to combat gaps for their acquisition workforce including their contracting and business personnel pools and their engineering force. Within the State of Ohio, Wright-Patterson Air Force Base (WPAFB) is the largest single-site employer. With 26,270 workers, the base employs a significant number of individuals within the STEM career fields.

Given a current workforce numbering in the tens of thousands, an emphasis on skill development efforts for the entire current WPAFB workforce would be unmanageable within the scope of this case study. Accordingly, the examples

224   *Global case studies*

provided in this case focus on investments made in the future workforce in the vicinity of WPAFB.

Organizations located on WPAFB support multiple programs for investing in the future STEM workforce, with efforts for students in kindergarten through grade 12 in addition to undergraduate and graduate programs of study. These take the form of out-of-school programs, outreach conducted during regular school hours (K-12), summer mentoring programs, and job shadowing opportunities. Information regarding many of these opportunities are available at http://www.oeof.org/pages/edout.html, https://teamafrl. afciviliancareers.com/opportunities/scholars, and https://careers.state.gov/ intern/pathways.

The WPAFB Educational Outreach Office facilitates partnerships within the K-12 community to increase students' awareness of STEM-related career options. The Wright Scholar Research Assistant Program, a summer internship program, provides hands-on experience for high school juniors and seniors in laboratory-based environments. Mentors for this program are selected from the scientists and engineers at the Air Force Research Laboratory (AFRL). Similarly, the Repperger Research Intern Program provides experiential learning opportunities for graduate and undergraduate students each summer. Yet another program, the Pathways Internship Program, offers Federal employment experience with periods of work and study for students enrolled as degree seeking students in academic, technical and vocational courses at a two- or four-year college or university, graduate, or professional school.

3D modeling and simulation skills to support the future STEM workforce

The 711 Human Performance Wing (HPW), located at WPAFB, aims to advance human performance in air, space, and cyberspace through research, education, and consultation. As one of many labs housed under the 711 HPW, the Gaming Research Integration for Learning Laboratory® (GRILL®) conducts training research through the use of 3D modeling, simulation, and game engine technologies. As an extension of this focus, in 2011 the GRILL® began mentoring high school students recruited through the Wright Scholar Research Assistant Program.

The GRILL® team's role as mentors for Wright Scholars began as a one-time project in the summer of 2011, when they were identified as the team to assist in the development of a capstone project to integrate 3D modeling tools into a high school course. The team chose to leverage their mentor role for the Wright Scholars as a means to accomplish this task. With the ultimate goal of developing a capstone project that was not only usable by schools but would increase student interest in science, technology, engineering, and mathematics (STEM) education, the team evaluated numerous technologies and selected those that would be both affordable and usable by the schools. Video game engines, 3D modeling tools, and remotely controlled (RC) cars were quickly integrated into projects to engage students. The student interest in the use of these technologies was apparent from the beginning, and the GRILL® continued to support students each summer in the years that followed.

During the summers, the team hosted high school and undergraduate students through summer internship vehicles, and began to increase the number of middle and high school teachers who spent a summer residency in the GRILL®. Summers allowed for multi-week, in-depth collaboration between the GRILL® team and the teachers in the residency. During these periods, teachers developed content that they would take into their classrooms, and the GRILL® team supported teachers as they learned about the technology and how to seamlessly integrate it into their methods.

Fairly quickly, the GRILL® STEM efforts grew to include more than 15 school districts in the area. By 2015, more than 1,000 students locally were engaged with these new technologies in their classrooms each school year, gaining experience with everything from programming to CAD/3D modeling tools to game engines.

As early as 2013, many of the participating schools were located upward of an hour outside of the Dayton area. Throughout the school year, interactions with the teachers were far fewer due to time and other constraints, including travel distance. Although the content was published to the GRILL® website (http://gamingresearchintegrationforlearninglab.com), and available to teachers (free-of-charge), it was becoming apparent that year-round support of teachers in the rural classrooms would require additional resources.

Simply stated, the time and personnel required to maintain an engineer mentor presence in the classrooms were lacking. For a teacher to be comfortable and relatively autonomous in the use of the new technologies (e.g., programming tools, 3D modeling, game engines), two or three consecutive summer residencies of 9-weeks each were required. Experience has shown that sustained support for teachers over the course of a 2–3 year period yields the most impact in terms of a teacher possessing the skills to integrate technology fully throughout their curriculum.

Space constraints in the summer, travel distance, and the availability of funds threaten to reduce access to these experiences. The GRILL® team acknowledged the need for a model that could provide continued engineering support for teachers in their own classrooms. Such sources would have to be found in the vicinity of the school district for it to be feasible. If such sources were available they would have significant potential to complement the training activities and content that the GRILL® has to offer for teachers.

Common skills requirements, complementary capabilities: identifying viable partners

During this same time period, representatives at the West Central Ohio Workforce Development Initiative, concentrated in nearby counties in Ohio, were working together to increase awareness of job opportunities in their area.

226 *Global case studies*

Through the development of a new website (www.hometownopportunity. com), the initiative members hoped to connect current and future workforce members with opportunities available across multiple industries: agriculture and food processing, education, healthcare, manufacturing, professional services, as well as transportation and logistics. In a short amount of time, more than 200 organizations were represented on the website. Detailed descriptions were uploaded to depict the type of skills required and the various types of opportunities that the employers offered to the local workforce.

As a result of the outreach to school districts in the area in which the West Central Ohio Workforce Development Initiative was focused, GRILL® staff became aware of the Hometown Opportunity website. Many of the local manufacturing employers rely on mechanical and electrical engineers and those skilled in CAD/CAM programming, machine programming, and project management. Although one might not immediately equate the skills required for manufacturing firms located in rural towns and villages with those required of scientists and engineers working research and development within federal laboratories, the overlap was significant. Through the use of the 3D modeling tools, game engines, and open-ended, project-based learning content, the GRILL® content addresses both the skills the lab's future workforce needs to persist in their undergraduate programs of study and also those skills required by the local manufacturing industry. The firms, local to the vicinity of the rural school districts, represented a strong potential resource for engineering support for the classroom.

Balanced scorecard: communicating common objectives & shared initiatives

Five years into the mentoring effort, the number of collaborating partners had grown significantly and more potential partners (external organizations) had been identified. Locally there were multiple organizations with the authority and resources to garner an impact, especially if aligned with the GRILL® team's efforts. The team wished to leverage the **Balanced Scorecard (BSC)** approach for a strategic look at the program and potential growth as well as to communicate the objectives with potential partners and to help identify specific initiatives where each might fit in.

Originally developed to achieve advanced measurement for management personnel, the BSC approach provided a means to map strategy to four perspectives: customer, learning and growth, financial, and internal processes. Further, the approach allowed for a breakdown of objectives, measures, targets, and initiatives within each of the three perspectives, therefore enabling firms to more effectively manage their intangible assets.

Segmentation of the GRILL® program into the traditional four perspectives for the balanced scorecard approach (customer, learning and growth, financial, and internal process perspectives) required an upfront decision regarding which of the stakeholders would be designated as the "customer". Following the example of organizations with socially focused programs, the GRILL® team designated the end recipient of the program's investment (students) as the customer. Certainly, multiple versions of the BSC could be undertaken, including an internally focused version in which the AFRL was defined as the "customer". However, given that the purpose of this BSC was to support communication with potential external collaborators, a focus on the future workforce (students) as the "customer" would be most clear and advantageous. In this way, the "customer" or targeted audience in the analysis is one that is common with the external collaborators.

The GRILL® team had to make a similar decision regarding the focus for the learning and growth perspective. Given that in the BSC approach, this perspective is focused on putting the pieces in place to sustain the evolving efforts, it made the most sense to focus on investment in the local Teacher workforce. The likelihood of Teachers bringing the 3D modeling and related technologies into the classroom content is significantly lessened if they lack the skills and support, not to mention the necessary resources for purchasing the technologies for the classroom. Achieving the desired impact on the future workforce will be impossible without the integration of new content and technologies in the classrooms. Hence, the objectives identified under the learning and growth perspective focused on the increased recruitment and support of teachers. Initiatives in support of these objectives emphasized partnerships to incentivize teacher involvement through opportunities for professional development and education as well as partnerships to secure technologies for classrooms.

Regarding the financial perspective, stakeholders at the AFRL are the focus. In the case of the GRILL®, fiscal constraints deem it impossible to invest dollars in technology purchases for the classrooms. Constraints such as this highlight areas in which it may be advantageous to leverage additional external partnerships. Objectives related to the financial perspective may focus on sustainability of investments, matching investment to maintain technology currency, and achieving gains in impact from a teaching and skills perspective without significantly increasing cost for the partners. The GRILL® team's investment largely focused on mentoring resources they brought to bear on the problem, with equipment purchases reserved potentially for other contributors. It is important to note that schools can achieve significant gains in terms of technology currency relative to the real world and the workforce, but investments in technology within the classroom and in teacher training are never final. Once the classrooms adopt technologies, districts will need to invest resources to maintain currency between industry and the classroom.

Last but not least, objectives related to the internal process perspective focus on increasing the capacity to capture data on the impact, increasing student awareness of the use of 3D modeling and engineering tools and their applicability to STEM degrees and local workforce needs, and better mechanisms to connect interested students into follow-on internships, jobs, and educational opportunities both within the lab and beyond.

228 *Global case studies*

Balanced scorecard: initial outcomes

Having identified the objectives, measures, targets, and potential collaborative initiatives associated with the GRILL® outreach program, the team was poised to discuss areas where partners within the West Central Ohio Workforce Development Initiative might make sense. The process of articulating and modifying the objectives and initiatives helped to characterize and organize the ongoing efforts in the minds of the GRILL® team members. Further, it helped the team recognize where their strengths were and helped illuminate those initiatives which were best suited for external organizations. Initial discussions with local industry members were successful, resulting in a pilot of support of a local teacher and his classroom by an engineer from a local healthcare manufacturing firm.

Final remarks

The present case study aims to demonstrate how loosely coupled public–private partnerships can help to meet the demands associated with ensuring a skilled workforce in financially constrained environments. Economic development within a particular region relies heavily on the workforce and their associated skills. Areas rich in multiple employers from similar or complementary sectors have much to offer in the way of real-world learning opportunities. This case illustrates how employers may have common needs in terms of training for their workforce, and that by exploring those skills requirements can help to identify potential areas for collaboration. Partnerships among area employers can increase the availability of trained workforce members without significant increases in expenditures.

Within the State of Ohio and across the U.S., county and state-level economic development offices have great potential for assisting firms in the identification of others in their vicinity attempting to tackle similar workforce development problems. In this example, the extensive documentation undertaken as part of the West Central Ohio Workforce Development Initiative reduced the time required to identify via partnership options and areas of common interest.

The ability to identify and leverage partnerships across organizational boundaries is a competitive advantage in today's highly competitive global economy. Multinational firms who are able to develop strategic partnerships for sustainable workforce development will be rewarded in their ability to maintain a culture of innovation and technological competence at a lower cost than their global competitors.

Questions for discussion

1 What roles do corporations play in the achievement of sustained, inclusive, and sustainable economic growth? Do corporations' roles differ from those of public institutions?
2 In what ways can corporations capitalize on loosely coupled systems for workforce development?
3 Other than the Balanced Scorecard approach, are there other strategic management approaches that would help to articulate goals and streamline communication regarding common objectives?
4 What recommendations would you have for a firm who is interested in identifying strategic partnerships to assist with the development of a highly killed workforce?

References

ATD. 2013. "$164.2 Billion Spent on Training and Development by US Companies." Retrieved July 29, 2016, from https://www.td.org/Publications/Blogs/ATD-Blog/2013/12/ASTD-Releases-2013-State-of-the-Industry-Report.

ATD. 2015. "2015 State of the Industry." Retrieved July 29, 2016, from https://www.td.org/Publications/Research-Reports/2015/2015-State-of-the-Industry

International Trade Organization. 2016. "Ohio Exports, jobs, and foreign investment." Retrieved July 29, 2016, from http://www.trade.gov/mas/ian/statereports/states/oh.pdf.

Kaplan, Robert S. 2010. Conceptual Foundations of the Balanced Scorecard. Working paper. Retrieved August 26, 2016 from http://www.hbs.edu/faculty/Publication%20Files/10-074.pdf.

OECD. 2015. OECD Science, Technology and Industry Scoreboard 2015: Innovation for growth and society. OECD Publishing, Paris. DOI: http://dx.doi.org/10.1787/sti_scoreboard-2015-en.

OECD. 2016. Skills Matter: Further Results from the Survey of Adult Skills, OECD Skills Studies. OECD Publishing, Paris. DOI: http://dx.doi.org/10.1787/9789264258051-en

Ohio Development Services Agency. 2016. "Ohio Major Employers-Section 1." Retrieved July 29, 2016, from https://development.ohio.gov/files/research/b2001.pdf.

United Nations. 2015. "Sustainable Development Goals: Sustainable Development Knowledge Platform." Retrieved July 01, 2016, from https://sustainabledevelopment.un.org/?menu=1300.

United States Government Accountability Office. 2015. Actions Needed to Guide Planning Efforts and Improve Workforce Capability (GAO-16-80). Washington, D.C.: U.S. Government Printing Office.

Winner, Jennifer, Kimberly Puckett, Leesa Folkerth, Amelia Malone, and Jerred Holt. 2014. Modeling and simulation challenge problems in high school classrooms and internships: Lessons learned. Paper presented at the Inter-service/Industry Training, Simulation, and Education Conference, Orlando, FL.

230 *Global case studies*

Privilege Capital: increasing shareholding values through market expansions

Martina Roskova, Managing Partner, Privilege Capital

Introduction

From the moment the alarm rang in the early morning, you knew that this was going to be a monumental day. After securing your first post-graduation job with a reputable advisory firm in Prague, you have eagerly anticipated your first day in the office. As you board the train on the way to work, you think of how your undergraduate studies in international business and finance might help you as you commence your new career. Investment banking is an exciting field, but the classroom can only teach so much about how things really work. Based on your employment interview, you know that for the first six months you will be working with a senior financial advisor in the firm so that you can get a clear understanding of how the business works and where your strengths lie.

As you enter the home office of Privilege Capital, you are greeted by your new supervisor. "We are very happy to have you working with us," she says, while handing you a packet of information. Included in the packet are logistical concerns like access badges, as well as various forms to fill out to finalize system access. After completing the various forms, you turn to the following paper which serves as a first day introduction for all new employees. As you are eager to get started, you read with great interest the pages that follow.

First day welcome packet

Privilege Capital is an independent advisory firm specializing in cross-border market expansions, private equity, and shareholding advice with a prime focus on serving the acquisitive, organic growth, and shareholder value maximization of acquiring firms. The company's headquarters are located in Prague, the Czech Republic, and the firm mainly focuses on acquisition and expansion projects, particularly leveraging its strong experience in market expansion in the European Union (the "EU") and Central and Eastern European region (the "CEE"), primarily the Czech Republic, Slovakia, Poland, and Hungary. The key mission of Privilege Capital is to maximize the shareholder values of the corporation. That is achieved through successful development, formulation, and execution of market expansion strategies through cross-border acquisitions, mergers, direct equity investments, and other similar transactions. Privilege Capital in its advisory capacity directly represents leading European and global corporations, entrepreneurs, and private equity investors in the execution of their expansion strategies.

Global case studies 231

Market expansions: accessing the European Union through the establishment of operations in Central and Eastern Europe

Privilege Capital bases its experience on advisory services in CEE market expansion for multinational corporations for the period after the 1989 political revolution as well as for mid- to large-size businesses and corporations for the period after the 2004 accession of Eastern European countries into the EU single market. The year 1989 led to major changes in the political landscape across the CEE region, and to the implementation of the free market economic system and to the privatization of state-owned businesses which created a high market potential for direct investment. The primary motivation of western companies for entering the newly opened CEE market was to expand their customer base and gain the "first mover advantage". The CEE region, as an emerging market, has been characterized by fast growth, low costs, lower income skilled labour, a favourable geographic location, and pro-investment oriented governments. The direct investment especially in the case of **greenfield investments** contributed to job creations, provided mutual profits to both the investors and investment country economies, and therefore have been encouraged by the governmental investment incentives in the form of tax relief, in addition to other cost saving advantages. After the integration of the CEE countries into the single EU market, the market opportunities have become even more attractive for both western European companies and other overseas enterprises. The CEE countries have remained cost competitive while offering easy access to western EU countries' customer base. As an example, Privilege Capital has assisted U.S. based mid- to large-size manufacturers and suppliers for the automobile industry which were driven by their need to serve their current or potential western European customers more efficiently and were looking for opening manufacturing sites, primarily through acquisitions, in the Czech Republic. Privilege Capital has recommended to its overseas clients (i.e. American and Asian corporate investors) that the most efficient way for setting up their businesses and commencing their business in the CEE, is to acquire existing companies in Eastern Europe. The newly acquired subsidiaries help to achieve a stronger competitive position for the whole company in the EU market. Although traditionally the market expansions in the CEE region have been cost-driven, today investment decisions in the CEE region are like any other cross-border expansion implemented in the world. By the basic business rule, all companies are aiming to maximize shareholder value. The focus on profitable growth, sustainable competitive advantage, and further market penetration are being achieved via implementation of the company's global growth strategies.

Preparation and execution of the CEE market entry requires, like any other global expansion, depth of knowledge of the local political, economic and business environment. The advisory process for market expansion starts with a feasibility study covering all aspects of market entry, which includes a detailed SWOT analysis focused on strengths, weaknesses, opportunities and threats of

232   *Global case studies*

all related areas including taxation, accounting, economic, political and industrial aspects related to the local market. The market entry decision-making process also involves analysis and/or identification of suitable acquisition targets for manufacturing site locations. Investment in the form of acquisitions are typically preferred options for most companies as they enable a quicker start in the foreign target market and offer shorter payback periods which help to create immediate income for investors. On the other hand, greenfield investments typically require a stronger management involvement, a higher resource commitment and a higher risk exposure. Most corporations decide on choosing the greenfield investment option only when a suitable acquisition entry is not available. Not all potential acquisition plans are executed for a number of reasons ranging from a lack of suitable acquisition targets in specific industries to a failure of transaction closure. Although a well prepared and properly executed market strategy of an acquisition is crucial, equally important is a post-acquisition development of corporate governance with the acquired subsidiary that should not only implement proper controlling, managing and monitoring functions, but also focus on respecting cultural sensitivities. Corporate governance serves as a framework for interchanges and relationships, including mobilization of investments, information transfer and adequate management. In practice, both Anglo-Saxon and German (i.e. "Continental") models of corporate governance are being implemented by foreign investors in the CEE, depending on investor preference.

Privilege Capital's role in international mergers, acquisitions, and buy-outs

Acquisitions, mergers and buy-outs have become an increasingly important means of reallocating resources in the global economy and for executing global corporate strategies. For some firms, such as private equity groups, pursuing acquisitions and divestitures is the primary corporate strategy. Therefore, the private equity advisory function involves the preparation and execution of both acquisitions and sales of companies. Privilege Capital serves a broad range of corporate customers. In addition to the typical roles of financial and strategic investors, entrepreneurs, investment bankers and advisors, most senior managers will likely be involved in strategic transactions of acquisition, merger or joint ventures during their careers. They could, at a minimum, receive an acquisition bid from another company or need to obtain financing through private equity or venture capital investors. Cross-border mergers and acquisitions are quite a common phenomenon today and investment procedures and decision-making processes are standardized to those in the domestic markets. The few differences and specifics are further outlined below.

In cross-border acquisition projects, Privilege Capital represents both categories of buyers, i.e. strategic and financial buyers, serving primarily private equity investors. Strategic buyers are usually operating companies in the industrial or service sectors, that are acquiring other companies in order to expand their operations, increase their profit margins and enhance their competitive advantages. Strategic buyer target companies are based either in their own sectors of operation (for example direct or indirect competitors, suppliers, customers) or compete in complementary sectors. The goal for strategic buyers is to identify companies whose products or services can synergistically integrate with their existing businesses to create incremental and long-term shareholder value. This involves, for example, offering existing production to new customers or markets in order to increase revenue and profits in absolute numbers as well as to improve profitability margins. Financial buyers are entities that acquire shares in companies with the aim of realizing a return on their investment via exit with an average holding period of from four to seven years. The exit is realized either via a sale to a strategic or another financial buyer, or via initial public offering. Financial buyers are primarily private equity and venture capital firms, but also consist of family offices or high net worth individuals looking to diversity their investment holdings. But **strategic investors** also can act as pure **financial investors** in cases when their investments are aimed only at a financial return, with acquired firms typically being located outside of their own operating sectors. Financial investors can also act as strategic investors in cases where acquisitions increase the existing businesses in their portfolio.

As these two groups of buyers have different goals for their investments, the approach to the acquisition and post-acquisition process may also differ. In the acquisition process, strategic buyers sometimes spend more time on the preparatory and approval stages. There is also a differentiation in terms of geographic preference. Since most strategic buyers are expanding globally, financial investors have a narrower geographic focus, typically making a decision on a country or region prior to initiating their investments. Strategic buyers typically spend more time focusing on synergy and integration capabilities. Financial investors focus on both the company and the industry in which it operates, and value targets based on standalone cash-generating capabilities and earnings growth potential. The implementation of **synergistic effects** are sometimes strong motivation to purchase the company, and could in some cases lead to the offering of a higher purchase price for the target company by strategic investors. The business model of financial investors doesn't typically lead to an increase in the purchase price. The investment horizon could also have an impact on valuation. Strategic buyers plan to keep a newly purchased business indefinitely as they often integrate the acquired company into their existing business. Financial investors, on the other hand, have a fixed investment horizon.

Privilege Capital's advisory role is involved in all of the preparation stages of an expansion project, as illustrated in Exhibit 8.13.

Preparation of a market entry strategy involves understanding the market trends and the creation of the market entry mode. This is followed by a proactive review of acquisition opportunities, the preparation of preliminary investment analysis, including economic and financial models for the selected target company, the development of an acquisition strategy, and the preparation

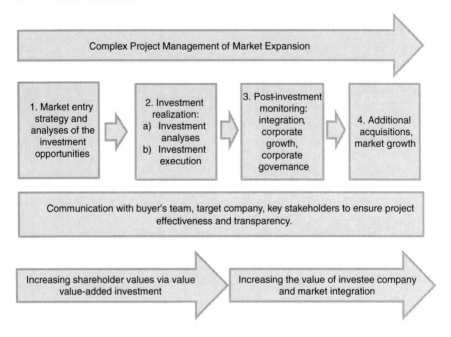

Exhibit 8.13 Complex project management of market expansion

of negotiation tactics with the target's owners. The investment realization stage involves investment analysis (such as the evaluation of the aspects of legal, accounting, tax, commercial due diligence, market and company risk assessment) and investment execution, consisting of investment proposal preparation, transaction structuring (i.e., the arrangement of local debt financing), structuring of transaction terms (assuring that all terms are covered in the legal documentations), negotiation of the contractual terms and closure of the transaction. Post-investment monitoring consists of business integration, enforcement of shareholders' rights, assistance in the creation of strong visibility for the acquiring group in the market to keep the highest level of market reputation, cooperation in the company's growth, monitoring the investment in line with the market context, regular valuations and evaluation, and reviewing and accessing new market opportunities. The post-investment stage for financial investors also includes initiation and execution of add-on acquisitions, focus on other growth areas, exit preparation and execution. Financial investors are in most cases looking for growth through add-on acquisitions. These add-on investments are in most cases executed by the already invested company, in which the business is integrated.

Private equity financing of international acquisitions

Financial acquisitions typically belong to the private equity category. Private equity investors acquire a shareholding stake in private companies that are not quoted on a stock exchange and are distinguished by their active investment model, in which they seek to deliver operational improvements in its portfolio companies over the targeted investment period. Private equity funds are set up with different categories and sizes. Although private equity investors could acquire minority shareholding stakes, in most cases they purchase majority shareholdings or execute leveraged buy-outs. The majority of equity funds invest in buy-outs either of medium-sized enterprises or established companies in traditional industries. The private equity-type transaction consisting of smaller investment sizes in start-up, high-potential and entrepreneurial companies typically driven by technological innovation, will typically fall into the category of Venture Capital. While private equity firms are in general acquiring companies in any industry, venture capital funds focus on new and innovative industries, for example information technology, biotechnology, and clean energy. A special category of venture capital is "seed funds" that invest in entrepreneurial start-ups that just have a business idea.

Private equity funds are raised for a specific period of around eight years, of which the first four are used for investment and remaining years are utilized for investment monitoring and exit. Private equity funds are structured as advisory companies with set criteria and raised for selected geographic regions. Capital for private equity can be raised from private or institutional investors. The majority of private equity investors consist of institutional and accredited investors who can commit large sums of money for longer, but well-defined periods of time.

Private equity investors prefer to invest in high growth industries with stable and fairly predictable cash flows, and not in highly cyclical or commodity related industries, or in industrial sectors that are under consolidation. The following characteristics are preferred for the targeted companies: sustainable competitive advantage, solid and growing market position in markets offering high potential, high barriers of entry (i.e. companies not easily substituted by new entries), strong brand awareness, professional and credible management. Additional factors include a wide distribution network, a diversified supplier-customer base and highly competitive products. Other desirable characteristics include companies that are outperforming the industry average, market leaders with high growth potential for both organic as well as acquisitive growth, and companies consolidating in fragmented industries. In certain cases, preferred characteristics for acquisition include companies with good business fundamentals, but where a significant discount in purchase value is possible owing to temporary financial trouble. Strong exit potential is a key in all investments. Typical private equity investment transaction candidates include assertive market players who are either consolidating in regional markets, developing new products, expanding to new export markets, extending production capacities, or planning to acquire competitors in a fragmented market. Other transactions could involve companies in the pre-IPO phase, planning an IPO at a later stage or non-core companies of the large conglomerates that are being spun-off. A separate category is transactions initiated by

236 *Global case studies*

management teams who are looking for private equity investors to back up their management buy-outs (the "MBO").

The structure and financing of buy-out transactions are in principle the same worldwide. The financing of a buy-out transaction is structured through the legal establishment of a newly incorporated company (the "NEWCO") that raises financing and subsequently acquires the entire share capital of the target company. After the transaction is completed, the NEWCO is merged with the acquired company and the debt facility is then repaid by the acquired operating company. The funding for buy-out transactions is provided through a combination of debt, equity and mezzanine facilities. The equity portion for a typical transaction averages 30% of the total acquisition transaction value and is provided by the equity investors (or in MBO transactions partly by management), debt (senior debt for the transaction and revolving facility of the acquired company) is provided primarily by regional banks or banking syndications. Mezzanine financing is raised through specialized mezzanine funds (independent funds or bank-related groups). Mezzanine financing consists of a subordinated debt instrument with equity linkage, ranks between senior debt and equity financing in terms of risk and return, and is contractually and structurally subordinated to senior debt. As a return component, mezzanine financing incorporates cash interest, paid in capitalized interest, and warrants. The equity part of the investment is unsecured, as the equity investors are taking an active controlling and monitoring role in their transactions through active board representation.

Business valuation techniques applied in the valuation of businesses in cross-border transactions

Valuation of businesses in cross-border transactions globally does not differ in their key approaches and techniques. For the valuation of any business, a detailed knowledge of the business and related industry is required. The valuations incorporate economic, political, and industrial specific risks and growth potential. Valuations of companies are very subjective and no valuation will ever give the "correct" company value. The valuation techniques instead provide guidance of what a company might be worth and at best provide a range in which the true valuation is likely to reside. At the end of the day, a company is only worth what someone is prepared to pay for it. By definition, the fair market value is the price that is agreed upon in a sale transaction between a willing, knowledgeable and unpressured buyer and seller. The true value for a private company which is being sold or acquired is therefore determined through a process of negotiation. Valuation techniques and approaches are complex in their details, but relatively straightforward in their objectives and applications. A key valuation technique used globally by both strategic and financial investors is the discounted cash flow (the "DCF") valuation approach. DCF valuation is also superior to other valuation methods since it is based on the fundamental determinant of corporate value, (i.e. cash).

A company's value is driven by its ability to generate cash flow over the long term. Furthermore, a company's cash-flow generating ability and hence its value creation ability is driven by long-term growth and returns that the company earns on invested capital relative to its cost of capital.

In DCF calculations, the value of the company equals the discounted value of expected future free cash flow. Free operating cash is the total amount of cash the company generates from the operating activity after funding purchases of fixed assets and any required increases in working capital. Free operating cash flow consists of earnings before interest, taxes and amortization ("EBITA"), plus taxes on EBITA and depreciation charges, adjustments by non-cash items, subtracted investments in operating working capital and less capital expenditure. It does not incorporate any financing-relating cash flows such as interest expense or dividends. Free cash flow is the appropriate cash flow because it reflects the cash flow generated by the company's operations that is available to all the company's capital providers, both debt and equity. In the financial models, free cash flow is derived from the historical earnings and is forecasted for both the explicit, typically 5-year period, and infinite period. The explicit period is the period for which detailed cash flow forecasts are completed, while infinite period cash flow (called the "continuing" or "terminal" value) is calculated as a lump sum value based on assumptions for growth and return rates. The future forecasted cash flow is discounted by the appropriate discount rate to derive net present value. The usual approach to discounting future cash flow is to use the weighted average cost of capital (the "WACC") that reflects the opportunity cost of capital to both equity and debt investors and equals the rate of return that the investors could expect to earn on other investments of equivalent risk less any tax benefits received by the company (i.e. the tax shield provided by interest expense). In summary, the stages of discounted cash flow valuation approach start with historical analysis of cash flows, are followed by cash flow forecasting, terminal value calculation, calculation of appropriate discount rate and concluded by reaching the enterprise value (the "EV") of the business consisting of equity and debt value.

In a large majority of valuations, a comparative valuation is being used as a complementary to the discounted cash flow technique. Comparative valuation calculations, such as comparative transactions or comparative companies are in most cases based on EV/EBITDA (enterprise value/earnings before interest, tax, depreciation and amortization) multiples or EV/turnover multiples. The comparative transactions approach is becoming more difficult to apply owing to the limitations of transaction data available on private companies. For comparative companies, the data is usually derived from U.S. public companies with an appropriate market or country-related discounts. In addition to cash based and comparative valuations, there is a range of other valuation techniques, such as asset-based and dividend-based, but these techniques are not as highly used in practice.

As mentioned earlier, the decision-making process could have an effect on valuation, as strategic buyers focus on synergy and integration capabilities and

238   Global case studies

could derive to higher valuation relative to financial investors valuing their target firms based on standalone cash-generating capability and expected earnings growth. Some investors could perceive other "hidden" value in companies after incorporating considerations of better performance owing to stronger management, or expectations that when the company is "unbundled" the parts individually are worth more than the whole.

Reasons behind successes and failures in expansion projects

Completed transactions are publicly announced. However, there is a large majority of transactions that are not executed successfully due to a number of reasons. Any expansion projects from initial considerations through final acquisition require a significant allocation of resources in terms of expenses and time. The process of successful acquisition closure could take several months, from three months, in the best ideal situation, up to six months. There have been cases where strategic investors have taken much longer to execute acquisitions. Although confidentiality for any transaction is crucial, it is not typically strictly enforced. A lengthy acquisition process with limited confidentiality in place could have a negative impact on supplier and customer relationships and could also create high uncertainties for employees. In most cases, during the sale process, any benefits that the new buyers could bring to the business are not communicated to employees, but the probability of sale is spread through internal gossip. The company's owners could have the best intentions for selling the business, but there could be a number of parties involved that are not in favour of the transaction. For example, managers afraid of losing their positions, minority shareholders, and other stock-holders could have an interest in breaking the deal. Additional difficulties are associated with due diligence. Some investors decide not to proceed with their deals after the due diligence process incorporating accounting, tax, legal and in some cases industry-specific due diligence performed by external advisors. The due diligence process should serve as a verification rather than investigation process and is performed after the seller and the buyer agree on the major terms of the transaction. In practice there are cases when investors are entering due diligence without a strong intention of transaction completion. These could be strategic competitors searching for data or financial investors deciding between transactions. It is therefore crucial for both parties to share the most comprehensive detailed information on the business prior to the due diligence stage. Most transactions fail in the last stages of negotiation, sometimes owing to personal hubris. As mentioned earlier, the main motivation behind market expansion and acquisition is the creation of value for shareholders. However, the completion of a transaction doesn't guarantee the increase in shareholder value. The success of an acquisition transaction must be evaluated over time in the post-acquisition stage. Most acquisitions don't deliver expected value because purchasers had paid unreasonably high purchase price owing to a number of reasons ranging from overbidding in sale or tender situations, to

Global case studies 239

overestimating synergies, poor transaction preparation, an unprofessional due diligence process, and an overly optimistic view of the market potential and company growth prospects in the final valuation. Also in the case of a profitable business target, there could be difficulties in business integration or disruptions in relationships with customers, employees, or suppliers that could have an impact on the business overall.

The lessons learned from prior acquisitions is that the most successful deals result from highly disciplined and professional deal making incorporating transparent, truthful, and open information from all parties involved throughout the whole process.

Your next move

As you finish reading your welcome packet, you sit back in your chair and quickly link the various topics covered in the introductory paper with your undergraduate studies. "This will really be great. Applying what I have learned in college over time with an expert in the field!" you say to yourself.

Just then you are startled by a knock on your cubicle wall. "Good Morning!" says your supervisor. "As it turns out, the person who was going to be working with you today called in sick. We are short staffed, and we will need you to meet with a new potential client this morning. I realize that this is unusual for your first day, but we were impressed with your background so much that we thought this would be a good learning experience for you.

"A representative from a large chemical company is scheduled to be here in one hour's time. We are not sure what their intentions are yet and would like for you to meet with them to assess the situation," your supervisor continues. "Things move quickly in investment banking and if we were to cancel our appointment we would certainly lose our opportunity for their business. The chemicals industry has had much consolidation in recent years and has been the recipient of some unwanted press from protesters concerned about the environment and the suitability of the products offered for consumption. So you are getting your first at-bat earlier than expected, but we know that you are up to the challenge."

Questions for discussion

1 Compile a list of questions for the meeting. Specifically consider the following:
  a How might you assess what type of investor this company is?
  b How might you assess preferred markets for entry?
  c How might you determine suitability for acquisition versus greenfield expansion?
  d How might you determine the extent of public opinion of any proposed purchase?
2 Prepare a list of follow-up due diligence items needed from the prospect.

240   *Global case studies*

3   What additional information is needed now to assess the various targeted firms?

4   What instructions would you provide the client in order to ensure that the process is kept fully confidential? Or is there benefit to informing employees early of any possible moves?

Glossary

Absolute uniformity: proposes that accounting methods be standardized regardless of the different circumstances of different users

Advising Bank: bank in the letter of credit process that is typically in the home country of the exporter. This is an important distinction, as the advising bank is the bank that is known to the seller

Agent middlemen: market participants that represent the firm's interests and arrange for the distribution of goods for a fee

Arm's length pricing: company practice of charging the same price for affiliates or parents as they do for third-party buyers

Average cost pricing: where the firm identifies both the variable and fixed costs of production

Back to Back Loans: see Parallel loans

Balanced Scorecard (BSC): a strategic planning and management system traditionally focusing on four perspectives (i.e. the customer, learning and growth, financial performance, and internal processes)

Banker's acceptance: when the bank would agree to accept the time draft for a fee

Basel Accords: series of international banking agreements administered by the Bank for International Settlements in Basel, Switzerland

Bill of lading: receipt given by the carrier to the shipper acknowledging receipt of the goods being shipped, and specifying the terms of the delivery

Brexit: New colloquialism termed for Britain voting to leave the European Union. This process was officially launched after a June 2016 referendum vote where 52% of the British public voted to leave the EU. The UK officially requested to leave the EU on March 29, 2017.

Bulldog bonds: foreign bonds issued in Great Britain

Cash conversion cycle: length of time (usually expressed in days) between the purchasing of raw materials until the receipt of cash after the finished goods have been sold (inventory days on hand + accounts receivable days on hand − accounts payable days on hand)

Circumstantial uniformity: use of different accounting practices according to the variations in the circumstances of economic facts and conditions

242 *Glossary*

Clean letters of credit: where the presentation of any documentation is not required, other than the bill of exchange, to obtain payment

Collective bargaining: negotiations of wages or other terms of employment by an organized body of employees

Confirmed letter of credit: where the advising bank is committed to honor the payment of the credit, provided that the beneficiary meets the terms and conditions of the credit

Constant dollar accounting: goal here is to report assets, liabilities, expenses, and revenues in terms of the same purchasing power

Copyrights: exclusive legal right given to an originator or an assignee to print, publish, perform, film, or record literary, artistic, or musical material

Corporate inversions: when an MNC relocates its legal domicile to a lower tax nation, usually while retaining its material operations in its higher tax country of origin (see also tax inversions)

Cosmopolitanism: the ideology that all human beings belong to a single community, based on a shared morality

Cost method (of accounting): the parent carries an unsubstantial investment in the subsidiary and only reports income from the subsidiary when the subsidiary declares a dividend to the parent

Cost-plus pricing: where an additional amount is added to the cost of production to determine appropriate pricing at the next level of distribution

Culture shock: a pronounced reaction to the psychological disorientation caused by moving to a totally different environment

Current cost accounting: the emphasis is on money it would take to replace assets because of price increases

Demurrage fees: fees for storage of the exporter's goods at the foreign loading dock

Distribution chain: market participants within distribution systems required to get goods to market (producer, wholesaler, distributor, and retailer)

Documentary letters of credit: where the bank will require the presentation of documentation in order to obtain payment such as the invoice, customs documents, proof of insurance, a packing list, etc.

Draft: demand for payment from the buyer at a specified time (i.e. sight and time drafts)

Dual equity issue: is split up into two parts, one sold domestically and the other overseas

Dumping: occurs when exporting nations purposely underprice their goods for foreign markets only to displace domestic competition and gain market share, with the ultimate objective of raising prices when that position is well established

Equal Credit Opportunity Act (ECOA): U.S. law enacted in 1974 making it unlawful for any creditor to discriminate against any applicant, with respect to any aspect of a credit transaction, on the basis of race, color, religion, national origin, sex, marital status, or age (provided the applicant has the capacity to contract)

Glossary 243

Ethnocentric: firm markets its goods and services in foreign markets using the same marketing mix that is used in the domestic markets (i.e. literally viewing things from the home country perspective)

Ethno-domination: when distribution channels are dominated by specific ethnic groups within the country

Eurocurrency: is any freely convertible currency (including the U.S. dollar) that is held in a bank outside the country of its origin

Euroequity issue: when shares are sold solely outside the country of the issuer

Euromarkets: three main types of financial markets consisting of Eurocurrency markets, Eurobond markets, and Euro-equities markets

Exchange risk: risk inherent in currency price movements which may erode profitability

Excise taxes: taxes levied on luxury goods or activities (see also sin taxes)

Expatriates: home country nationals who live and work in foreign countries

Export management companies: firms which provide distribution services for firms under contract

Expropriation: political risk of confiscation of privately owned assets by domestic government

Extended market order: concept described by economist F.A. Hayek concerning the pitfalls of government intervention intended to ameliorate supposed ills in the general economy

Extraction tax: taxes levied upon producers of mined, extracted, or harvested resources (see also severance tax)

Financial accounting: is oriented toward external users and is concerned with providing relevant information about the activities of the enterprise

Financial investors: firms desiring to purchase existing firms in unrelated industries

Fisher effect: an economic theory proposed by economist Irving Fisher that describes the relationship between inflation and both real and nominal interest rates. The Fisher effect states that the real interest rate equates to the nominal interest rate minus the expected inflation rate.

Foreign sales agents: market participants that sell a product line in international markets

Four P's of marketing: product, price, promotion, and placement

Freight forwarders: logistics experts involved with shipment of goods

Functional currency: the currency of the primary economic environment in which the entity operates

Geocentric: standardization of the marketing mix, which allows a given firm to offer the same product or service in different markets, and to use essentially the same marketing approach to sell the product or service globally.

Global strategy: strategy that achieves cost advantages through centralized operations with global reach

Globalization: process by which businesses or other organizations develop international influence or start operating on an international scale

244 *Glossary*

Gray market exports: when individuals or entities take advantage of a firm's pricing policies that account for market variations in demand and acceptable prices

Greenfield investment: new market expansion via new business start-up rather than via existing business acquisition

Harrell & Kiefer country plotting matrix: technique for comparing the attractiveness of a given country/market with the competitive strengths of the business

Home country nationals: employees who are citizens of the country where the headquarters are located

Horizontal integration: combines firms which are at the same stage of the production cycle

Host country nationals: local employees who are citizens of the country where the subsidiary exists

Interest rate parity: a theory in which the differential between the interest rates of two countries remains equal to the differential calculated by using the forward exchange rate and the spot exchange rate techniques.

International firm: firm that takes advantage of knowledge and capabilities of the managing parent company through world-scale expansion and adaptations

Intra-company pooling: financing technique that seeks to optimize the total availability of resources on a worldwide or area-group basis

Irrevocable letter of credit: can only be modified or revoked with the consent of the beneficiary

Juridic domicile: where foreign affiliates of parent corporations formed as subsidiaries receive different tax treatment because they are incorporated within the borders of a different nation (i.e. income is not taxed by their home country if it is not earned or received within that country)

Kanban: Just-In-Time inventory (JIT) system

Lagging: policy of creating deliberate delays with respect of outflows or inflows

Leading: policy of accelerating outflows or inflows

Letter of credit: is a written commitment by a bank, made at the request of a customer (the buyer), to effect payment or honor drafts of the seller, if the seller complies with certain specific conditions

Lockouts: when the employer closes or locks the plant, and bars workers from entering

Managerial accounting: is concerned with the information needs of the internal users of an enterprise who require detailed information on all of its business activities

Managerial grid: classic example of managerial classification by Blake and Mouton

Market capitalization: the value of total stocks outstanding at a particular point of time (stock price multiplied by shares outstanding)

Glossary 245

Merchant middlemen: market participants who take title to goods and trade them on their own behalf

Mittelstand: category of medium-sized family-owned German businesses that have achieved much export-oriented success

Multinational firm: firm that builds flexibility to respond to national differences through strong, resourceful, and entrepreneurial operations

New product: Most expensive but potentially most rewarding as new product and message is created to meet demands of a new market

Offshoring: process of obtaining a good or a service from an international source primarily to lower costs

Oligopolistic markets: market condition when a few large firms hold the largest portion of the market for certain goods or products

One-step method: records international transactions using the spot rate for the foreign currency in effect on that day

Outsourcing: process of obtaining a good or a service from an outside provider (whether domestic or international)

Parallel loans: when blocked funds are lent out to a local company, who arranges an equivalent loan to the parent company overseas (also known as Back to Back Loans)

Personal selling: individual salespeople communicate the qualities and characteristics of the products to prospective customers

PESTL Analysis: evaluation technique for markets which include political, economic, sociocultural, technological, and legal environment considerations

Piracy: the illegal and unauthorized means to obtain goods, such as copying software

Polycentric: firms attempt to customize the marketing mix in each market in an attempt to meet specific needs of customers in each market

Product adaption: firm modifies its existing product line to take into account the cultural, legal, or economic differences between domestic and foreign markets

Product adaptation/message adaptation: both the product and the message are changed to meet conditions in foreign target markets where both the characteristics of the market and the use of the product differ from those in domestic spheres

Product adaptation/message extension: product is changed but the message is extended

Product creation: innovation of a product which might be within a firm's area of expertise but was not included in the current product line

Product extension: firm markets the same product abroad as it does at home

Product extension/message adaptation: company changes the message communicated to its consumers

Product extension/message extension: marketing the same product with the same message

246 *Glossary*

Progressive taxation: system of taxation where the more you earn the more you pay

Promotion: reaching potential consumers and providing them with information on the product's existence, attributes, and the needs it satisfies

Promotion message: firm can either extend its message from existing markets or adapt its message to the target market, which yields a scenario of five different overall product and promotion strategies for the international enterprise (product extension/message extension; product extension/message adaptation; product adaptation/message extension; product adaptation/message adaptation; and new product)

Promotional mix: includes advertising, personal selling, and sales promotions

Protectionism: government intervention in trade markets to protect specific industries in its economy

Publicity/Public relations: firm's relationship with entities in its markets other than the buyers of its product, which include non-consuming members of society as well as agents from the various arms of government

Purposive uniformity: varies the determination of accounting practices and standards according to both diversity of users and circumstances

Quota: a specified amount of a product that a government will permit to be imported

Rationalization: when a subsidiary changes its purpose for production from manufacturing for its own market to manufacturing a limited number of component parts for use by several or all subsidiaries

Red chip stocks: issued on the Hong Kong stock exchange, but are controlled by mainland China

Re-export: where goods are imported to a given country and then small changes or additions are made to goods and then are exported to other markets (typically the re-exporter has favorable trade policies compared to those of the original exporting country)

Regulation Q: interest rate ceilings imposed by the US Government in 1966

Reporting currency: the reporting currency of the parent company

Resident buyers: market participants that work in foreign markets to acquire goods

Reverse culture shock: when issues arise after an expatriate is repatriated back to the home culture

Revocable letter of credit: can be modified or revoked by the issuing bank without notice or consent from the beneficiary

Revolving letter of credit: when multiple transactions are undertaken by the same parties, this is established exactly the same as the original letter of credit but with shorter periods for shipment, and the ability to substitute documents specific to the current transaction

Sales promotions: activities pursued by a firm in an attempt to generate interest in the company's products, greater levels of sales, and enhanced distributor effectiveness

Samurai bonds: foreign bonds issued in Japan

Glossary 247

Severance tax: see extraction tax

Shackle Possibility Curve: economic model theorized by George Lennox Sharmin Shackle illustrating the universe of potential value choices that might exist for a given situation

Shunto: Spring wage offensive; time in Japan when wage negotiations take place

Sight draft: draft requiring payment when the importer receives the goods

Sin taxes: see excise taxes

Sociocultural factors: are customs, lifestyles and values that characterize a society. Some examples are religion, attitudes, economic status, class, language, politics and law. These factors can affect quality of life, business and health.

Sogo shosha: enormous general trading companies in Japan that control much of the import and export trade market (e.g., Sumitomo, Mitsubishi, Toyota Tsusho, and Mitsui)

Stand-by letter of credit: This form of letter of credit is a bank guarantee, where the beneficiary (seller/exporter) can claim payment if the principal (buyer/importer) does not fulfill their obligations

Strategic investors: firms acquiring existing companies within the same industry where they are looking to expand operations, enhance competitiveness, or increase profit margins

Subjectivity of value: is a theory of value which advances the idea that the value of a good is not determined by any inherent property of the good, nor by the amount of labor necessary to produce the good, but instead value is determined by the importance an acting individual places on a good for the achievement of his desired ends

Synergistic effects: situations where the combined value or effect is greater than the sum of the parts

Target return levels: corporate profitability goal where a company wants to achieve a specific return level in relation to costs or to the original investment

Tariffs: taxes imposed at the borders of a country

Tax havens: locations offering low tax rates in an effort to attract investment

Tax inversions: see corporate inversions

Technology development: three stages of development are invention, innovation, and diffusion

Technology transfer: process by which knowledge is diffused through learning from its place of origin and introduction to other world markets

Third-country nationals: employees who are citizens of neither the country of the subsidiary or the headquarters

Time draft: draft where credit is extended to an importer for a specified period of time

Trademarks: exclusive legal right to protect knowledge that is embodied in a product that can be sold

248 *Glossary*

Transferable letter of credit: when the beneficiary can request that the letter of credit be transferred to another beneficiary for execution

Transfer pricing: the determination of appropriate prices to be charged between different branches of the same firm that are conducting business between each other

Translation: the process of restating financial statements into a uniform currency

Transnational strategy: strategy that develops global efficiencies, international flexibility, and worldwide learning simultaneously

Turnkey projects: contracted projects that encompass all elements of the project, usually including training

Turnover: is another term for sales in the United Kingdom, while in the United States, it refers to the renewal or replenishment of inventory stock

Two-step method: accounts for gains or losses in transactions by separating the activities of business activity and currency exchanges

Unitary taxes: taxes imposed by a specific state on the basis of an MNC's multi-state or worldwide profits, not merely those profits generated by operations in that state

Value-added tax (VAT): tax that is assessed only upon the value added to products at each level of production

Vertical integration: combines the stages of production typically done by different companies

Water's edge taxation: concept embraced by many multinationals which limits states to taxing only income from operations within the United States, not from global sales

Webb-Pomerane Act: A U.S. law passed in 1918 that exempted certain exporters' associations from certain antitrust regulations (namely Sherman and Clayton antitrust laws)

Wildcat strikes: when the workers strike during the life of an existing contract and give little or no notice

Xenophobia: intense or irrational dislike or fear of people from other countries

Yankee bonds: foreign bonds issued in the United States

Zaibatsu: large Japanese conglomerates that also have trading companies as integral components

Index

Page numbers in **bold** denote Exhibits.

3D modeling tools 224–5

absenteeism 149
absolute uniformity 82
accounting 72–92; auditing 91–2; cash method 75; consolidation 85, 87–8; depreciation 75; disclosure differences 76–7; for expropriation 90–1; factors affecting 73–4; foreign currency transactions 83–7, **86**, **87**; harmonization 81–3; for inflation 88–9; planning and control of 91; policy formation 80–1; reserves 74–5; segmentation of 77–9, **78**, **79**; social reporting 79–80; transfer pricing and costing 89–90; valuation differences 75–6
accounting profession 80, 81
Acme Industries *see* market share case study
acquisitions 230–40, **234**
Adler, Nancy 125
advertising programs 26–7
advising banks 57
agent middlemen 34
Agros bottled water *see* export market selection case study
Air Force Research Laboratory (AFRL) 224
allowances, expatriate employees 123, 124
Alternext 67
American Institute of Certified Public Accountants (AICPA) 81

American stock exchange (AMEX) 69
Amsterdam 67
Andorra **107**
Anguilla **107**
Antigua & Barbuda **107**
antitrust laws 33
area simulation training model 122
arm's length pricing 31–2, 90, 107
Aruba **107**
Asian Financial Crisis 58
asset-based valuations 237
Association of Accountants and Auditors in Europe (AAAE) 82
attractiveness of global markets *see* export market selection case study
auditing 91–2
Australian stock exchange (ASX) **66**, 69
Austrian economic thought 216, 218–19, **218**, 221
autonomy: overseas managers 118; subsidiaries 144–6
average cost pricing 29

back orders 149
back-to-back loans 53
Bahamas 106, **107**
Bahrain **107**
Balanced Scorecard (BSC) 223, 226–8
Ball, Donald A. 143
banker's acceptances 56
Banque Commerciale pour l'Europe du Nord 62
Basel Accords 58

250 *Index*

Bavishi, V. B. 78–9
BCIU *see* Business Council for International Understanding (BCIU)
beer *see* export market selection case study
Belgium 67, 128
Belize **107**
benefits 116, 117, 128
Bermuda 106, **107**
bilingual employees 116
bills of lading 56
blocked funds management 50–3
bond issues 59–60, **60**
bonuses, expatriate employees 123, 124
border taxes 32, 99
bottled water *see* export market selection case study
brand name restrictions 22
Brazil 81
Bretton Woods arrangements 62
brewery case study *see* export market selection case study
Brexit 66
bribery 51, 75–6
British Virgin Islands 106, **107**
Brussels 67
BSC *see* Balanced Scorecard (BSC)
bulldog bonds 60
bundled technology 154
Business Council for International Understanding (BCIU) 122–3
business expenses 96, 104–5
business level strategies 10
business teaching, international 11–12, **12**
business valuation techniques 236–8
buy-outs 230–40, **234**

California, USA 107, 108
call-over method 67
Canada 32, 98, 102, **131**
capital budgeting 53–5
capital-intensive technology 158, 159
capital markets *see* international capital markets
Carlsberg beer *see* export market selection case study
carry-back and carry-forward periods, tax credits 104, 110

case studies 171; cooperative workforce development 222–9; hedging with foreign exchange 199–205, **200**, **201**, **203**; increasing market share 193–9, **196**, **197**, **198**; international real estate investor 213–21, **215**, **217**, **218**, **220**; market expansions 230–40, **234**; Myanmar 172–5, **174**; triple bottom line 205–12; *see also* export market selection case study
cash-based valuations 236–7
cash conversion cycle 46–7, **46**
cash flow 236–7
cash method of accounting 75
Cayman Islands 106
Cayman Islands Dominica **107**
Central and Eastern Europe (CEE) 230–40, **234**
centralized decision-making 144–6
centralized funds management 48–50
centralized information systems 164–5
centralized marketing 17, 18–20
Channel Islands **107**
China 10, **66**, 68, **100**, 151, 152, 161
China Securities Regulatory Commission 68
Choi, Frederick D. S. 78–9
circumstantial uniformity 82
class-struggle mentality 132
clean letters of credit 56
Coca-Cola 19, 24
codetermination 135
collective bargaining 128, 130–3
color cultural differences 22
commission brokers 65
communities, in triple bottom line 209–10
comparative valuations 237
compensation packages 116, 123, 127–9
competition, and pricing 30
competitiveness case studies 171; hedging with foreign exchange 199–205, **200**, **201**, **203**; increasing market share 193–9, **196**, **197**, **198**; Myanmar 172–5, **174**; *see also* export market selection case study
competitive strength analysis 183–6, **185**, **187**, **192**
confidentiality 238

confirmed letters of credit 57
conglomerates 10
conservatism, and accounting systems 74
consolidation of financial statements 85, 87–8
constant dollar accounting 89
consumer goods 18, 20, 27
consumer groups 77
continuing value calculation 237
convergence 6, **7**, 8–9, **8**
Cook Islands **107**
cooperative agreements 146
cooperative workforce development case study 222–9
Copenhagen 67
copyrights 22, 161
core competencies 10
corporate governance 232, **234**
corporate inversions 100
corporate level strategies 10
corporate policies 120
corporate reports 162–4, **164**
corporate tax rates 100, **100**
Costa Rica **107**
cost-based manufacturing systems 151
cost-based pricing methods 29–30, 31, 90
cost leadership 10
cost method 88
cost-plus pricing 29, 31, 90
country attractiveness analysis 183–6, **185**, **187**, **191**
credit, letters of 56–7
credit ratings 54, 60, 63
credits, tax 96, 102, 103–5, 110, 124
creditworthiness 58, 60, 73
cross-border acquisitions 230–40, **234**
cross-cultural marketing mistakes 24–6
cross-cultural training programs 122–3
cultural awareness training model 122
cultural differences, and marketing 20, 21–2, 26–7
cultural identity 6
culture shock 121
culture-specific training programs 122
Curacao & St. Maarten **107**
currency exchange 47–8, 55, 83–7, **86**, **87**; hedging with foreign exchange case study 199–205, **200**, **201**, **203**

current cost accounting 89
current/noncurrent method of translation 85, **86**
current-rate method of translation 85, 86, **86**, **87**
customers, in triple bottom line 206–8
Cyprus **107**; *see also* export market selection case study

data protection 165–6
DCF *see* discounted cash flow (DCF) valuation
decentralized decision-making 144–6
decentralized information systems 164–5
decentralized marketing 17, 18–20
decision-making authority: centralized versus decentralized 144–6; overseas managers 118
deemed paid credits 103–4
demand, and pricing 30
demurrage fees 56
Denmark 67
depreciation 75
design of local production systems 143, 147–8, 158–9
differential wage policies 128–9
differentiation 10
diffusion of technology 154
disclosure 76–7
discounted cash flow (DCF) valuation 236–7
discretionary authority: overseas managers 118; subsidiaries 144–6
distribution chains 33–4
distribution decisions 33–5
divergence 6, **7**, 8–9, **8**
diversification: related 10; unrelated 10
dividend-based valuations 237
documentary letters of credit 56
double taxation 102, 109
Dow Jones Industrial Average 65
drafts 56
dual equity issues 64
due diligence process 238
dumping 31

earnings before interest, taxes and amortization (EBITA) 237
economic growth trends 2, **3**, **4**

252 Index

Edgarscan 77
Egypt 81
Elanco 212
Eli Lilly and Company 205–12
Eli Lilly and Company Foundation 209
empathy 121
employee participation in management 135
employees, in triple bottom line 208–9
ENA juice *see* export market selection case study
energy from non-conventional sources 96
environmental responsibility 211–12
equipment maintenance 143
equities markets 64–9, **66**
equity method 88
Estonia 67
ethical issues 125–6, 208–9
ethnocentric approach: logistics 148; marketing 19; staffing 126, **127**
ethnocentric views of employees 116
ethno-domination of distribution channels 35
Eurocurrencies 61–2
Eurodollars 61–2
Euroequity issues 64
Euromarkets 61–4
Euromonitor International Database 179
Euronext Stock Exchange 66–7, **66**
European Central Bank (ECB) 68
European Union: accounting standards 83; Brexit 66; industrial relations 134; market expansions case study 230–40, **234**
evaluation, of managers 146–7
exchange market hedge 47; case study 199–205, **200, 201, 203**
exchange risk 47–8
excise taxes 32, 98, 99
expansion projects 230–40, **234**
expatriate employees: managers 117–26, 146–7; taxation 109–10, 123
expenses, business 96, 104–5
explicit period cash flow 237
Export Express program, US 55
Export-Import Bank, US 55
export management companies 34

export market selection case study 176–88, **180**; country attractiveness/competitive strength analysis 183–6, **185, 187, 191, 192**; market size analysis 179, **181, 189**; PEST analysis 179–83, **182, 190**
export orientation 51
Export Working Capital program, US 55
expropriation 54, 90–1
external audits 91–2
externalizing 156–8, **157**
extraction taxes 98, 99

facilitative payments 51, 75–6
fair value accounting 89
families of expatriate employees 118, 121, 123, 124
FASB *see* Financial Accounting Standards Board (FASB), US
fatalism, and accounting systems 74
FDI *see* foreign direct investment (FDI)
federal deposit insurance schemes 63
female expatriate managers 125
financial accounting 72–3
Financial Accounting Standards Board (FASB), US 81, 86–7, **87**
financial deregulation 58
financial investors 232–3, 234, 236, 238
financial markets, national 59–60, **60**
financial reports 162
Financial Times (FT) Index 65
financing: private equity 233, 234–6; *see also* international capital markets; working capital management
Finland 67
Fisher effect 214, 221
fixed costs of production 29
floor brokers 65
foreign currency transactions 47–8, 55, 83–7, **86, 87**; hedging with foreign exchange case study 199–205, **200, 201, 203**
foreign direct investment (FDI) 2–6, **5**
foreign-earned income, individual 109–10, 124
foreign exploitation 129
foreign market entry case studies: Myanmar 172–5, **174**; *see also* export market selection case study

Index 253

foreign sales agents 34
foreign statement translation 85–6, **86, 87**
foreign tax credits 102, 103–5, 110, 124
France 35; accounting 81; financial deregulation 58; manufacturing productivity **131**; social reporting 80; stock market 66–7; taxation 97, **100**
Frankfurt 59, 64, **66**, 67–8
Free Market 67
free operating cash flow 237
freight forwarders 34
fringe benefits 116, 117, 128
front-end technology 154
functional currency 86–7, **87**
functional dimension of international business 12, **12**
functional level strategies 10–11
function structure 113–14
Futures and Options market, London 67

Galbraith, J. K. 219
Gaming Research Integration for Learning Laboratory (GRILL) 224–8
gender equality 125
General Motors 24
Geneva 59
geocentric approach: logistics 148; marketing 19; staffing 126, **127**
Germany 10; accounting 81; codetermination 135; job security 129; labor-management relations 128, 132; manufacturing productivity **131**; social reporting 80; stock market **66**, 67–8; taxation 99, **100**
Gibraltar **107**
global consumer convergence spectrum 6, **7**, 8–9, **8**
global efficiency versus local responsiveness and flexibility 6–9, **7, 8, 9**
globalization 1, 2–6
global strategic orientation 7–8, **7, 9,** 166–7
GNI *see* gross national income (GNI) per capita trends
goals, business 9
gray market exports 32–3
Great Britain *see* United Kingdom

greenfield investments 231, 232
Grenada **107**
GRILL *see* Gaming Research Integration for Learning Laboratory (GRILL)
gross national income (GNI) per capita trends 2, **4**
Guernsey **107**

hard technology 153
harmonization of accounting practices 81–3
Harrell & Kiefer country plotting matrix 185, **185**, 186, **187**
hedging with foreign exchange case study 199–205, **200, 201, 203**
holidays 116
home country nationals 118, 119, 146
home replication strategic orientation **7, 8, 9**
Hong Kong 59, 64, **66**, 68, **107**
host country nationals 118, 119, 120, 146
hybrid plant design 158

IAA *see* Inter-American Accounting Association (IAA)
IASB *see* International Accounting Standards Board (IASB)
Iceland 67
IFAC *see* International Federation of Accountants (IFAC)
illegal activities 75–6
illness 149
ILO *see* International Labor Organization (ILO)
import duties, and transfer pricing 32
income exclusion provisions of tax law 110
income taxes 96, 99, 109–10, 124
in-country reports 163
India **66**, 69, **100**, 151; *see also* market share case study
indirect foreign tax credits 103–4
industrial espionage 161
industrial products 18, 20, 27
industrial relations 126–35, 137–8; codetermination 135; collective bargaining 128, 130–3; ethnocentric staffing 126, **127**; geocentric staffing

254 *Index*

126, **127**; job security and layoffs 129; labor productivity 129–30, **131**, 149; MNC tactics 133–4; polycentric staffing 126, **127**; unions 127–8, 129, 130–5; wages and benefits 127–9, 132–3

infinite period cash flow 237

inflation 50, 55, 88–9

information management 161–6, **164**

in-house lunch programs 149

innovation 154

intellectual training model 122

Inter-American Accounting Association (IAA) 82

interest rate parity 221

interest rates 47, 60, 214, 216, **217**; Euromarkets 62–3

internal audits 91, 92

internalizing 155–6, 158–9

Internal Revenue Service, US 32, 95, 105, 107

International Accounting Standards Board (IASB) 82

International Assembly of Collegiate Schools of Business (IACSB) 12

international business teaching 11–12, **12**

international capital markets 57–69; bond issues 59–60, **60**; emergence of 58–9; Euromarkets 61–4; national financial markets 59–60, **60**; stock markets 64–9, **66**

International Federation of Accountants (IFAC) 82

International Financial Reporting Standards Board 82

International Labor Organization (ILO) 134

International Maritime Organization 152

international real estate investor case study 213–21, **215**, **217**, **218**, **220**

International Trade Administration 223

International Trade Loan program, US 55

interpreters 116

intra-company pooling 48–50

intra-company transfers 31–2

invention 154

inventory control 150

Ireland **100**, 106, **107**

irrevocable letters of credit 56–7

Isle of Man **107**

Italy 75, 99, **100**

Japan 10, 34–5; accounting 74, 81; bond issues 60; financial deregulation 58; fringe benefits 128; job security 129; *kanban* system 151; labor-management relations 128, 132–3; manufacturing productivity **131**; stock market 65, **66**; taxation **100**; transnational data flows 166

Jersey **107**

job security 116, 129

joint ventures 121, 146

Jordan **107**

juice *see* export market selection case study

juridic domicile principle 101, 109

just-in-time (JIT) system 151

kanban system 151

Kuala Lumpur 68–9

labeling requirements 22

labor contracts 131, 132

labor-intensive technology 158, 159

labor issues 126–35, 137–8; codetermination 135; collective bargaining 128, 130–3; ethnocentric staffing 126, **127**; geocentric staffing 126, **127**; job security and layoffs 129; labor productivity 129–30, **131**, 149; MNC tactics 133–4; polycentric staffing 126, **127**; unions 127–8, 129, 130–5; wages and benefits 127–9, 132–3

Lachmann, Ludwig 218

lagging 50

language barriers 116

Latvia 67

layoffs 129

leading 50

lead managers 59–60

Lebanon **107**

letters of credit 56–7

Liberia **107**

licensing 156, **157**

Liechtenstein 106, **107**

lifetime employment 129
Lilly Pharmaceuticals 205–12
local image 120
localism 6
local operations system design 143,
    147–8, 158–9
local responsiveness and flexibility versus
    global efficiency 6–9, **7**, **8**, **9**
lockouts 131–2
logistics 142–3, 148, 149, 151
London 59, 64, 65–6, 67
Luxembourg **107**

Macau **107**
McCulloch, Wendell H., Jr. 143
maintenance 143, 150
Malaysia 68–9
Maldives **107**
Malta **107**
management buy-outs (MBOs) 235–6
management information systems (MIS)
    161–6, **164**
managerial accounting 72
Managerial Grid questionnaire 135, **136**,
    140
managerial staffing 117–26, 146–7
manufacturing productivity 129–30, **131**,
    149
maritime piracy 152
Maritime Silk Road program, China 152
market-based reports 163
market capitalization 65, **66**, 67, 68
market entry case studies: Myanmar
    172–5, **174**; *see also* export market
    selection case study
market expansions case study 230–40,
    234
marketing 16–37; adaptation versus
    standardization 17–18, **36**; centralized
    versus decentralized 17, 18–20;
    checklist 40–4; cross-cultural mistakes
    24–6; distribution decisions 33–5;
    pricing decisions 28–33; product
    decisions 20–4; promotion decisions
    23–8
market-penetration pricing 31
market share case study 193–9, **196**, **197**,
    198
market size analysis 179, **181**, **189**

Marshall Islands **107**
materials handling 148
matrix structure 114
Mauritius **107**
Menger, Carl 216, **218**
Menger satisfaction scale 216, **218**
merchant middlemen 34
mergers and acquisitions 230–40, **234**
message adaptation strategies 23, 24
message extension strategies 23–4
Mexico 151
mezzanine financing 236
middlemen 34
minimum wage legislation 127
mission statements 9
"Mittelstand" 10
Monaco **107**
monetary/non-monetary method of
    translation 85, **86**
money market hedge 47
Montserrat **107**
Moody's credit ratings 54, 60
Moscow Nardony Bank 62
motivation, employee 116, 117, 123,
    127–9
multi-domestic strategic orientation **7**, 8,
    9
Myanmar case study 172–5, **174**

NASDAQ Nordics **66**, 67
national financial markets 59–60, **60**
nationalism 6
nationalization 90–1
national stock markets 64–9, **66**
Nauru **107**
Nestle 78, **79**
Netherlands 67, 80, 81, 128
Netherlands Antilles 106
newly incorporated companies 236
new product marketing strategy 24
New York 59, 64–5
Niue **107**
nonproprietary technology 154
NOREX alliance 67
Norway 67, 166
Norwegian Sovereign Wealth Fund 6

objectives, business 9
obsolete technology 154

256   *Index*

OECD *see* Organization for Economic
Cooperation and Development
(OECD)
off-the-balance-sheet items 75–6
Ohio, USA 223–8
oligopolistic markets 30
One Belt, One Road program, China
152
one-step method of accounting 83–4
operations and production management
141–51, 161–8; control 143–7;
designing local operations systems
143, 147–8, 158–9; global versus
international strategy 166–7;
information management 161–6, **164**;
just-in-time system 151; production
technology choice 158–9; productive
activities 148, 149–50; rationalization
143; supply 142–3; supportive
activities 148, 150–1; worldwide
standardization 142–3
operations reports 162–3
ordinary shares 65
organizational ethics 208–9
organizational structures 113–14
Organization for Economic Cooperation
and Development (OECD) 134,
222–3
orphan drugs 96
outsourcing 156–8, **157**
overseas assignments 117–26
over-the-counter markets 67

Panama 106, **107**
parallel loans 53
Paris 59, 64, 66–7
patent monopolies 160
patents 160–1
Pathways Internship Program 224
people, in triple bottom line 206–10
personal selling 27–8
PEST analysis 179–83, **182**, **190**
pharmaceuticals 205–12
Photos Photiades Breweries (PPB) *see*
export market selection case study
piracy 152
PISA *see* Program for International
Student Assessment (PISA)
placement decisions 33–5

planet, in triple bottom line 211–12
plant design 143, 147–8, 158–9
political risks 54, 90–1
polycentric approach: logistics 148;
marketing 19; staffing 126, **127**
Portugal 67
predatory pricing 31
preferred shares 65
preventive maintenance 150
price escalation 30
price-fixing 33
pricing decisions 28–33
pricing methods 29–32
privacy of personal information 165–6
private equity financing 232–3, 234–6
Privilege Capital 230–40, **234**
product adaptation strategies 22–4
product creation strategies 23
product decisions 20–4
product extension strategies 22, 23
production management *see* operations
and production management
production rationalization strategy 143
production system design 143, 147–8,
158–9
productive activities 148, 149–50
productivity, labor 129–30, **131**, 149
product structure 114
profits, in triple bottom line 210–11
profits, repatriation of 50–4
Program for International Student
Assessment (PISA) 223
progressive taxation 94–5, 96
promotion, employee 115
promotional mixes 24
promotion decisions 23–8
promotion messages 23–4
proprietary technology 154
publicity 28
public–private sustainable linkages
222–9
public relations 28
public sector workforce development
223–8
purchasing 150
purposive uniformity 82

quality control 143, 150
quality standards 149–50

Quarterly Journal of Austrian Economics 219

radical subjectivism 218–19
rationalization 143
raw materials 142–3, 148, 149–50, 151
recruitment 114–15
red chip stocks 68
regional accounting associations 82–3
regional harmonization of accounting practices 82–3
regional structure 114
Regulation Q 62
related diversification 10
religious festivals 116
remittances 50–4
repatriation of employees 121, 124–5
repatriation of profits 50–4
reporting currency 86–7, **87**
Repperger Research Intern Program 224
research and development 154–5
reserves 74–5
resident buyers 34
Revenue Act 1962, US 101–2
reverse culture shock 121, 124–5
revocable letters of credit 56
revolving letters of credit 57
Russia **100**

safety standards 22
St. Kitts & Nevis **107**
St. Vincent & Grenadines **107**
salaries 116, 117, 123, 124
sales promotions 28
sales staff 27–8
salvage value 75
Samoa **107**
samurai bonds 60
San Marino **107**
Sarbanes-Oxley Act 2002, US 77
SBA *see* Small Business Administration (SBA), US
scheduling problems 149
science, technology, engineering, and mathematics (STEM) careers 223–8
Securities and Exchange Commission (SEC), US 65, 76–7, 81
seed funds 235
segmentation of accounting 77–9, **78**, **79**

selection, employee 115, 120–1, 146
self-awareness training model 122
selling groups 34
sensitivity training 122
severance taxes 98, 99
Seychelles **107**
Shackle, George Lennox Sharmin 219–21, **220**
Shackle possibility curve 219–21, **220**
Shanghai **66**, 68
Shenzhen **66**, 68
shunto, Japan 133
sickness 149
sight drafts 56
Silicatec *see* hedging with foreign exchange case study
simulation skills 224–5
Singapore 59, **66**, 69, 106, **107**
sin taxes 98
Small Business Administration (SBA), US 55
social reporting 79–80
sociocultural factors, and accounting systems 74
soft technology 153–4
sogo shosha, Japan 34
Sony Corporation 77–8, **78**
South Korea **66**, 69
Soviet Union 61–2
spring wage offensive, Japan 133
staffing 114–26, 137, 148; absenteeism 149; compensation packages 116, 123, 127–9; ethnocentric 126, **127**; geocentric 126, **127**; managerial 117–26, 146–7; motivation 116, 117, 123, 127–9; polycentric 126, **127**; promotion 115; recruitment 114–15; repatriation of employees 121, 124–5; selection 115, 120–1, 146; training 27–8, 115–16, 122–3, 222–9
Standard & Poor's 500 Index 65
Standard & Poor's credit ratings 54, 60
standardization: of marketing 17–18, **36**; of operations and production 142–3
stand-by letters of credit 57
Steelcase Inc. 27–8
stereotype avoidance 121
Stockholm 67
stock markets 64–9, **66**

258   *Index*

strategic investors 232–3, 236, 237–8
strategic orientations 6–9, **7**, **8**, **9**, 166–7
strategy formulation processes 9–11
strikes 131, 132, 133
structural global dimension 11–12, **12**
subjectivism 218–19
subjectivity of value 216, 219, 221
supply systems 142–3, 148, 149, 150, 151
supportive activities 148, 150–1
Survey of Adult Skills 224
sustainability case studies 171; cooperative workforce development 222–9; international real estate investor 213–21, **215**, **217**, **218**, **220**; market expansions 230–40, **234**; triple bottom line 205–12
sustainable development goals 222
Sweden 67
Switzerland 75, 77, 81, **107**
synergistic effects 233

Taiwan 64, 68; *see also* market share case study
target return levels 30
tariffs 32, 99
taxation 48, 54, 94–111; business expenses 96, 104–5; compliance and enforcement 99–105; corporate tax rates 100, **100**; credits 96, 102, 103–5, 110, 124; deductions and allowances 96; deemed paid credits 103–4; double 102, 109; evasion 32, 99; excise taxes 32, 98, 99; expatriate employees 109–10, 123; extraction taxes 98, 99; of foreign branches and subsidiaries 100–1; incentives for international business 108–10; income taxes 96, 99, 109–10, 124; of individual foreign-earned income 109–10, 124; juridic domicile principle 101, 109; policy 94–5; progressive 94–5, 96; tariffs 32, 99; tax havens 105–6, **107**; tax treaties 102, 105, 124; transaction taxes 97–8, **97**; and transfer pricing 32, 106–8; of transnational data flows 166; unitary taxes 107–8; of U.S. controlled foreign corporations 101–2; of U.S.

possessions corporations 108; value-added taxes (VAT) 97–8, **97**; and wages 127; water's edge 108
technical assistance 151
technology 130, 153–61, 168; definition 153–4; development 154–5; and financial markets 58; licensing 156, **157**; pricing 159–60; production technology choice 158–9; protecting 160–1; transfer 155–60, **157**; turnkey projects 156
temporal method of translation 85, 86, **86**, **87**
terminal value calculation 237
third-country nationals 118–19
time drafts 56
tobacco taxation 32, 98
Tokyo 59, 64, 65, **66**
Tonga **107**
trade acceptances 56
trademarks 161
trading post system 68
training, employee 27–8, 115–16, 122–3, 222–9
transaction taxes 97–8, **97**
transferable letters of credit 57
transfer pricing 31–2, 53, 89–90, 106–8, 160
translation of financial statements 85–6, **86**, **87**
transnational strategic orientation 7, **7**, **9**
treaties, tax 102, 105
Treaty of Versailles 134
triple bottom line case study 205–12
Tung, Rosalie 117
Turks & Caicos **107**
turnkey projects 156
turnover 75
two-step method of accounting 84

unbundled technology 154
underwriters 59–60
unions 127–8, 129, 130–5
unitary taxes 107–8
United Kingdom: accounting 89; bond issues 60; Brexit 66; and Euromarkets 62; financial deregulation 58; labor-management relations 128, 132; manufacturing productivity **131**; stock

market 65–6; taxation **100**; turnover 75
United Nations 222, 224
United States: accounting for expropriation 90–1; accounting for inflation 89; accounting policymaking 81; bond issues 60; consolidation rules 87–8; cooperative workforce development case study 222–9; corporate tax rates **100**; depreciation 75; disclosure 76–7; distribution systems 34; and Euromarkets 61–2; facilitative payments 75–6; financial deregulation 58; foreign currency transactions 84; gray markets 33; hedging with foreign exchange case study 199–205, **200**, **201**, **203**; labor-management relations 131–2; manufacturing productivity **131**; Regulation Q 62; Sixteenth Amendment to Constitution 109; stock market 64–5; taxation of controlled foreign corporations (CFCs) 101–2; taxation of expatriate employees 109–10, 124; taxation of foreign branches and subsidiaries 100–1; taxation of possessions corporations 108; tax credits 96, 102, 103–5, 110, 124; tax deductions 96; tax incentives for international business 108–10; tax law 95, 99; tax treaties 102, 124; training expenditure 222; transfer pricing 32, 33, 90, 107–8; turnover 75; unitary taxes 107–8; Webb-Pomerane Act 34; working capital loans 54–5
unrelated diversification 10
US Virgin Islands **107**

valuation 75–6; business valuation techniques 236–8
value-added taxes (VAT) 97–8, **97**
value creating activities 10

values-based leadership case study 205–12
Vanuatu **107**
variable costs of production 29
venture capital 232–3, 235
vertical integration 147

wages 116, 117, 123, 124, 127–9, 132–3
water's edge taxation 108
Webb-Pomerane Act, US 34
weighted average cost of capital (WACC) 237
West Central Ohio Workforce Development Initiative 226, 228
wildcat strikes 132
women, overseas assignments 125
work councils, Germany 132
workforce development case study 222–9
working capital management 45–55, **46**; blocked funds management 50–3; cash conversion cycle 46–7, **46**; exchange risk 47–8; financial analysis 53–5; foreign currency considerations 47–8, 55; and inflation 50, 55; intra-company pooling 48–50; letters of credit 56–7; parallel loans 53; political risks 54; repatriation of profits 50–4; sources of funds 54–5; tax considerations 48, 54; transfer pricing 53
work injuries 149
work stoppages 149, 150
World Trade Organization (WTO) 98
Wright-Patterson Air Force Base (WPAFB), Ohio, USA 223–4
Wright Scholar Research Assistant Program 224–8

xenophobia 1

yankee bonds 60

zaibatsu 248

About the authors

Riad A. Ajami is currently Professor of International Business and Global Strategy and Director, Center for Global Business at Wright State University. Professor Ajami previously held the position of Professor of International Business (with tenure) and Director, International Business Program at the Fisher College of Business at Ohio State University. Prior to joining Raj Soin College of Business, Professor Ajami held the position of Charles A. Hayes Distinguished Professor of Business and Director, Center for Global Business Education and Research at the University of North Carolina, Greensboro (UNCG). Before joining UNCG Professor Ajami held the position of Benjamin Forman Chair Professor of International Business and Director, Center for International Business and Economic Growth at the Rochester Institute of Technology. He has had visiting appointments as the Dr. M. Lee Pearce Distinguished Professor of International Business and Economic Cooperation, School of International Studies at the University of Miami; School of Business Administration at the University of California, Berkeley; the Wharton School, University of Pennsylvania; and the Harvard Center for International Affairs at Harvard University; Hautes Etudes Commercials – HEC (Grande Ecole of Management), France; American University of Beirut; Istanbul University; and a distinguished faculty affiliate at Audencia (School of Management), France.

Dr. Ajami received his Ph.D. from Pennsylvania State University in International Business, Strategic Management and Oil Economics.

Currently, Dr. Ajami is the Editor-in-Chief of the *Journal of Asia-Pacific Business* and serves as an editorial board member of *Competitiveness Review*, *Journal of Global Marketing*, *Journal of Transnational Management Development*, and other leading international, academic business journals.

Dr. Ajami is also the co-author of *The Psychology of Marketing: Cross-Cultural Perspectives* (Gower Publishing, 2010), *Customer Relationship Management:*

A Global Perspective (Gower Publishing, 2008), and *The Global Enterprise: Entrepreneurship and Value Creation* (2007, The Haworth Press). He is also a frequent contributor to a number of books on the subject of International Business. He has had articles published on International Business in the *Wall Street Journal*, *Journal of International Business Studies*, *Management International Review*, *Strategic Management Journal*, *Journal of International Management*, and other leading international, academic business journals. Professor Ajami has appeared on national television and radio, including, among others, Nightline, the PBS News Hour, NBC News, CNN, National Public Radio and CBS Radio. Dr. Ajami was a principal and co-founder of the consulting firm Management International: Consultants and Advisors, based in Luxembourg and New York City.

G. Jason Goddard is currently Vice President at Wells Fargo, where he has been a commercial lender for over 20 years. Mr. Goddard is currently senior learning strategist for business credit in Business Banking University, and works in Winston-Salem, NC. He obtained his MBA from the Bryan School at the University of North Carolina at Greensboro. Mr. Goddard is currently adjunct professor of practice at Wake Forest University and part-time lecturer at UNC-G. He is the Assistant Editor of the *Journal of Asia-Pacific Business*, where he has authored numerous articles. Mr. Goddard teaches the investment real estate course at the School of Business at Wake Forest University each spring and fall semester. Mr. Goddard also teaches the subject annually at the RMA-ECU Commercial Real Estate Lending School at East Carolina University in Greenville, NC, and he has had numerous articles published in the national RMA Journal. He has also taught undergraduate and MBA courses in international business and international finance at UNC-G, and has coordinated the America in the Global Economy lecture series at UNC-G. Mr. Goddard has twice led a group of UNCG MBA students on the study abroad program in Paris, France, and has taught annually in Ludwigshafen Germany at the University of Applied Sciences. Mr. Goddard has also taught Customer Relationship Management, an elective in the UNC-G MBA program, and Market Psychology, an elective in the Wake Forest MALS program. Mr. Goddard is co-author of the following text books: *International Business: Theory and Practice*, Second Edition (M.E. Sharpe Publishers, September 2006); *Customer Relationship Management: A Global Perspective* (Gower Publishing, May 2008); *The Psychology of Marketing: Cross-Cultural Perspectives* (Gower Publishing, October 2010); *Real Estate Investment: A Value Based Approach* (Springer, July 2012); and *International Business: A Course on the Essentials*, (M.E. Sharpe, October 2013). You can follow him on Twitter @GJasonGoddard.

Taylor & Francis eBooks

Helping you to choose the right eBooks for your Library

Add Routledge titles to your library's digital collection today. Taylor and Francis ebooks contains over 50,000 titles in the Humanities, Social Sciences, Behavioural Sciences, Built Environment and Law.

Choose from a range of subject packages or create your own!

Benefits for you
- Free MARC records
- COUNTER-compliant usage statistics
- Flexible purchase and pricing options
- All titles DRM-free.

Benefits for your user
- Off-site, anytime access via Athens or referring URL
- Print or copy pages or chapters
- Full content search
- Bookmark, highlight and annotate text
- Access to thousands of pages of quality research at the click of a button.

REQUEST YOUR FREE INSTITUTIONAL TRIAL TODAY

Free Trials Available
We offer free trials to qualifying academic, corporate and government customers.

eCollections – Choose from over 30 subject eCollections, including:

Archaeology	Language Learning
Architecture	Law
Asian Studies	Literature
Business & Management	Media & Communication
Classical Studies	Middle East Studies
Construction	Music
Creative & Media Arts	Philosophy
Criminology & Criminal Justice	Planning
Economics	Politics
Education	Psychology & Mental Health
Energy	Religion
Engineering	Security
English Language & Linguistics	Social Work
Environment & Sustainability	Sociology
Geography	Sport
Health Studies	Theatre & Performance
History	Tourism, Hospitality & Events

For more information, pricing enquiries or to order a free trial, please contact your local sales team:
www.tandfebooks.com/page/sales

The home of Routledge books

www.tandfebooks.com